Classical Subjects Crea

French for Children

Primer B

Learn more than how to order a croissant

Joshua Kraut, PhD

with David Spieser, PhD

French for Children Primer B

Version 1.0

ISBN: 978-1-60051-296-4

Classical Academic Press
515 S. 32nd Street
Camp Hill, PA 17011

www.ClassicalAcademicPress.com

Illustrations by Jason Rayner
Book design by Lenora Riley

PGP.11.21

TABLE OF CONTENTS

*These sections are continued from *FFCA*. See page 5 for a note about this.

CD Track & Audio File Information

CD Track	Audio File	Chap.	Page
1	01_01	1	9
2	01_02	1	10
3	01_03	1	10
4	01_04	1	11
5	01_05	1	11
6	01_06	1	15
7	01_07	1	20
8	02_01	2	21
9	02_02	2	22
10	02_03	2	22
11	02_04	2	22
12	02_05	2	27
13	02_06	2	32
14	03_01	3	33
15	03_02	3	34
16	03_03	3	34
17	03_04	3	34
18	03_05	3	38
19	03_06	3	44
20	04_01	4	45
21	04_02	4	46
22	04_03	4	46
23	04_04	4	46
24	04_05	4	47/51
25	04_06	4	56
26	05_01	5	60
27	06_01	6	65
28	06_02	6	66
29	06_03	6	66
30	06_04	6	66
31	06_05	6	71
32	06_06	6	74
33	07_01	7	75
34	07_02	7	76
35	07_03	7	76
36	07_04	7	76
37	07_05	7	80
38	07_06	7	84

CD Track	Audio File	Chap.	Page
39	08_01	8	85
40	08_02	8	86
41	08_03	8	86
42	08_04	8	86
43	08_05	8	91
44	08_06	8	96
45	09_01	9	97
46	09_02	9	98
47	09_03	9	98
48	09_04	9	98
49	09_05	9	100
50	09_06	9	101
51	09_07	9	101
52	09_08	9	101
53	09_09	9	102
54	09_10	9	108
55	10_01	10	118
56	11_01	11	119
57	11_02	11	120
58	11_03	11	120
59	11_04	11	120
60	11_05	11	125
61	11_06	11	130
62	12_01	12	131
63	12_02	12	132
64	12_03	12	133
65	12_04	12	133
66	12_05	12	133
67	12_06	12	142
68	12_07	12	144
69	13_01	13	145
70	13_02	13	146
71	13_03	13	146
72	13_04	13	146
73	13_05	13	150
74	13_06	13	155
75	13_07	13	156
76	14_01	14	157

CD Track	Audio File	Chap.	Page
77	14_02	14	158
78	14_03	14	158
79	14_04	14	158
80	14_05	14	165
81	14_06	14	170
82	15_01	15	171
83	15_02	15	172
84	15_03	15	172
85	15_04	15	172
86	15_05	15	184
87	15_06	15	186

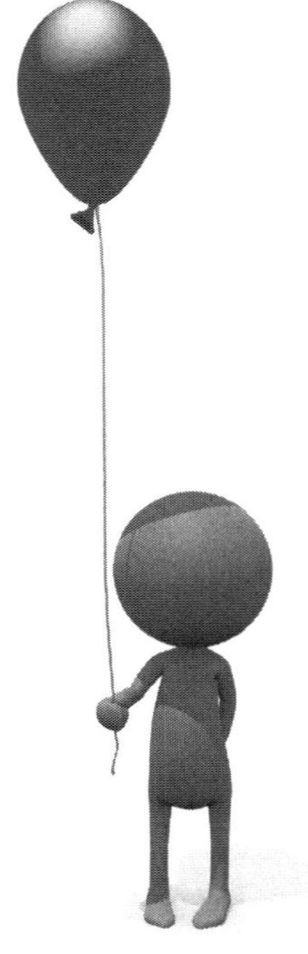

Suggested Schedule

There are seventeen chapters in *French for Children Primer B*, thirteen of which are content chapters and four are review. Doing one chapter per week (content and review chapters) will allow you to finish the course in approximately half of an academic year. Alternatively, if you complete one content chapter every two weeks, taking just one week per review chapter, the course will take a full year—thirty weeks.

Weekly Schedule

The following is a basic weekly schedule, to be modified as necessary by the teacher. Note that days two and five call for longer sessions.

Day One (approx. 30 mins.)

Listen to the audio file of the opening dialogue and have students follow along in the text. Take a few minutes (not too long) to ask students what they've understood from the dialogue and what they think is going on. Total comprehension at this stage is not essential; students should be encouraged to guess at the details of the plot or simply the meaning of new vocabulary items based on context. Present the vocabulary and the paradigm (grammar chant). Students should chant through the paradigm and vocabulary two or three times, using the recorded audio files (and/or teachers' pronunciation) as a guide. (Optional step 1: At this point, the video can be played up to the point at which the instructor reads through the chant and the vocabulary, but the video should be stopped after that.) Then, ask students to skim back over the dialogue to see if they understand more of the French. Again, do not take too long for comprehension questions at this stage; the dialogue will be revisited later. (Optional step 2: Students can take turns reading different parts in the dialogue, one or two lines each. This activity is meant to help students read the French and develop good French pronunciation more than to stage a drama, since students may not understand every word of the dialogue.)

Day Two (approx. 55–65 mins.)

Review the paradigm (grammar chant) and vocabulary and have students chant them again one or two times. Watch the video (either picking up where you left off from day one or viewing it in its entirety). The videos are approximately forty-five minutes to an hour in length. While you should feel free to stop them and rewind at any time, be aware that they may take a while to get through with frequent interruptions.

Day Three (approx. 30 mins.)

Start with a quick chant of the paradigm and vocabulary. Then spend some time explaining the grammar page, paying special attention to the examples. If you see an italicized sentence, be sure to emphasize it (you may consider having students circle these and other key sentences with a colored pencil for future reference). Ask comprehension questions, such as "What two words do you need to turn a positive sentence into a negative one in French?" or "What is an irregular verb?" After this, begin the worksheet, or assign it as homework.

Day Four (approx. 30 mins.)

Again, start the day with a quick chant of the paradigm and vocabulary. Next, the worksheet should either be started or completed. Check students' work and go over any corrections with the students. Grammar should be reviewed and retaught as necessary. One means of reviewing grammar can be to view the video again to ensure comprehension of key grammatical topics for that chapter.

Day Five (approx. 50 mins.)

Students should take the quiz without looking back at the rest of the chapter. When the quiz has been completed, go over the answers together and review any trouble spots. Finally, go back and listen to the opening dialogue once more, having students follow along in the text. Discuss what is happening, and identify vocabulary/grammatical points that help in understanding the dialogue. Translate the dialogue together.

Biweekly Schedule

The following is a basic biweekly schedule spread over seven class meetings, to be modified as necessary by the teacher.

Day One (approx. 30 mins.)

Listen to the opening dialogue and follow along in the text. Take a few minutes (not too long) to ask students what they've understood from the dialogue, and what they think is going on. Total comprehension at this stage is not essential; students should be encouraged to guess at the details of the plot or simply the meaning of new vocabulary items based on context. Present the vocabulary and the paradigm (grammar chant). Students should chant through the paradigm and vocabulary two or three times, using the recorded audio files (and/or teachers' pronunciation) as a guide. (Optional step 1: At this point, the video can be played up to the point at which the instructor reads through the chant and the vocabulary, but it should be stopped after that.) Then, ask students to skim back over the dialogue to see if they understand more of the French. Again, do not take too long for comprehension questions at this stage; the dialogue will be revisited later. (Optional step 2: Students can take turns reading different parts in the dialogue, one or two lines each. This activity is meant to help students read and develop good French pronunciation more than to stage a drama, since students may not understand every word of the dialogue.)

Day Two (approx. 55–65 mins.)

Review the paradigm (grammar chant) and vocabulary and have students chant them again one or two times. Have students watch the video (either picking up where you left off from day one, or else in its entirety). The videos are between forty-five minutes and an hour in length. While you should feel free to stop them and rewind at any time, be aware that they may take a while to get through with frequent interruptions.

Day Three (approx. 30 mins.)

Start with a quick chant of the paradigm and vocabulary. Then spend some time explaining the grammar page, paying special attention to the examples. If you see an italicized sentence, be sure to emphasize it (you may consider having students circle or highlight these and other key sentences for future reference). Ask comprehension questions, such as "What two words do you need to turn a positive sentence into a negative one in French?" or "What is an irregular verb?" Go back and listen to the opening dialogue once more, having students follow along in the text. Discuss what is happening, and identify vocabulary/grammatical points that help in the understanding of the dialogue (a full translation is not necessary at this time—target in particular those sections of the dialogue that employ grammatical notions discussed in the Grammar section). If time remains, have students begin the worksheet.

Day Four (approx. 30 mins.)

Again, start the day with a quick chant of the paradigm and vocabulary. Next, the worksheet should be started. Students may consult the chapter to complete this section. Grammar should be reviewed and retaught as necessary. One means of reviewing grammar can be to view parts of the video again to ensure comprehension of key grammatical topics for that chapter.

Day Five (approx. 30 mins.)

The worksheet should be completed and reviewed. Trouble spots should be addressed. Students should prepare for taking the quiz by playing vocabulary games (e.g., flash cards, bingo, charades, etc.).

Day Six (approx. 30 mins.)

Have students take the quiz, noting that they are not to look back at the previous sections of the chapter.

Day Seven (approx. 30 mins.)

Review the quiz. Then, return a final time to the opening dialogue, having students listen to the audio file and follow along in the text. Translate the dialogue together. Discuss what is happening and identify vocabulary/grammatical points that help you understand the dialogue. Students may be encouraged to read aloud and to do their best to "act the part" if they feel so inclined.

Introduction

Welcome back for another exciting course in French! *French for Children Primer B* (*FFCB*) picks up right where the previous volume—*French for Children Primer A* (*FFCA*)—left off. In fact, if you look at the table of contents in this book, you'll see that some of the "series" of grammatical themes simply continue on here. For example, we're beginning in chapter 1 with part 2 in our discussion of irregular verbs—that's a continuation of part 1 from *FFCA*. You'll come across other grammatical units that began in *FFCA* and are expanded upon in this book, so if you see a part 3 of some unit that appears to be missing the first two parts, make sure you have a look back at *FFCA*!

Just as a reminder, then, there are two types of chapters in this book: *lesson chapters* and *review chapters*. Review chapters bring together the information you've seen in the previous few chapters, and give you an opportunity to test your knowledge. Lesson chapters are where you learn things for the first time.

In each lesson chapter, you will see a few things: At the top of each page in the lesson chapters, you will see different titles. The title that is BIGGER THAN THE REST tells you which part of a chapter you are in. The four main parts of each lesson chapter are: Memory, Grammar, Worksheet, or Quiz. Let's take a look at what you'll find in each of the different parts.

Memory

Dialogue

The dialogues in this book continue to tell the tale of Jean and Aurélie, whom you met in *FFCA*. As in that book, the dialogues in this book introduce you to some of the new vocabulary that you'll be learning in each lesson chapter. Feel free to read over the chapter's vocabulary list before reading the dialogue if you desire, but we do not recommend that you try to memorize the vocabulary letter-for-letter before attempting to read the dialogues.

The most rewarding way to approach the dialogues may simply be to *jump right in and try to figure out what words mean by their context.* The mix of French and English within the dialogues continues in this book, though with more emphasis on the French. As with *FFCA*, this mixture of languages should make it possible for you to decipher the new French words in each chapter. Even if you can only narrow it down to a guess (for example: "I think this word must be some kind of food," or "I think this word is an action that means to go somewhere"), that's a great start. This will give you a "feel" for the word even before you study the vocabulary more deeply (see item 3 in this list). There are translations of all of the dialogues in the back of the teacher's edition of *FFCB* (see Appendix A: Dialogue Translations).

Chant

The French word **chant** means the same thing as the English word "chant," so you already know what this is! In each chapter we ask you to chant a certain set of words or phrases. Why? The goal is to help you and your mouth get used to forming the sounds of these words. You can listen to the audio files of the chants. The chants and their translations are also included in their own appendix (appendix B) at the end of this book.

Vocabulaire

There are approximately ten vocabulary words in each chapter. After reading through the dialogue and trying to figure out the new words ahead of time, we recommend that you spend a few minutes committing these words to memory every day that you are working on the chapter. Memorize the vocabulary, and following the chapter will be easy as pie. Don't memorize it, and you'll be flipping pages back and forth the whole time to look up what the words mean! As a way of making memorizing the vocabulary easier, try creating flash cards and having someone quiz you with them.

Grammar

This section is where we discuss the inner workings of French grammar—and how to use it. Pay close attention to a few different *icons* that may appear on the pages of the Grammar section:

***Remarque*:** The French word **remarque** looks like an English word you may know—"remark." In this book, when you see the **Remarque** icon, this means that you will be given a little bit of extra information to remember about the grammar rule you've just learned.

***Renvoi*:** A **renvoi** is a sort of reminder to go back to a subject that has already been mentioned. For example, if we are talking about something in chapter 7, which uses some of the information from chapter 2, there will be a **Renvoi** icon in chapter 7, which tells you "Turn to chapter 2 if you need to refresh your memory."

Worksheet

The Worksheet is just what the name says it is: worksheet exercises where you can put your brain to the test and see if you can use the grammar lesson to complete the charts, sentences, and word puzzles you'll find. For the Worksheet, feel free to flip back and forth between the exercises and the pages in the Grammar section in case you get stuck; the idea is to learn as you go. Answers to the exercises from both the Worksheet and the Quiz sections are found in *French for Children Primer B Answer Key*.

An additional note on the answer key: In *FFCA*, for present-tense verb phrases, such as **je parle**, we supplied two translations: "I speak/I am speaking." Both translations were included in the answer key. In *FFCB*, we will no longer provide both translations since we'll be introducing even more expressions that could be translated multiple ways. It would be too complicated, for instance, to list four different possible translations for a sentence that combined a present-tense verb and another one of these expressions! However, specifically on the topic of the verb translations, you can rest assured that both translations are still appropriate unless it is clearly a situation in which one seems more natural than the other. The key is simply to know in the back of your mind when you'd use one translation and when you'd use the other.

Quiz

Finally, the end of each lesson chapter contains a Quiz section. This section is similar to the Worksheet, except this time you're *only* supposed to use your brain—no looking back at the Grammar section, the Worksheet, your flash cards, your notes, nothing, zero, zip, **rien** (**rien** is French for "nothing"). Of course, **la police** won't come to your house if you do go back and look, but the point is that *if you still need to go back to previous pages for help, you have not really learned the lesson*, and so you should probably not go on to the next chapter until you can pass the quiz with either a perfect score or only one or two answers wrong. And, of course, once you're done with the quiz, we highly recommend going back to the opening dialogue and reading it through once more—probably much faster, and more enjoyably this time!—to cement in all of the new things you've learned.

La dictée

At the end of every Quiz section we've included an exercise called a **dictée**—a dictation exercise. Traditionally in this exercise, the teacher reads a short sentence slowly, a few words at a time, and the students copy down, or transcribe, what they hear. You can hear the sentences read on the CD or audio file. (Check the CD Track & Audio File Information page for the list of the **dictée** associated with each chapter.) If the teacher feels comfortable doing so, he or she may read the sentences aloud as well, including perhaps a faster repetition (one which approaches a normal speech rate) the second time.

Transcribing spoken French is especially helpful since, as you'll see, there are many letters that you may not hear pronounced, but which are important to include in the written form nonetheless. In fact, the **dictée** has a rich tradition in francophone culture, believe it or not—a bit like our spelling bees. Today in the francophone world there are **dictée** competitions in many different regions, and they attract both schoolchildren and adults! Our hope is that these "spoken puzzles" will be challenging and instructive for you as well.

Here are a few practical tips regarding **dictées**:

First, you should feel free to incorporate the **dictées** in the Worksheet section if you find that more helpful, or if it works more neatly with your schedule. Second, as for the marking of the **dictées** (assuming they are being used in a Quiz), the instructor should be generous with "partial credit" in these exercises. It can be quite challenging to get the entire sentence exactly right, so having a breakdown of how students can obtain points for each sentence—rather using an all-or-nothing scheme—would be preferable. One could award points, for example, for each correctly spelled word.

Treasures in the Back of the Book: New Material in *FFCB*

Far, far away, in the back of this book, you will find several things:

Appendices

The appendices contain some of the same information you will learn from the book's regular lesson chapters, but it is condensed and organized into charts in the appendices to make it easier to search through. There is a preposition appendix (appendix E; prepositions appear throughout this book), verb appendix (appendix C) with verb conjugations, and a past participle appendix (appendix D; also see chapter 11).

Glossaries

The alphabetical glossary contains all of the vocabulary items in this book, along with their translations, presented in one long, alphabetical list. Think of this section as a "mini-dictionary" that contains the words for both *FFCA* and *FFCB*. For nouns, you will see the clues to determining the noun's gender in the glossary entry. In the glossary by chapter—you guessed it—all of the vocabulary words from *FFCB* are listed by the chapter in which they first appear. This glossary can be a very handy tool when you're studying your vocabulary. You will also find a categorical glossary that divides the book's vocabulary, along with the Conversation Journal words and phrases, into various categories based on how they are used.

CHAPITRE UN

DIALOGUE [01_01/TR. 1]

In case you're just joining us or can't quite recall what was happening in the dialogue sections in FFCA, *we have been following the story of Jean, a field mouse, and Aurélie, a dairy cow, who were mistakenly released into the wild after zookeepers mistook them for protected species. They have been trying to find their way back to the zoo and at this point in the story have joined up with a somewhat eccentric village miller and his son. The miller and his son are on their way to the local fair, which happens to be on the way to the city.*

Aurélie, Jean, the miller's son, and the miller—still carrying his donkey—set off for the fair. The miller manages to walk at a surprising pace, given his load, and soon he has gone some distance ahead of the others. Jean and Aurélie begin talking with the boy as the miles go by.

JEAN, *speaking to the miller's son.* **Alors! Comment t'appelles-tu?**

THIBAULT. **Je m'appelle Thibault—et vous? Comment vous appelez-vous?**

JEAN. **Moi, je m'appelle Jean.**

AURÉLIE. **Et je suis Aurélie—enchantée!**

THIBAULT. **Enchanté! Je suis content de marcher avec vous.**

JEAN. **Nous sommes contents aussi.** The road is a long one, and we're glad for the company. Plus, we weren't quite sure we could trust your dad's . . . errr . . . well . . . judgment. . . . *Jean points ahead to the miller, who is still huffing and puffing as he carries his donkey.*

THIBAULT. **Ah non, ça va, ça va. Il aime ses animaux, c'est tout. Et il aime beaucoup son âne!** He's just making sure it doesn't get too tired.

JEAN. Well, it's still nice to go along with you.

AURÉLIE. **Et vraiment . . . nous avons un peu peur de voyager . . . nous habitons dans le zoo!**

JEAN. Yes, you see, and we are not used to traveling like most folks. **Toi, tu voyages beaucoup?**

THIBAULT. **Non. C'est dommage. J'ai envie de voyager. J'ai envie de visiter beaucoup d'endroits.**

AURÉLIE, *not believing that people actually want to travel on purpose.* ***Vraiment? Où?***

THIBAULT. Oh, I don't know. **Beaucoup d'endroits sont intéressants . . . la plage, les montagnes . . . la ville, peut-être? Tout le monde dans mon village parle de la grande ville. "Oh, la ville, elle est magnifique!"** They say, "**La ville, elle est grande**

et belle!" The farthest I've been, though, is just the next town over where the market is, so how should I know? **Mais vous, vous êtes de là-bas. Vous pensez que la ville est si belle?**

JEAN. **Hmmm . . . tu as des bonnes questions.** You know, it's been so long since I was out walking around there. **Nous sommes toujours dans le zoo, alors c'est difficile pour nous d'avoir une idée.**

AURÉLIE. **J'ai une idée.**

THIBAULT AND JEAN. What is it?

AURÉLIE. **Nous visitons la ville ensemble!**

THIBAULT. Hey, Jean, what do you think of that?

JEAN. **Oui! Je pense que c'est une bonne idée. Aurélie, tu es une vache intelligente!** But I'm afraid it will be quite a challenge getting back . . . **si nous réussissons**, I'll be glad to see the city **avec toi, Thibault! Allons-y!**

Chant (ahem, rap) [01_02/Tr. 2]

To Be or Not to Be

Les garçons: Je suis beau. (Yo!)
Les filles: Je suis belle. (Belle!)
Tu es beau. (Yo!)
Tu es belle. (Belle!)
Il est beau. (Yo!)
(Et elle est belle, belle, belle, belle!)
Nous sommes beaux. (Yo!)
Vous êtes beaux. (Yo!)
Vous êtes belles. (Belles!)
Ils sont beaux (Yo, yo!)
(Et elles sont belles, belles, belles, belles!)

Être (to be) [01_03/Tr. 3]

Person	Singular	Plural
1st Person	**je suis** (I am)	**nous sommes** (we are)
2nd Person	**tu es** (you are)	**vous êtes** (you are)
3rd Person	**il/elle est** (he/she/it is)	**ils/elles sont** (they are)

Vocabulaire [01_04/Tr. 4]

Français	Anglais
être, je suis	to be, I am
voyager, je voyage	to travel, I travel
visiter, je visite	to visit, I visit
avoir envie de, j'ai envie de	to feel like/to want, I feel like/I want
un endroit	a place
une idée	an idea
ensemble	together
intelligent/bête	smart/dumb
content[1]**/triste**	happy/sad
difficile/simple	difficult/simple[2]

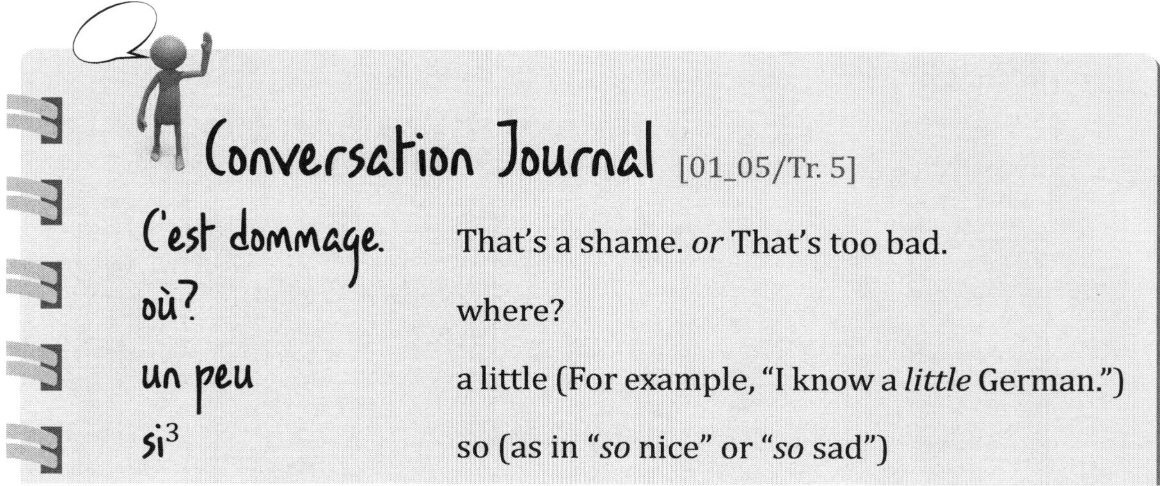

Conversation Journal [01_05/Tr. 5]

C'est dommage.	That's a shame. *or* That's too bad.
où?	where?
un peu	a little (For example, "I know a *little* German.")
si[3]	so (as in "*so* nice" or "*so* sad")

Renvoi

Don't remember what *infinitives* are? See **chapitre** 3 of *FFCA*!

1. In **chapitre** 13 of *FFCA*, you learned the word **heureux**, which also means "happy." **Content** is simply a synonym for **heureux**; there are no precise rules governing when to use which word, though some contexts (too many to list here!) do tend toward one usage over the other. One major example of this is when the sentence is **negative**: Saying "I'm not happy" with **content** usually means "I'm a bit mad/ frustrated," whereas saying "I'm not happy" with **heureux** means you're actually feeling blue.
2. Do you remember the word **facile** from *FFCA* **chapitre** 12? In addition to "easy," it can also mean "simple." In French, **facile** and **simple** are synonyms, just as "easy" and "simple" are in English. So **difficile/facile** is a pair of opposites just as **difficile/simple** is.
3. You might remember from *FFCA* **chapitre** 9 that **si** means "if" in English. Well, here we're dealing with the same two letters—the same sound, even—but an entirely different word. **Si** in this week's **chapitre** means "so" as in "He's so smart!" We call words such as **si** (if) and **si** (so) *homonyms*. In English, we have homonyms, too, such as the word "lies." You can say, "He lies down on the sofa" or "He tells lies." It is a totally different word in each case!

Irregular Verbs, Part 2: Être

In *FFCA*, our first exposure to irregular verbs—Irregular Verbs, Part 1—introduced us to the verb **avoir** (to have). Our chant in this chapter contains the verb **être**, which means "to be." As you look at the different forms in the chant, you might notice something that seems curious: The word **être** doesn't seem very closely related to the forms **suis, es, est, sommes, êtes**, or **sont**, right? (OK, maybe **êtes** does look like **être**, but that's really the only one that does.) It doesn't seem to conjugate like the verb **parler** (to speak) does, for example. You have the infinitive, **parler**, and then you just go straight on down the line with the conjugations: **parle, parles, parle, parlons**, etc.

Well, there is no way around it: The verb **être**, like the verb **avoir**, is just one of those *irregular* verbs—verbs that change forms without following a normal pattern. In fact, **être** is one of the *most* irregular (or unpredictable) verbs that exists in French! That means that it will take a little extra practice to learn its forms (hint, hint). Be careful, also, about your pronunciation with this verb—there are many opportunities to say too much! In the following chart, we've put a line through all of the letters that should "keep quiet." Just to be sure you can recall them, have another listen to the chant on the audio file [01_03/Tr. 3].

Je sui~~s~~	**Nous somme~~s~~**
Tu e~~s~~	**Vous ête~~s~~**
Il/Elle e~~st~~	**Ils/Elles so~~nt~~**

Liaison

If you've learned one firm rule about pronunciation so far, it's been "Don't say too much!" People learning French often pronounce letters—especially at the ends of words—that are actually silent. We've seen many examples so far: From the **t** in **chat**, the **x** in **jeux** or **chevaux**, to the **m** and **p** in the word **champ**—there are far too many to list here! However, you should know that there are certain occasions when you may—in fact, when you *must*—pronounce the last consonant of a word. Occasionally when a word ends in a consonant, we will pronounce this last letter *when the following word begins with a vowel*. Now, even with the following word beginning in a vowel, this rule does not apply all of the time. It applies only under certain conditions.

We have a perfect example in this **chapitre**: the sentence "You are," or **vous êtes** in French. **Vous** is a subject pronoun, and **êtes** is a verb. The subject pronouns **nous, vous**, and **ils/elles** all end with an **s** that you normally wouldn't hear in sentences such as **Nous chantons** (We are singing). However, *when these subject pronouns find themselves next to verbs that begin with vowels, we always pronounce the final* ***s***. This is what is called a **liaison** (LEE-AY-ZAHN). **Liaison** is a French word we've borrowed in English. It means a connection or something that serves to connect, which makes sense since we're connecting consonants to vowels in this case.

You've just read about one of the biggest categories of **liaison**, that which links subject pronouns to verbs that begin with vowels. Here are a few additional examples of this type of **liaison**:

il<u>s</u> étudient	they study
elle<u>s</u> aiment	they like
nou<u>s</u> espérons	we hope

The other major category in which there is an obligatory liaison is between certain words and *nouns* that begin with vowels. There are three categories of words to which this applies: articles (see *FFCA* **chapitre** 7), numbers, and adjectives (see *FFCA* **chapitre** 12). Here are a few examples:

a friend = **u<u>n</u> ami** (article + noun)
two schools = **deu<u>x</u> écoles** (number + noun[4])
a little tree = **un peti<u>t</u> arbre** (adjective + noun)

There are even more rules governing **liaison** in French, but we will not go through all of them in this book.[5] You've learned the essential principles here for making sure you form a **liaison** when required; if you avoid all other **liaisons** (by not saying too much!), your pronunciation will still be perfectly acceptable. The best way to learn these **liaisons**, in any event, is to listen attentively to spoken French, such as in the audio files of the dialogues and chants for each chapter.

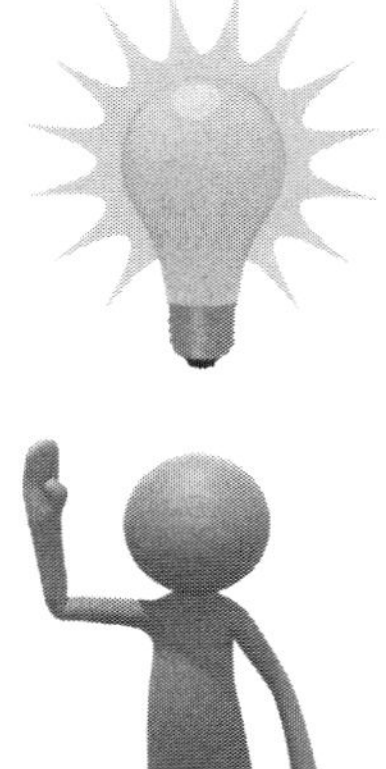

4. When the *x* is pronounced at the end of a word, before a vowel, it makes a *z* sound.
5. The rules to which we are referring govern when you can *choose* to form a liaison, not when you *must* do so.

Traduction

Of course, during Jean and Aurélie's absence from the zoo, their keepers have been searching all over for their escaped animals. Here are the two missing-animal posters that have been put up around town to help track them down. Translate Jean's poster from French to English; then translate Aurélie's poster from English to French!

Avis de Recherche!*

Il s'appelle Jean.
Il est une souris.
Il a onze ans.
Ses yeux sont bleus.
Son nez est rouge.
Ses oreilles sont petites.
Il est très intelligent et sympa.

____
____
____
____
____
____
____

Avis de Recherche!

Her name is Aurélie.
She is a cow.
She is eleven years old.
She is very funny.
Her eyes are green.
She has four big legs.
Her mouth is very big.

____
____
____
____
____
____
____

*Missing Person Notice

Say It Aloud!

The following are sentences that (we could imagine) come from Jean and Aurélie's meeting with Thibault. Fill in the blanks using the different conjugations you've learned for the verb **être**. Then, translate the sentences. Finally, say them out loud and compare your pronunciation to what you hear on the audio file [01_06/Tr. 6].

1. **Jean et Aurélie habitent dans le zoo. Le zoo ________________ dans la ville.**

   Translation: ____

   ____

2. **La maison de Thibault ________________ dans un petit village.**

   Translation: ____

   ____

3. **Ses sœurs ________________ jeunes. Elles ont cinq, sept, et neuf ans!**

   Translation: ____

   ____

4. **"Aurélie, tu ________________ intelligente!"**

   Translation: ____

   ____

5. **"Nous avons peur de voyager, alors nous ________________ contents de marcher ensemble."**

   Translation: ____

   ____

6. **Thibault a envie de marcher à la ville: "Moi aussi! Je ________________ très content de marcher à la ville avec vous. Vous ________________ très sympas."**

   Translation: ____

   ____

Grammaire

Circle the correct answer.

1. The verb **être** does not follow a normal pattern, so we call it:

   a. erratic.

   b. regular.

   c. irregular.

   d. unreliable.

2. When you say, "**Mes amis *sont* sympas,**"

   a. you cannot hear the **t**in **sont**.

   b. you cannot hear the **n** in **sont**.

   c. you cannot hear the **n** or the **t** in **sont**.

   d. you can hear all of the letters in **sont**.

3. If you saw a note lying on the ground that said, "**Merci! Je suis contente!**" the one thing you could be sure of is that:

   a. The author of the note is sad.

   b. The author of the note is a female.

   c. The author of the note is in trouble.

   d. The author of the note is mean.

4. How do you say, "I like to be at school" in French?

   a. **Il aime est à l'école.**

   b. **Je suis aimer à l'école.**

   c. **J'aime être à l'école.**

   d. **J'aime suis l'école.**

Nouveau Vocabulaire

Fill in the blank with the correct translation(s) for each word.

Français	Anglais
1. **être, je suis**	______________
2. **voyager, je voyage**	______________
3. **visiter, je visite**	______________
4. **avoir envie de, j'ai envie de**	______________
5. **un endroit**	______________
6. **une idée**	______________
7. **ensemble**	______________
8. **intelligent/bête**	______________
9. **content/triste**	______________
10. **difficile/simple**	______________

Ancien Vocabulaire

Fill in the blank with the correct translation(s) for each word.

Français	Anglais
1. **le genou**	______________
2. **regarder, je regarde**	______________
3. **la grange**	______________
4. **avoir besoin de, j'ai besoin de**	______________
5. **porter, je porte**	______________
6. **mignon**	______________

Français	Anglais
7. **méchant**	______________________
8. **l'eau**	______________________
9. **mais**	______________________
10. **un enfant**	______________________

Hide-and-Seek Conjugation

Somewhere in the following chart, there is a verb form from another verb that is trying to hide in this conjugation chart. It's playing hide-and-seek with you. Seek it out, circle it, and then add the correct conjugation for **être**. Make sure you write the translations for all the other conjugations, too (we've left space inside the chart so you can stick them right in there).

Remarque

In French, the game hide-and-seek is called **cache-cache**, which literally means "hide-hide" in English.

Person	Singular	Plural
1st Person	**je suis** ______________ (______________)	**nous sommes** ______________ (______________)
2nd Person	**tu es** ______________ (______________)	**vous avez** ______________ (______________)
3rd Person	**il/elle est** ______________ (______________)	**ils/elles sont** ______________ (______________)

Traduction: The Être Staircase

Translate the following sentences into French, and see if you can make it to the bottom of the staircase full of **être** verbs. Don't forget to make those adjectives agree with the subjects in gender and number!

I am happy. ______________________________

You are happy.______________________________

You are sad. ______________________________

He is sad. ______________________________

He is interesting. ______________________________

She is interesting. ______________________________

She is intelligent. ______________________________

We[6] are intelligent. ______________________________

We are funny. ______________________________

You[7] (**vous**) are funny. ______________________________

You are handsome. ______________________________

They are handsome. ______________________________

They are beautiful. ______________________________

6. We don't know the gender of "we" in this sentence, so let's imagine that "we" is a mix of males and females, then.
7. Again, let's assume that this is a mix of males and females.

Dictée!

Listen to the audio file [01_07/Tr. 7] of the **dictée** for this **chapitre**. On the lines provided, write down the three sentences you hear. You do not need to write translations for them, though it's good practice to think through what the English translation would be. You may stop and repeat the audio file several times as you're writing down the sentences.

1. ____

   ____

2. ____

   ____

3. ____

   ____

CHAPITRE 2 DEUX

DIALOGUE [02_01/TR. 8]

Suddenly, the miller stops dead in his tracks and cries out. The three companions soon catch up and see, approaching in the distance, the outline of a wolf walking toward them. As he nears, however, the four travelers realize that this is no ordinary predator.

THIBAULT. **Bonjour, Monsieur le Loup. Ça va?**

MONSIEUR LE LOUP. Ça va très bien, merci! Et vous, les amis? Vous allez où aujourd'hui? Vous allez aussi aux champs, peut-être?

JEAN. **Aux champs? Non . . . nous allons à la foire.**

MONSIEUR LE LOUP, *relieved.* **Aha! Ça c'est *très, très* bien.** The fields are so boring, anyway.

AURÉLIE. **Mais, monsieur? Alors, pourquoi vous allez aux champs?**

MONSIEUR LE LOUP. Moi? Euh . . . je vais aux champs pour . . . euh . . . pour le business . . . oui, c'est ça.

JEAN, *noticing the wolf's peculiar attire.* I see. **Mais j'ai une question. Pourquoi portez-vous un manteau?**

MONSIEUR LE LOUP. Ah, mon manteau . . . alors . . . ça . . .

THIBAULT. **Oui, Monsieur le Loup . . . et vous portez aussi un chapeau? Les loups portent des chapeaux?**

MONSIEUR LE LOUP. Mon chapeau? Alors, c'est pour . . . euh . . .

THIBAULT. And it looks like there's something written on your hat, too—**"Je suis Guillaume, le berger des moutons." Monsieur? Vous êtes berger?**

MONSIEUR LE LOUP. Oui . . . euh . . . oui! Et bien sûr, je m'appelle . . . Gérald—non—Guillaume! Je vais aux champs pour regarder mes moutons.

AURÉLIE. **Oh, il est très intéressant, le loup. J'ai envie d'aller avec Guillaume!**

MONSIEUR LE LOUP. Avec qui? Ah, non, non, non! C'est une mauvaise idée . . . besides, **tu vas à la foire**; I don't want to make you late . . . **vas-y, vas-y**!

JEAN, *growing more and more suspicious.* **Alors, Guillaume. Vous aimez être berger?**

MONSIEUR LE LOUP. Moi? Ah oui. [*smiles*] **J'aime les moutons. Ils sont filets mignons—mmm ahem—**[*coughs*] **excusez-moi—*très* mignons . . .**

Chant [02_02/Tr. 9]

Aller (to go)

Person	Singular	Plural
1st Person	**je vais** (I go)	**nous allons** (we go)
2nd Person	**tu vas** (you go)	**vous allez** (you go)
3rd Person	**il/elle va** (he/she/it goes)	**ils/elles vont** (they go)

Vocabulaire [02_03/Tr. 10]

Français	Anglais
aller, je vais	to go, I go
un manteau	a coat
un chapeau	a hat
une chemise	a shirt
un pantalon	pants
une chaussure/ chaussette	a shoe, a sock
un mouton	a sheep
un berger	a shepherd
une foire	a fair
un loup	a wolf
porter, je porte	to wear, I wear (Note: You've already learned that the verb **porter** means "to carry." It can also mean "to wear" as in "to wear clothing.")

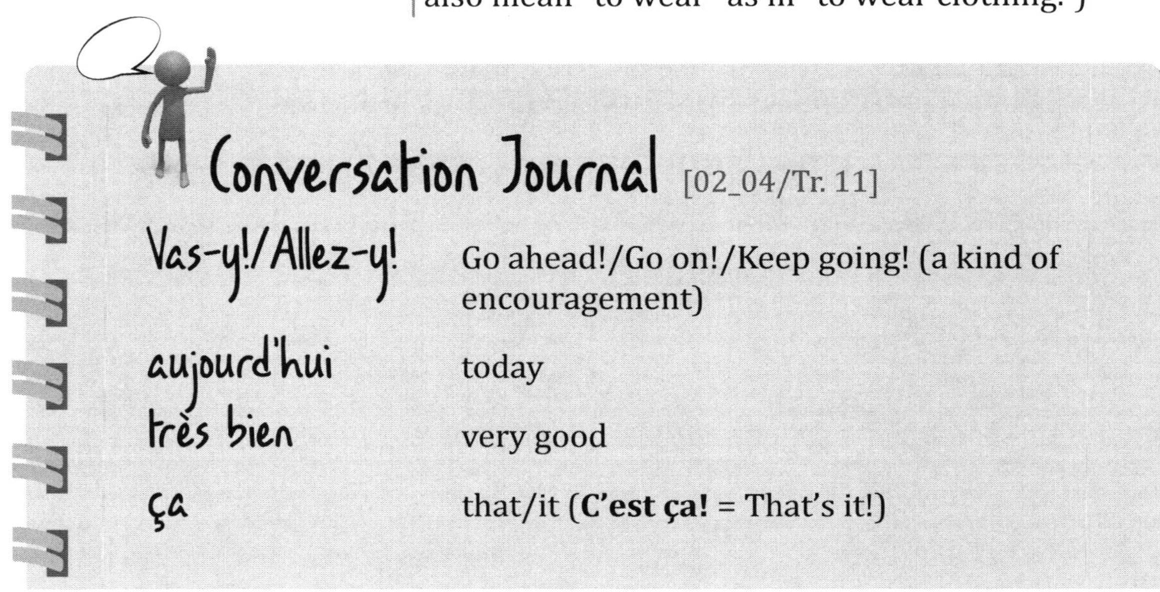

Irregular Verbs, Part 3: Aller

Encore (again)! Another irregular verb? That's right. In this **chapitre** we attack the verb **aller**, which means "to go." Looking at this **chapitre**'s chant, you might recognize at least one of the conjugations already. Do you remember the expression **allons-y** (see the *FFCA* **chapitre** 2 Conversation Journal), which means "let's go"? Now you can see the connection between **aller**, the verb that means "to go," and **allons-y**. In fact, in this **chapitre**'s Conversation Journal we add another couple of expressions with the verb **aller** to our collection: **Vas-y!** *or* **Allez-y!** As the Conversation Journal shows, this expression is a kind of encouragement meaning "Go ahead!" or "Go on!" **Vas-y** is just the *informal* form, and **allez-y** is the *formal* form (or *plural*, if you're talking to a group of people). Here again are the conjugations of **aller**, which you saw in the chant. Notice, as with other irregular verbs we've seen, that you can't guess what the conjugations would be just by looking at the infinitive, **aller**:

Renvoi

If you can't quite remember what *formal* and *informal* mean, check *FFCA* **chapitre** 5.

Renvoi

Allons-y is found in the Conversation Journal of *FFCA* **chapitre** 2.

Aller (to go)

Person	Singular	Plural
1st Person	**je vais** (I go)	**nous allons** (we go)
2nd Person	**tu vas** (you go)	**vous allez** (you go)
3rd Person	**il/elle va** (he/she/it goes)	**ils/elles vont** (they go)

The Acrobatic À

The verb **aller** is often accompanied by another little word that you already know: the word **à**, which can mean "to" or "at." That's logical enough, right? If you're going, you're usually going *to* a place—we don't just say, "I'm going the supermarket," or "I'm going my friend's house." It's better to say, "I'm going *to* the supermarket," or "I'm going *to* my friend's house." Well, it's the same in French:

Je vais *à* la plage.	I'm going *to* the beach.
Je vais *à* la maison.	I'm going *to* the house.
Je vais *à* la forêt.	I'm going *to* the forest.

Hmmm . . . that wasn't so bad. I guess we're finished, and we can move right on to the Worksheet section—enough with all of this grammar. **Allons-y!** But wait! Hold on just one minute here. Something smells fishy. All of those places look like *feminine* nouns: ***la* plage**, ***la* maison**, ***la* forêt**. What's going to happen when we try some sentences with *masculine* nouns, such as ***le* zoo**, ***le* lac**, or ***le* village**? Will everything stay the same? If we keep the word **à** in the same place, won't the sentence be—

Je vais *au* zoo.	I'm going to the zoo.
Je vais *au* lac.	I'm going to the lake.
Je vais *au* village.	I'm going to the village.

Oh là là! What just happened? Where did the word **le** go?

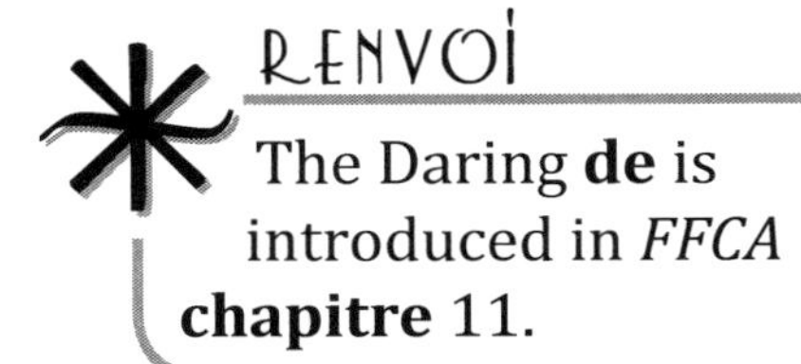
RENVOI

The Daring **de** is introduced in *FFCA* **chapitre** 11.

What we just experienced might remind you of another explosion that occurred in *FFCA*—that of the Daring **de**, which combined with different articles such as **le** and **les** to produce new words. In this chapter, we meet a distant cousin of the Daring **de**—another fairly exciting word, the Acrobatic **à**. When the word **à** jumps onto the word **le** in a sentence, we get the combination **au**. Every time. Do you want to see another example, then? Imagine we're at a friend's party, and someone asks us what we're doing:

Je parle au garçon. I'm talking to the boy.

Now, if we'd been talking to his sister, who was standing next to him, we would have just said:

Je parle à la fille. I'm talking to the girl.

There's nothing strange about that second sentence. In the first sentence, however, the Acrobatic **à** grabbed hold of the **le** in **le garçon**, and the resulting combination was **au garçon**.

The Acrobatic **à** has one more trick up its sleeve, too. It also leaps onto the plural article **les**. Watch what happens in these sentences:

Il visite les villages dans la forêt.	He's visiting the villages in the forest.
Il va aux villages dans la forêt.	He's going to the villages in the forest.

In the first sentence, you still see the word **les** because he is not visiting *to* the villages of the forest—he is visiting the villages *in* the forest. However, in the second sentence, he is going *to* the villages in the forest. **Il va (à + les) aux villages de la forêt.**

A quick chart to summarize the movements of the Acrobatic **à** will come in handy here:

Combination	Result	Examples
à + la	**à la**	**Nous allons à la maison.**
à + le	**au**	**Ils parlent au garçon.**
à + les	**aux**	**Les moutons vont aux champs.**

ATTENTION

You do not have to worry about the articles **un**, **une**, or **des**. Nothing special happens when **à** meets these articles. They remain the same: **Je parle à un oiseau. Je parle à une vache. Je parle à des animaux.**

We should also note that nothing in particular happens when the Acrobatic **à** meets an *indefinite* article such as **un**, **une**, or **des**:

Nous allons à une plage près d'ici. We're going to a beach near here.

Les animaux vont à un zoo dans la ville. The animals are going to a zoo in the city.

RENVOI

Do you remember definite and indefinite articles? If you need a little reminder about them, check out **chapitre** 8 of *FFCA*.

Both **à** and **de** are part of a group of words that we call *prepositions. A preposition is a little word that shows the relationship between other words in a sentence, such as a noun, by giving us information about its position, direction, or other properties.* An example of a preposition in English is the word "to," as in "to the forest." We could then attach that to a sentence like this: "The cow walks to the forest."

We've already seen a number of prepositions in *FFCA*:

à (to, at)	**devant** (in front of)
à côté (de) (next [to])	**loin (de)** (far [from])
avec (with)	**pour** (for)
dans (in)	**près (de)** (near [to], close [to])
de (of, from)	**sur** (on, on top of)
derrière (behind)	**vers** (toward)

Chant

Remplir (fill in) **le tableau** (the chart/table).

Person	Singular	Plural
1st Person	**je vais** (I go)	______ (we go)
2nd Person	______ (you go)	______ (you go)
3rd Person	______ (he/she/it goes)	______ (they go)
—	______ (Go on! Keep going!)	______ (Go on! Keep going!)

In the following sentences, fill in the blanks with the correct forms of the verb **aller** (to go). Remember, you can use the infinitive form **aller**, too! An example is provided below.

Exemple: L'oiseau et le renard vont à la montagne.

Remarque

In *FFCA*, present-tense verb phrases such as **vont à la montagne** were translated as "go to the mountain" *or* "are going to the mountain." The examples and answer key reflected both possibilities. In *FFCB*, we will no longer provide both translations since we'll be introducing even more expressions that could be translated multiple ways. It would be too complicated, for instance, to list four different possible translations for a sentence that combined a present-tense verb and another one of these expressions! However, you can rest assured that both translations are still appropriate unless it is clearly a situation in which one translation seems more natural than the other. The key is simply to know in the back of your mind when you'd use one translation and when you'd use the other.

1. **Le loup ______ aux champs.**
2. **Jean et Aurélie ______ à la ville.**
3. **Le meunier (the miller) ______ à la foire.**

4. **Le loup parle: "Tu ______________________ aux champs?"**

5. **Le meunier parle: "Non, je ______________________ à la foire."**

6. **Jean et Aurélie parlent: "Nous ______________________ à la ville."**

7. **Le loup parle à Jean et Aurélie: "Ah, vous ______________________ à la ville! Très bien!"**

8. **Thibault parle à Jean et Aurélie: "J'ai envie d' ______________________ avec vous!"**

9. **Finalement (finally), Thibault ______________________ à la ville avec Jean et Aurélie.**

Say It Aloud! The Acrobatic À

Remplir (Fill in) **les trous** (the holes) in the following sentences by circling the correct kind of Acrobatic **à**—that is: **à**, **à la**, **au**, or **aux**. (Hint: We've given you the gender of the noun—either masculine [m.] or feminine [f.]—that follows the preposition in each sentence. Sometimes you'll need it, sometimes you won't!) Once you've chosen the correct Acrobatic **à**, translate the sentences into English. Finally, go back and pronounce the complete sentence in French, comparing your pronunciation to what you hear on the audio file (02_05/Tr. 12).

1. **J'aime les endroits intéressants. J'aime aller __________ endroits (m.) intéressants.**
   [à / à la / au / aux]

   Translation: ____

2. **Vous allez __________ zoo (m.)?**
   [à / à la / au / aux]

   Translation: ____

3. **Je suis berger. Je vais __________ champs (m.)!**
   [à / à la / au / aux]

   Translation: ____

4. **Ma sœur est paresseuse. Elle reste __________ maison (f.).**
   [à / à la / au / aux]

   Translation: ____

5. **Tu parles __________ enfants (m.) méchants?**
   [à / à la / au / aux]

   Translation: ______________________________

6. **Mon frère va __________ une grande école (f.).**
   [à / à la / au / aux]

   Translation: ______________________________

7. **Tu restes __________ maison (f.) aujourd'hui?**
   [à / à la / au / aux]

   Translation: ______________________________

Grammaire

Circle the correct answer.

1. The words **à**, **de**, and **dans** are examples of a kind of word called a ___________.

   a. preposition

   b. conjunction

   c. article

   d. adverb

2. If you heard just the two words **au** and **aux** read aloud one after the other, the difference in pronunciation:

   a. would be like the difference between "oh" and "oaks."

   b. would be fairly small.

   c. does not exist.

   d. would be similar to the difference between "aw" and "ox."

3. Which two words will you *never* see next to each other in French?

   a. **aller** and **à**

   b. **aller** and **aux**

   c. **à** and **la**

   d. **à** and **le**

Nouveau Vocabulaire

Fill in the blank with the correct translation(s) for each word.

Français	Anglais
1. **aller, je vais**	______________
2. **un manteau**	______________
3. **un chapeau**	______________
4. **une chemise**	______________
5. **un pantalon**	______________
6. **une chaussure/chaussette**	______________
7. **un mouton**	______________
8. **un berger**	______________
9. **une foire**	______________
10. **un loup**	______________
11. **porter, je porte**	______________

Ancien Vocabulaire, Special Edition—Prepositions

Fill in the blank with the correct translation(s) for each word. No peeking at the list in this **chapitre**!

Français	Anglais
1. **à**	______________
2. **à côté de**	______________
3. **avec**	______________
4. **dans**	______________

Français	Anglais
5. **de**	______________________
6. **loin (de)**	______________________
7. **pour**	______________________
8. **près (de)**	______________________
9. **sur**	______________________
10. **vers**	______________________

Prepositional Family Reunion!

In the following sentences, the Daring **de** joins forces with its distant cousin, the Acrobatic **à** to form fantastic new **phrases**.[4] Isn't it handy to be able to say where people come from and where they are going to? Just as in the Worksheet section, the goal of this exercise is for you to pick the correct preposition from the choices below each blank and circle it. Check *FFCA* **chapitre** 11 if you run into trouble with the preposition **de**. Once you've chosen the correct preposition, translate the **phrases** into English.

1. **Les animaux vont ______________ grange (f.) ______________ forêt (f.).**
   de / de la / du / des **à / à la / au / aux**

   Translation: ____

2. **Ma famille marche ______________ village (m.) ______________ montagne (f.).**
   de / de la / du / des **à / à la / au / aux**

   Translation: ____

3. **Les oiseaux volent ______________ arbres (m.) ______________ champs (m.).**
   d'un / d'une / des **à / à la / au / aux**

   Translation: ____

4. **Une phrase** means "a sentence." As you say the word in the plural, though, don't forget that we drop the final **s** on **phrases**—*FRAHZ*." When you want to say the English word "phrase" in French, you'd say **une expression**. And then, to say "an expression," such as an idiom, or something like that, you . . . Hey! What are you doing still reading this footnote!? Go back to the Quiz!

4. **Notre chien va ________________ maison (f.) ________________ école (f.) pour**
   de / de la / du / des **à / à l' / au / aux**

   chercher notre petite sœur.

   Translation: ____

5. **Ils voyagent ________________ petit village (m.) ________________ grande ville (f).**
   d'un / d'une / des **à / à la / au / aux**

   Translation: ____

Où Vont-Ils? (Where Are They Going?)

Complétez les phrases (complete the sentences) **avec un sujet** (with a subject), unless there already is one (as in sentences 3 and 5), **et le verbe aller** (and the verb **aller**) in the appropriate form. You do not need to write out the full translation into English. **Voir l'exemple** (see the example):

Exemple: Oh no! I forgot my library book in our classroom. I need it for this weekend. Stay here. **Je vais à l'école!**

1. We've got our suntan lotion, snorkels, towels, and snacks—we're ready.

   ________________ ________________ **à la plage.**

2. How many of you have subway tickets? How about a map of downtown?

   Are you at least planning to visit some cool museums? No? That's too bad!

   ________________ ________________ **à la ville!** It doesn't happen that often!

3. **Fred** ________________ **à la maison**—he's had enough of work!

4. What's with all of your camping gear? Oh! I see. ________________

   ________________ **à la montagne.**

5. **Aujourd'hui Alexandre** ________________ **à l'école.** It's his first time, so he's very nervous!

6. ________________ ________________ **à la foire avec son âne sur sa tête?**

   Il est fou (crazy)**!**

Dictée!

Listen to the audio file [02_06/Tr. 13] of the **dictée** for this **chapitre**. On the lines provided, write down the three sentences you hear. You do not need to write translations for them, though it's good practice to think through what the English translation would be. You may stop and repeat the audio file several times as you're writing down the sentences.

1. ______________________________

   ____

2. ______________________________

   ____

3. ______________________________

   ____

CHAPITRE 3 TROIS

DIALOGUE [03_01/TR. 14]

JEAN, *who has had enough of the wolf's story.* **Monsieur le Loup, excusez-moi, mais nous ne sommes pas bêtes. Vous n'êtes pas berger.**

MONSIEUR LE LOUP, *laughing nervously.* **Bien sûr, vous n'êtes pas bêtes, ou stupides** . . . but you really don't think that I'm a shepherd? **Ha ha . . . alors, pourquoi pensez-vous que je ne suis pas berger?**

LE MEUNIER. Well, your appearance, for one. **Vous n'avez pas l'air d'un berger.**

MONSIEUR LE LOUP. I don't seem like a shepherd? **Aha . . . ben, c'est normal . . . puisque je suis nouveau. . . .**

THIBAULT. Hmm . . . I'm not sure I believe that one, either. **En plus, vous ne marchez pas comme un berger. Ce n'est pas leur manière de marcher à quatre pattes.**

MONSIEUR LE LOUP. Vraiment . . . euh . . .

JEAN. **Vous ne portez pas des vêtements de berger. Votre manteau, c'est un grand sac! Où est votre pantalon? Où sont vos chaussures?**

MONSIEUR LE LOUP. Well, I mean, I have them, they're just back in my—

AURÉLIE, *realizing what's happening.* **Oh là là! Vous ne parlez pas comme un berger! Pas du tout!**

MONSIEUR LE LOUP. Je ne parle pas comme un berger? Comment? How do you know that?

AURÉLIE. **Puisque votre manière de parler n'est pas gentille.**

MONSIEUR LE LOUP, *backing away slowly.* Well, friends, you'll have to excuse me. I really must be going. **Mes moutons sont délicieux—**ahem!**—un peu vieux, et ils ont besoin de moi pour trouver la grange. . . .**

JEAN. **Bien sûr.** Be off! But don't think that your costume is going to fool any sheep—let alone a real shepherd and his dogs. Besides, **les bergers n'ont pas de queue!**

MONSIEUR LE LOUP, *shouts as he is running away.* We'll see! **J'espère que les moutons ne sont pas intelligents comme vous!**

ATTENTION

Behold another word in the BAGS club (see *FFCA* **chapitre** 14): **Gentil** means "nice," which fits perfectly into our category "goodness." That means that **gentil** (which turns to **gentille** in the feminine) will come *before* the noun it describes.

CHANT [03_02/TR. 15]

Je ne mange pas de fromage. (I don't eat cheese.)

A lost poem from the miller's wife from her childhood (before imported cheese) . . .

Je ne mange pas de fromage.
Il n'est pas bon dans mon village.
Puisque je n'aime pas marcher loin,
Je reste ici, et mange le pain.

VOCABULAIRE [03_03/TR. 16]

Français	Anglais
avoir l'air (de), j'ai l'air (de)	to seem (like), I seem (like)
commencer, je commence	to begin/to start, I begin/I start
des vêtements	clothes
un sac	a bag
une patte	a paw, hoof, foot
une queue	a tail
une manière	a way, a manner
le pain	bread
ce	this, that[1]
comme	like (ex., "He looks *like* you.")

Conversation Journal [03_04/Tr. 17]

puisque	since (ex., "We're tired *since* we didn't sleep last night.")
pas du tout	not at all

1. In fact, **ce** is the word that begins the expression **C'est . . .** (**c'est** = **ce** + **est**), meaning "This is . . . " or "That is . . . "— or even "It is. . . ."

Negation

So far we've learned quite a few verbs in this book. We know how to say everything from "I sing" (**je chante**) to "you're swimming" (**tu nages**) to "they're mean" (**elles sont méchantes**). But what about saying, "I *don't* sing" or "you're *not* swimming" or "they're *not* mean"? In short, what we're asking is: How can we take a sentence and make it *negative*?

Now, when we call a sentence "negative," we don't mean that the sentence is mean-spirited or nasty. In speaking of a "negative" sentence, we simply mean that it includes a negative marker, such as the word "not." In English, different negative markers include words such as "not," "never," and "none." In the case of "not," the negative marker simply reverses the meaning of the same sentence without the marker. For instance, "You're swimming" and "You're not swimming" have opposite meanings; "They're mean" and "They're not mean" are opposites, too.

So how do we do this in French? Well, we'll let you be the judge of that. Consider the following sentences: What happens in a negative expression?

Positive Sentence	Negative Sentence
Je chante. (I sing.)	**Je ne chante pas.** (I do not sing.)
Tu nages. (You are swimming.)	**Tu ne nages pas.** (You are not swimming.)
Elles sont méchantes. (They are mean.)	**Elles ne sont pas méchantes.** (They are not mean.)

Hmmm . . . clearly we've added some words in the negative sentences. Which ones? We added these two: **ne** and **pas**. And **voilà**! That's how we make a negative sentence in French.

Now, this might seem odd. After all, French seems to take two words just to communicate one idea. In English, it's simpler—one idea, one word: "You are swimming" or "You are *not* swimming." So which word, you might ask, means "not" in French, then—**Ne** or **pas**? Well, the answer is really "both"—these words function as a pair. It turns out that *the negative words* ***ne*** *and* ***pas*** *form a sandwich around the verb*. Once you've surrounded the verb of a sentence with **ne** and **pas**, you've made it negative. Think of the words **ne** and **pas** like the two lenses in a pair of glasses. You need *both* lenses in order to see clearly, just as you need both **ne** and **pas** to understand clearly that the verb is negative:

I do not sing.

Sometimes **ne** changes to **n'**, as when the verb begins with a vowel sound. The following are some examples. Remember that sentences with an asterisk (*) are *incorrect*, and you will never hear them in French.

***Je ne aime pas les serpents.** → **Je *n'aime* pas les serpents.**
I do not like snakes.
***Vous ne avez pas peur des loups?** → **Vous *n'avez* pas peur des loups?**
You are not afraid of wolves?
***Ils ne habitent pas dans la maison.** → **Ils *n'habitent* pas dans la maison.**
They do not live in the house.[2]

Now, when you look back at the poem from the miller's wife in this **chapitre**'s chant, you should be able to spot what's happening each time there is a negative action.

REMARQUE

Actually, if you dig a bit deeper into the history of French, you'll see that the word **pas** is *not* originally part of negative sentences. This word actually means "a step" (as in "A journey of a thousand miles begins with a single *step*"). It is what you might call a "small quantity" word. Other small quantity words, such as "a point" (**point**) or "a drop" (**goutte**) also came to be included in negative expressions in French, though far less frequently than **pas**. In English, we have something similar in expressions such as, "I don't sing one *bit*" or "She doesn't speak a *lick* of Spanish." In French, though, the word **pas** is not optional like small quantity words are in English. Also, in English, using these small quantity words adds extra meaning ("She doesn't speak a lick of Spanish" is a bit stronger than simply saying "She doesn't speak Spanish"). In French, using **pas** is just the normal way to make a sentence negative—no extra strength or other meaning is added.

2. The last sentence contains the verb **habiter**, which does not look like it should create any funny business with an apostrophe since it begins with a consonant (**h**). Ah! But we said that when there is even a vowel *sound*, that the **e** from **ne** would be squeezed out—and **habiter** certainly does begin with a vowel sound, since the **h** is silent.

One last rule to remember with **ne** and **pas** is that you will almost never hear the *indefinite articles* **un**, **une**, or **des** *just* after a negative verb.[3] So, if you have a sentence such as **J'ai une voiture** (I have a car), which you want to make negative, you can kiss the word **une** good-bye! ***Un**, **une**, and **des** are replaced by the word **de** in a negative sentence.* Take a look at the following examples of The Disappearing Articles **Un** and **Une**:

> **RENVOI**
> To refresh your memory on definite and indefinite articles, go back to *FFCA* **chapitre** 8.

J'ai une voiture. I have a car.	POOF!	**Je n'ai pas de voiture.** I do not have a car.
Il regarde un oiseau. He's looking at a bird.	POOF!	**Il ne regarde pas d'oiseau.** He's not looking at a bird.
Nous avons une grange. We have a barn.	POOF!	**Nous n'avons pas de grange.** We do not have a barn.
Vous avez des frères. You have brothers.	POOF!	**Vous n'avez pas de frères.** You do not have brothers.

The Curious Haves, Part 5

As Jean, Aurélie, Thibault, and his father, the miller, speak to the shepherd, they realize more and more that he doesn't look, talk, or act quite like a shepherd does. In short, he doesn't *seem* like a shepherd (which is, of course, understandable, given who he really is). How does the miller put it? He says, "**Vous n'avez pas l'air d'un berger**" ("You don't *have the air of* a shepherd"). **Voilà**, another case of the verb **avoir** (to have) being used in a most curious way in French—for the expression "to seem." So, then, whether it's to seem like some thing (a shepherd, a rock star, a good idea, or a pepperoni pizza) or to seem some way (dangerous, amazing, funny, or difficult), for both of these expressions we use **avoir l'air (de)** in French:

Il a l'air d'un gentil garcon.	He seems like a nice boy.
Tu n'as pas l'air méchant.	You don't seem mean.
Tu as l'air sympa.	You seem nice.
Ton chien a l'air d'un loup!	Your dog seems like a wolf!

3. Really, when we say "*just* after the verb," we mean if the word **un**, **une**, and **des** is part of the *object* of the verb. The object of a verb is simply the thing or person that is receiving the action of the verb: "My sister broke (← verb) an expensive sculpture (← object) yesterday," or "Who stole (← verb) my pet giraffe (← object)!?" You'll notice in the exercises that sometimes you do see **un**, **une**, or **des** appear in negative sentences, just not as part of the object of the verb.

Say It Aloud!

There are three things that you need to do to each of the following sentences:

1. Make the sentence *negative*. (Of course, the rule you just learned for **pas de** will not apply everywhere; it is used only when there is **un**, **une**, or **des** right after the verb.)
2. Translate the *negative* sentence into English.
3. Go back and pronounce the *negative* French sentence you created in step one, comparing your pronunciation to the audio file (03_05/Tr. 18). An example is provided below.

Exemple: **Nous commençons un jeu.**

Negative: Nous ne commençons pas de jeu.

Translation: We are not starting a game.

RAPPEL

In this example, the word **un** was changed to **de** because the sentence is *negative*.

1. **Nous portons des vêtements intéressants.**

   Negative: ______________________

   Translation: ______________________

2. **Notre chat mange notre pain!**

   Negative: ______________________

   Translation: ______________________

3. **Je porte mon fromage dans un sac.**

   Negative: ______________________

   Translation: ______________________

4. **Tu chantes comme un oiseau.**

   Negative: ______________________

   Translation: ______________________

5. **Elle nage comme un poisson.**

   Negative: ______________________________

   Translation: ______________________________

6. **Ils ont l'air gentil.**

   Negative: ______________________________

   Translation: ______________________________

7. **Vous travaillez beaucoup.**

   Negative: ______________________________

   Translation: ______________________________

Negative Mess

Put the words in the following sentences back in the correct order before you translate them into English.

1. **loup Le ville ne va à la pas.**

   Correct Order: ______________________________

   Translation: ______________________________

2. **pantalon Le n' pas a de loup.**

   Correct Order: ______________________________

   Translation: ______________________________

3. **l'air Le n' gentil pas loup a très.**

   Correct Order: ______________________________

   Translation: ______________________________

4. **champs Aurélie pas ne va aux.**

   Correct Order: ______________________________

   Translation: ______________________________

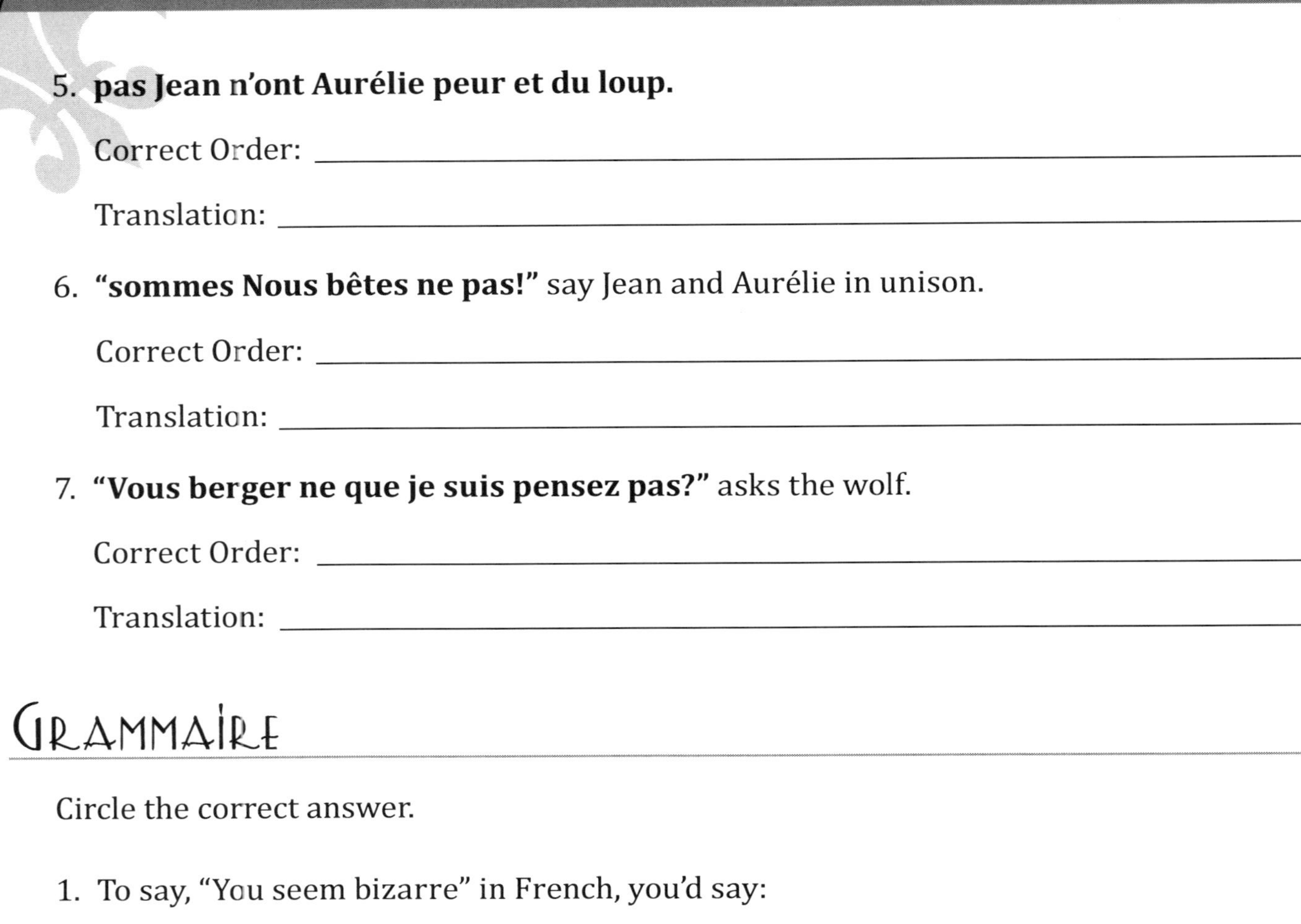

5. **pas Jean n'ont Aurélie peur et du loup.**

   Correct Order: ______________________________

   Translation: ______________________________

6. **"sommes Nous bêtes ne pas!"** say Jean and Aurélie in unison.

   Correct Order: ______________________________

   Translation: ______________________________

7. **"Vous berger ne que je suis pensez pas?"** asks the wolf.

   Correct Order: ______________________________

   Translation: ______________________________

Grammaire

Circle the correct answer.

1. To say, "You seem bizarre" in French, you'd say:

   a. **"Tu as air bizarre."**

   b. **"Tu as un air bizarre."**

   c. **"Tu as l'air bizarre."**

   d. **"Tu es l'air bizarre."**

2. If a French person asked you to join him for an appetizer of **escargots** (**un escargot** = a snail; pronounced *ES-KAR-GO*), you would probably say:

   a. **"Je ne pas manger des escargots."**

   b. **"Je ne mange des escargots."**

   c. **"Je mange ne des escargots."**

   d. **"Je ne mange pas d'escargots."**

   (Then again, you might say yes if you were adventurous . . . they're great with butter!)

3. If your neighbors insisted they had found your dog, but your family only owned cats, you could protest:

   a. "**Nous n'avons pas de chien!**"

   b. "**Nous ne avons pas de chien!**"

   c. "**Nous navons pas de chien!**"

   d. "**Notre chien ne voyage pas!**"

4. The wolf in our tale is not wearing a real coat, like a shepherd would, of course; he is wearing something more like a big old bag. How could we say, "He's not wearing a coat"?

   a. "**Il ne porte pas un manteau.**"

   b. "**Il ne porte pas de manteau.**"

   c. "**Il ne porte pas manteau.**"

   d. "**Il ne porte pas les manteaux.**"

Nouveau Vocabulaire

Fill in the blank with the correct translation(s) for each word.

Français	Anglais
1. **avoir l'air (de), j'ai l'air (de)**	________________
2. **commencer, je commence**	________________
3. **des vêtements**	________________
4. **un sac**	________________
5. **une patte**	________________
6. **une queue**	________________
7. **une manière**	________________
8. **le pain**	________________
9. **ce**	________________
10. **comme**	________________

Ancien Vocabulaire

Fill in the blank with the correct translation(s) for each word.

Français	Anglais
1. **qui?**	________________
2. **un chapeau**	________________
3. **quoi?**	________________
4. **où?**	________________
5. **un endroit**	________________
6. **réussir, je réussis**	________________
7. **le genou**	________________

Français	Anglais
8. **pourquoi?**	____________
9. **porter, je porte***	____________
10. **comment?**	____________

*Be sure to include both meanings of this word!

Negatives, Part I

Circle the best *negative* response to the following questions. Then, translate that response.

Exemple: **Tu as envie d'aller à la plage?**

a. **Non, je ne pas ai envie d'aller à la plage.**

b. **Non, j'ai ne pas envie d'aller à la plage.**

(c.) **Non, je n'ai pas envie d'aller à la plage.**

Translation: No, I don't feel like going to the beach.

1. **Le fromage est dans le sac?**

   a. **Non, le fromage nest pas dans le sac.**

   b. **Non, le fromage est pas dans le sac.**

   c. **Non, le fromage n'est pas dans le sac.**

   Translation: ____________

2. **Ta sœur commence à l'école aujourd'hui?**

   a. **Non, ma sœur ne commence pas à l'école aujourd'hui.**

   b. **Non, ma sœur commence pas à l'école aujourd'hui.**

   c. **Non, ma sœur ne commence à l'école aujourd'hui.**

   Translation: ____________

3. **Votre chien a sept pattes!?**

   a. **Non, notre chien n'a sept pattes!**

   b. **Non, notre chien n'ont pas sept pattes!**

   c. **Non, notre chien n'a pas sept pattes!**

   Translation: ____________

4. **Le pain a l'air délicieux?**

   a. **Non, le pain ne pas a l'air délicieux.**

   b. **Non, le pain a ne pas l'air délicieux.**

   c. **Non, le pain n'a pas l'air délicieux.**

   Translation: ______________________________

Negatives, Part 2

In this last section, you no longer have the choice of three answers. You must create the answer yourself. That is, don't just rephrase the question—answer it negatively! After you write the *negative* response in French, translate it into English in the space provided.

1. **Tu aimes ma manière de chanter?**

   Negative Answer: ______________________________

   Translation: ______________________________

2. **Vous portez des nouveaux vêtements?**

   Negative Answer: ______________________________

   Translation: ______________________________

3. **Je mange comme un cochon?**

   Negative Answer: ______________________________

   Translation: ______________________________

Dictée!

Listen to the audio file [03_06/Tr. 19] of the **dictée** for this **chapitre**. On the lines provided, write down the three sentences you hear. You do not need to write translations for them, though it's good practice to think through what the English translation would be. You may stop and repeat the audio file several times as you're writing down the sentences.

1. ______________________________

2. ______________________________

3. ______________________________

CHAPITRE 4 QUATRE

DIALOGUE [04_01/TR. 20]

At the end of the first leg of their long journey, the four travelers finally reach the town hosting the market. But even as they approach, the gatekeeper at the main entrance grows increasingly suspicious. He doesn't like the look of our four voyagers, and he has no shortage of questions for them upon their arrival. . . .

LE GARDIEN, *motions to the travelers to come off the road next to his watchtower; a huge, growling dog stands at his side.* Over here, **s'il vous plaît!**

AURÉLIE, *whispers to Jean.* **Oh là là, il a l'air méchant.**

JEAN, *whispering back.* **Je suis d'accord!**

LE GARDIEN. Quoi!? Est-ce que tu parles de moi?

JEAN. **Non, monsieur.**

LE GARDIEN. J'espère que non.

JEAN. **Elle . . . elle . . . parle de votre chien. Elle pense qu'il est mignon.**

LE GARDIEN. Bruno!? Mignon!? Hmph . . . , *forgetting his job for a moment,* **Je ne pense pas, mais peut-être. Il a des beaux yeux. Et ses pattes . . . elles sont mignonnes . . . Hum hum!** *remembering his duty,* **Où est-ce que vous allez?**

LE MEUNIER. Ben, nous allons au marché, monsieur.

LE GARDIEN. Et pourquoi est-ce que vous allez à notre marché?

LE MEUNIER. Parce que nous avons envie d'acheter des choses ici. S'il vous plaît, Monsieur, quand est-ce que le marché termine aujourd'hui?

LE GARDIEN. Hmmm . . . bientôt! Mais, vous avez l'intention d'acheter quoi ici? Des chevaux? Des vaches? Nous n'avons pas beaucoup de chevaux et de vaches!

THIBAULT. **Non, non. Nous avons besoin d'acheter des fruits et des légumes, c'est tout.**

LE GARDIEN, *turning his attention back to* ***le meunier***. **Et vous, monsieur. Pourquoi est-ce que vous portez votre âne sur la tête?**

LE MEUNIER, *who has been getting tired of so many questions, especially the last one, replies.* **Encore une question! C'est assez! Oui, je porte mon âne sur la tête. Est-ce que c'est un problème!? Et vous, pourquoi est-ce que vous ne portez pas votre chien sur la tête? Combien de questions est-ce que vous avez? Nous sommes fatigués! Nous avons faim! Nous avons envie d'entrer!**

LE GARDIEN, *surprised*. **Bon, euh, je suis désolé. Entrez, entrez!**

Chant [04_02/Tr. 21]

Est-ce que tu chantes? (Do you sing?)

Est-ce que tu chantes? *Oui, beaucoup.* (Do you sing? *Yes, a lot.*)

Et tu chantes quoi? *Je chante le blues.* (And what do you sing? *I sing the blues.*)

Pourquoi est-ce que tu chantes? *Je ne suis pas content!* (Why do you sing? *I'm not happy!*)

Quand est-ce que tu chantes? *Maintenant!* (When are you singing? *Now!*)

Ah . . . au revoir, alors! (Ah . . . good-bye, then!)

Vocabulaire [04_03/Tr. 22]

Français	Anglais
acheter, j'achète	to buy, I buy
entrer, j'entre	to enter, I enter
être d'accord, je suis d'accord	to agree, I agree
terminer, je termine	to terminate/finish, I terminate/finish
le marché	the market
un fruit	a fruit
un légume	a vegetable
une chose	a thing
fatigué	tired
encore	again, more

Asking Questions with Est-ce Que

In this **chapitre**, you should let your curiosity run wild. Why? How? What are we talking about? Exactly! If you're *asking* such things, you're ready to begin working, since this **chapitre** is all about *questions*. In this Grammar section, you will learn how to ask questions in French using three important ingredients. The first ingredient is the expression **est-ce que**. **Est-ce que** is used at the beginning of a sentence when you need to ask a question to which the response will be "yes" or "no." For example:

***Est-ce que* votre frère est à la maison?**	Is your brother home?
***Est-ce que* vous aimez voyager?**	Do you like traveling?

The word **que** (in **est-ce que**) becomes **qu'** when the word that follows it begins with a vowel, as we've seen before with words such as **le** or **de**:

Est-ce *qu'ils* aiment les oiseaux?	Do they like birds?
Est-ce *qu'elle* habite dans la forêt?	Does she live in the forest?

Attention

Est-ce que is pronounced, approximately, *ESS-KUH*, with no **t** in the middle. Listen to the audio file for the Worksheet exercise Ask It Aloud! The Guardian's Checklist (04_05/Tr. 24) to hear this word in action.

Asking Questions with Question Words, Part I

The second possible ingredient in asking questions is the different *question words* that French uses:

Question Word	Translation	Book & Chapitre
comment?[1]	how?	*FFCA* 3
combien?	how many? *or* how much?	*FFCA* 9
qui?	who?	*FFCA* 13
quoi?	what?	*FFCA* 13
pourquoi?	why?	*FFCA* 15
où?	where?	*FFCB* 1
quand?	when?	*FFCB* 4

1. Remember, you learned in *FFCA* that this word can mean "how" as in the question, "How do you know?" but it can also mean, "Excuse me?"—a question one asks when one does not understand something.

If this list seems like **déjà vu** (something you've already [**déjà**] seen [**vu**]), that's because it mostly is! We've listed the words in order of their appearance in *FFCA* and this book. We'd encourage you to take a short break from this **chapitre** to refresh your memory by flipping back through the various chapters to see these words used in context.

Using these six question words is not much more complicated than the yes or no questions you saw earlier in this **chapitre**. We will explore the general rule now, though there are some exceptions—especially for the words "who" (**qui?**) and "what" (**quoi?**)—that you will see in Asking Questions with Question Words, Part 2 in **chapitre** 6. For now, what you really need to learn is the following structure for questions:

the question word + **est-ce que** + a normal sentence . . . ?

For example:

Quand est-ce que tu manges?	When do you eat?
Comment est-ce que vous allez à la ville?	How are you going to the city?

For **combien?** we have to add **de**:

Combien *de* frères et *de* sœurs est-ce que tu as?	How many brothers and sisters do you have?
Combien *de* villes est-ce que vous visitez?	How many cities are you visiting?
Où est-ce qu'ils habitent?	Where do they live?

Try your hand at it! How would you say, "Where does he live?" The answer is at the bottom of the page.[2]

____?

Question word + **est-ce que** *OR* **est-ce qu'** + normal sentence . . . ?

Great! Before moving on to our third and final ingredient in asking questions, let's do a quick review. So far you have learned that:

1. You can ask a yes or no question by using the expression **est-ce que** at the beginning like this:

   Est-ce que Jean parle à Aurélie? Is Jean speaking to Aurélie?

2. **Où + est-ce qu' +** [normal sentence] **il habite?**
   Où est-ce qu'il habite? [Question word]

2. You can ask a question for other kinds of information with a question word, such as "who," "what," "when," "where," "why," or "how" by sticking the question word just before **est-ce que**, like this:

   Pourquoi est-ce que le loup porte un manteau? Why is the wolf wearing a coat?

Inversion

The final type of question leaves out the expression **est-ce que**. Instead, we'll use a different ingredient, called *inversion*. Why is it called that? It is called inversion because *instead of using* ***est-ce que****, you simply invert the subject and the verb—you reverse their order.* So, instead of asking, "**Comment est-ce que tu vas?**" (How are you doing?), you just ask, "**Comment vas-tu?**" (How are you doing?).

Other examples of inversion include:

Où sont les oiseaux?	Where are the birds?
Où est la ville?	Where is the city?
Pourquoi avez-vous peur?	Why are you afraid?

Now, when would you use this construction instead of using the **est-ce que** construction? Well, usually you can ask a question using *either* inversion *or* the regular old way with **est-ce que**. For example, with the last question above, instead of asking **Pourquoi avez-vous peur?** we might have asked **Pourquoi est-ce que vous avez peur?** In most cases, where the choice is optional, using inversion (usually!) sounds a bit more formal or fancy.[3] In fact, inversion is becoming less and less frequent in spoken French, though it remains in use in writing.

Notice we added a little hyphen between the verb and the subject pronoun; that applies to all subject pronouns (**je**, **tu**, **il**, **elle**, **nous**, **vous**, etc.).

The last thing to know about inversion is that when you use the third-person singular subject pronouns (**il** and **elle**), you may need to add more than just a little hyphen. When the verb ends with a vowel, we actually throw in the letter **t**, like this: "**Comment va-t-il?**" ("How is he?") or "**Combien a-t-elle?**" ("How many does she have?"). This is not such a crazy rule if you think about it: Inserting a **t** sound helps distinguish the verb from the pronoun when you're speaking, since otherwise you'd have to pronounce two vowels right next to each other and that might seem as though they are running together as a single word.

---

3. This is not always the case. Asking **Comment vas-tu?** (how are you?) instead of **Comment est-ce que tu vas?** does not make one sound formal; it is the normal way to ask this question, in fact. This is the case with some common expressions that use inversion. It is true, for example, of questions asking where things are, such as in the two examples on this page (**Où sont les oiseaux?** and **Où est la ville?**).

Question Words

Fill in the English equivalents of the French question words in the following chart.

Question Word	Anglais	Question Word	Anglais
comment?	____________	**pourquoi?**	____________
combien?	____________	**où?**	____________
quoi?	____________	**quand?**	____________
qui?	____________		

Question Confusion

The following are several French questions that are all mixed up. Put them back in order and translate them.

1. **lac le est Où?**

   Correct Order: ____________

   Translation: ____________

2. **français tu Est-ce que es?**

   Correct Order: ____________

   Translation: ____________

3. **Est-ce qu' fatigués sont ils?**

   Correct Order: ____________

   Translation: ____________

4. **vas Est-ce que tu au marché?**

   Correct Order: ____________

   Translation: ____________

5. **choses Combien achètes de tu est-ce que?**

   Correct Order: ____________

   Translation: ____________

6. **marché le termine est-ce que Quand?**

   Correct Order: ____________________

   Translation: ____________________

7. **est-ce que Pourquoi allez vous au marché?**

   Correct Order: ____________________

   Translation: ____________________

Ask It Aloud! The Gatekeeper's Checklist

The following is a list of questions that the **le gardien** (the gatekeeper/guard) of the village normally asks people trying to enter. Translate the questions into French. For this exercise, always use the **vous** form for "you," especially since **le gardien** doesn't normally know the people who are coming into the town. Then, go back and practice asking each French question aloud. Check your pronunciation with the audio file (04_05/Tr. 24).

1. Why are you here?

   Translation: ____________________

2. Where are you going in the village?

   Translation: ____________________

3. Are you staying here?

   Translation: ____________________

4. How many animals do you have?

   Translation: ____________________

5. How are you traveling?

   Translation: ____________________

6. Do you have friends here?

   Translation: ____________________

RAPPEL

Listen closely to the pronunciation of **est-ce que** on the audio file for this **chapitre**'s opening dialogue (04_01/Tr. 20), either by itself, or combined with a question word. The letter **t** is silent! In fact, the two words **est-ce** often end up blending together into one long sound—like saying the letter *s*.

Grammaire

1. If you hear a French speaker ask you a question beginning with "**Est-ce que . . .** " you know that she is:
   a. looking for a yes or no answer.
   b. looking for you to tell her the *reason* for something.
   c. looking for you to respond with **parce que**.
   d. looking for trouble.
2. To ask, "Why are the cats eating flowers?" you would say:
   a. "**Pourquoi les chats est-ce que mangent des fleurs?**"
   b. "**Pourquoi mangent les chats est-ce que des fleurs?**"
   c. "**Pourquoi est-ce que les chats mangent des fleurs?**"
   d. "**Est-ce que les chats mangent des fleurs?**"
3. To ask, "Why do the cats eat flowers?" you would say:
   a. "**Pourquoi les chats est-ce que mangent des fleurs?**"
   b. "**Pourquoi mangent les chats est-ce que des fleurs?**"
   c. "**Pourquoi est-ce que les chats mangent des fleurs?**"
   d. "**Est-ce que les chats mangent des fleurs?**"
4. To ask "Why is the cat eating flowers?" you would say:
   a. "**Pourquoi le chat est-ce que mange des fleurs?**"
   b. "**Pourquoi mange le chat est-ce que des fleurs?**"
   c. "**Pourquoi est-ce que le chat mange des fleurs?**"
   d. "**Est-ce que le chat mange des fleurs?**"

5. Considering your answers to questions 2, 3, and 4, it is clear that **Pourquoi est-ce que . . .** can mean:
   a. Why do . . .
   b. Why are . . .
   c. Why do . . . ? *and* Why are . . . ? *and* Why is . . . ?
   d. Why is . . .

Nouveau Vocabulaire

Fill in the blank with the correct translation for each word.

Français	Anglais
1. **acheter, j'achète**	____________
2. **entrer, j'entre**	____________
3. **être d'accord, je suis d'accord**	____________
4. **terminer, je termine**	____________
5. **le marché**	____________
6. **un fruit**	____________
7. **un légume**	____________
8. **une chose**	____________
9. **fatigué**	____________
10. **encore**	____________

Ancien Vocabulaire

Fill in the blank with the correct translation for each word.

Français	Anglais
1. **le dos**	____________
2. **avoir l'air (de), j'ai l'air (de)**	____________
3. **une chaussette**	____________
4. **une chaussure**	____________
5. **jaune**	____________
6. **vert**	____________

Français	Anglais
7. **laisser, je laisse**[4]	______________
8. **le fleuve**	______________
9. **le lac**	______________
10. **la plage**	______________

Question Pileup

Behold, a tragic situation: The sentences are all crunched together after a gigantic question pileup. See if you can separate each line into distinct words again to form a clear question. Then, translate that question into English. We've provided you with an example:

Exemple: **Pourquoiest-cequ'ilportesonânesurlatête?**
Question: **Pourquoi est-ce qu'il porte son âne sur la tête?**
Translation: **Why is he carrying his donkey on his head?**

1. **Oùestlemarché?**

 Question: ______________

 Translation: ______________

2. **Combiend'animauxavez-vous?**

 Question: ______________

 Translation: ______________

3. **Quandest-cequ'ellevaàlamaison?**

 Question: ______________

 Translation: ______________

4. You learned in *FFCA* **chapitre** 13 that **laisser** does not mean to simply leave a location—it means to leave behind an object, person, etc. In **chapitre** 9 of this book you'll learn a verb that does mean simply "to leave a location": **partir**.

4. **Pourquoiest-cequ'ilslaissentleurfromageici?**

   Question: ______________________________

   Translation: ______________________________

5. **Est-cequ'elleaimesonécole?**

   Question: ______________________________

   Translation: ______________________________

6. **Pourquoicherchez-vouslaville?**

   Question: ______________________________

   Translation: ______________________________

7. **Commentest-cequevousallezauvillage?**

   Question: ______________________________

   Translation: ______________________________

Questions about Jean et Aurélie

Use your knowledge of French questions to choose the best response to each of the following questions. Many of the choices (a, b, c, d) are *true* statements about the story of Jean and Aurélie, but only one of those choices will clearly respond to the question, so be sure to circle the correct response.

1. **Comment est-ce que Jean, Aurélie, le meunier, et Thibault vont au village?**

   a. **Ils ont une voiture.**

   b. **Ils vont aujourd'hui.**

   c. **Ils marchent.**

   d. **L'âne du meunier porte Jean, Aurélie, et Thibault sur son dos.**

2. **Pourquoi est-ce que Thibault va avec Jean et Aurélie?**

   a. **Il marche.**

   b. **Il a envie de voir la ville.**

   c. **Il a deux amis.**

   d. **Il va avec une souris et une vache.**

3. **Est-ce que le gardien [gatekeeper/guard] du village a un chien?**

   a. **Oui, et il s'appelle** (his name is) **Bruno.**

   b. **Non. Bruno n'a pas de chien.**

   c. **Non. Le gardien [gatekeeper/guard] n'a pas de chien.**

   d. **Non. Bruno n'est pas le gardien.**

4. **Où vont Jean et Aurélie?**

   a. **Au zoo.**

   b. **Le fromage.**

   c. **Une souris et une vache.**

   d. **À la montagne.**

5. **Le meunier a beaucoup d'enfants. Combien d'enfants est-ce qu'il a?**

   a. **Quatre.**

   b. **Il aime beaucoup ses enfants.**

   c. **Dans le village.**

   d. **Ils ont des yeux verts.**

Dictée!

Listen to the audio file [04_06/Tr. 25] of the **dictée** for this **chapitre**. On the lines provided, write down the three sentences you hear. You do not need to write translations for them, though it's good practice to think through what the English translation would be. You may stop and repeat the audio file several times as you're writing down the sentences.

1. ______________________________

   ____

2. ______________________________

   ____

3. ______________________________

   ____

CHAPITRE 5 CINQ

Here we are at the end of an exciting unit! You've learned how to say, "I am" (**je suis**) and "I go" (**je vais**) using two extremely common verbs. To boot, you figured out how to say, "I am not!" and "I'm not going!" thanks to our **chapitre** on negatives using **ne** and **pas**. You also started to see how to ask questions in French with the famous expression **est-ce que**, accompanied by our seven question words, and also by using inversion. Before reviewing these concepts in more detail, it's time to take a deep breath and . . . keep breathing in . . . a little bit more . . . now *quick*! Recite all of your vocabulary words as you exhale! (Don't forget to breathe when you need to, though—we wouldn't want you passing out.)

	French	English
☐	**être, je suis**	______ ______
☐	**voyager, je voyage**	______ ______
☐	**visiter, je visite**	______ ______
☐	**avoir envie de, j'ai envie de**	______ ______
☐	**un endroit**	______
☐	**une idée**	______
☐	**ensemble**	______
☐	**intelligent/bête**	______
☐	**content/triste**	______
☐	**difficile/simple**	______
☐	**aller, je vais**	______ ______
☐	**un manteau**	______

	French	English
☐	**un chapeau**	______
☐	**une chemise**	______
☐	**un pantalon**	______
☐	**une chaussure/ chaussette**	______
☐	**un mouton**	______
☐	**un berger**	______
☐	**une foire**	______
☐	**un loup**	______
☐	**avoir l'air (de), j'ai l'air (de)**	______ ______
☐	**commencer, je commence**	______ ______
☐	**des vêtements**	______
☐	**un sac**	______
☐	**une patte**	______

	French	English
☐	une queue	____________
☐	une manière	____________
☐	le pain	____________
☐	ce	____________
☐	comme	____________
☐	acheter, j'achète	____________ ____________
☐	entrer, j'entre	____________ ____________
☐	être d'accord, je suis d'accord	____________ ____________

	French	English
☐	terminer, je termine	____________ ____________
☐	le marché	____________
☐	un fruit	____________
☐	un légume	____________
☐	une chose	____________
☐	fatigué	____________
☐	encore	____________

My List of Words to Master

So that you can easily review the words you are having difficulty remembering, write them down on the lines provided below.

SENTENCES

Write five sentences using words you have put on your list of words to master.

1. ____

____

____

2. ____

____

____

3. ____

____

____

4. ____

____

____

5. ____

____

____

Grammaire

The Verb *Être* ("to be," Chapitre 1)

Conjugation

Fill in the chart below with the conjugated forms of the verb **être** (to be).

Person	Singular	Plural
1st Person	______________ (I am)	______________ (we are)
2nd Person	______________ (you are)	______________ (you are)
3rd Person	______________ (he/she/it is)	______________ (they are)

Eavesdropping

Let's pretend we're listening in on a couple of conversations between French speakers. Translate their conversations in the space provided on the right. Then, listen to the conversations on the audio file (05_01/Tr. 26).

1. *The Unhappy Pair*

   "Je suis content."
   Translation: ______________________________

   "Pourquoi est-ce que tu es content?"
   Translation: ______________________________

   "Parce que nous sommes ensemble!"
   Translation: ______________________________

   "Vraiment? Je suis triste."
   Translation: ______________________________

   "Pourquoi est-ce que tu es triste?"
   Translation: ______________________________

   "Parce que tu es méchant!"
   Translation: ______________________________

2. *Look on the Bright Side*

"Voilà! Nous sommes à la mer!"
Translation: ___

"Non, non, Monsieur! Vous êtes au lac. Le lac est petit, il n'est pas grand!"
Translation: ___

"Mais la mer est bleue!"
Translation: ___

"Oui, monsieur, mais le lac est aussi bleu. Donc [therefore *or* so], **c'est un lac."**
Translation: ___

"D'accord, d'accord, [OK, OK] **mais la mer a une plage!"**
Translation: ___

"Oui, mais le lac a aussi une plage!"
Translation: ___

"Mais . . . alors, où est le lac?"
Translation: ___

"Le lac est dans la forêt."
Translation: ___

"Et où est la forêt?"
Translation: ___

"La forêt est à côté des champs."
Translation: ___

"Et où sont les champs?"
Translation: ___

"Les champs sont près des montagnes."
Translation: ___

"Et où sont les montagnes?"
Translation: ___

"Ben, les montagnes sont à côté de la mer."
Translation: ___

"Donc, nous sommes près de la mer!"
Translation: ___

The Verb *Aller* ("to go," Chapitre 2)

Conjugation

Fill in the chart below with the conjugated forms of the verb **aller**, "to go." Be sure to translate the phrase from the **chapitre** 2 Conversation Journal as well.

Person	Singular	Plural
1st Person	______________ (I go)	______________ (we go)
2nd Person	______________ (you go)	______________ (you go)
3rd Person	______________ (he/she goes)	______________ (they go)
—	______________ Go ahead!/Go on!/Keep going!	

Three Strikes and They're Out!

Out of the following five sentences, three contain mistakes. Your job is to cross out each of the mistakes and then write the corrected sentence in the space provided. But be careful! The three sentences with mistakes might have more than one mistake in each sentence! Once you've fixed all of the mistakes, translate *all* of the sentences.

1. **Aujourd'hui, nous allons à la plage.**

   Corrected Sentence: ______________

   Translation: ______________

2. **Vous aller à le zoo?**

   Corrected Sentence: ______________

   Translation: ______________

3. **Je vas à la maison.**

   Corrected Sentence: ______________

   Translation: ______________

4. **Elle va au marché.**

   Corrected Sentence: ______________

   Translation: ______________

5. **Tu vais à les champs avec les moutons?**

   Corrected Sentence: ______________

   Translation: ______________

Negation with *Ne* and *Pas* (Chapitre 3)

Go Fish . . . for Negatives!

The following four sentences are missing some negative words (**ne**, **n'**, **pas**, or **de**). Fish around in the pond below and stick the right words in the blanks in order to complete the sentences by making them negative. Then translate the sentences into English in the space provided below. (Hint: You can cross off a negative word every time you use it.)

1. **Aurelie et Jean _______ sont _______ au zoo.**

   Translation: ____

2. **Le loup _______ porte _______ _______ chaussures.**

   Translation: ____

3. **La mère de Thibault _______ a _______ _______ fromage.**

   Translation: ____

4. **Vous _______ allez _______ à la montagne?**

   Translation: ____

5. **Je _______ vais _______ à la maison.**

   Translation: ____

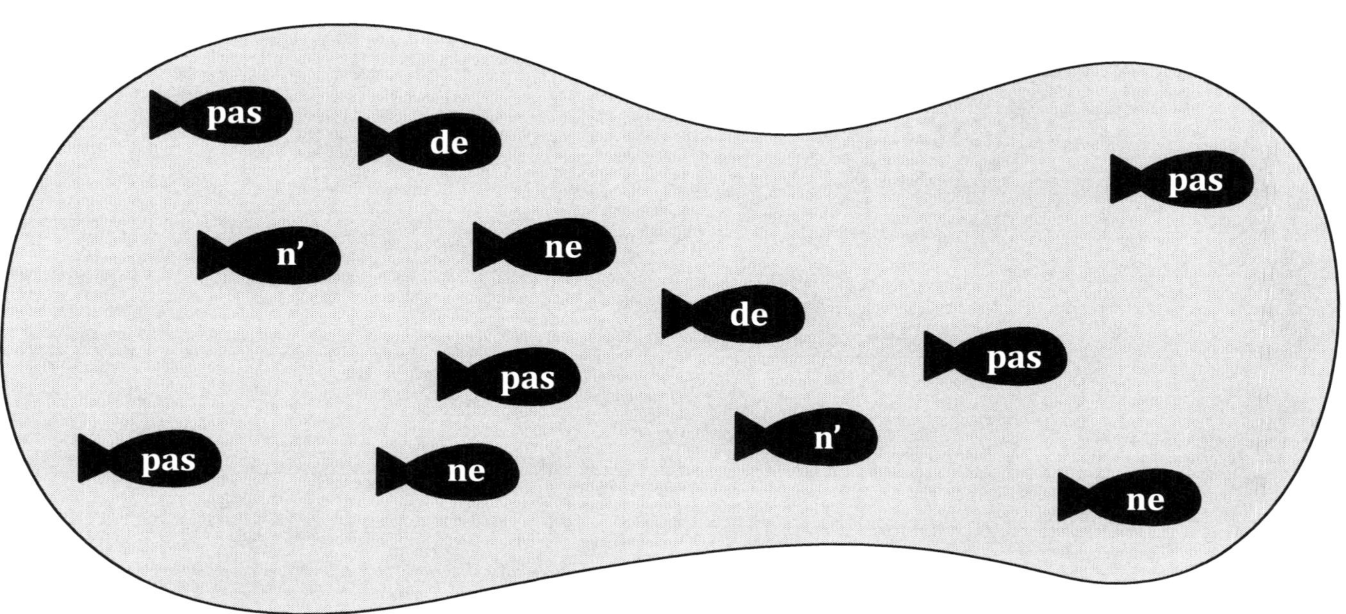

Questions: *Est-ce Que* (Chapitre 4)

You Ask the Questions!

In this last review exercise, it's your turn to ask questions for once. We provide you with an answer, and you must create a question that would produce that answer. The kind of question word you should use is to the right of the answer, in parentheses. As you see in the following example, we give you the answer as a statement: "We have three brothers." Using the kind of question listed in parentheses, you must come up with the question that produces the statement.

Exemple:

Nous avons trois frères. (How many?)
Question: Combien de frères est-ce que vous avez?

1. **Je vais à la ville à trois heures** [three o'clock]**.** (When?)

   Question: ______________________________

2. **Ils travaillent au marché.** (Where?)

   Question: ______________________________

3. **Elle achète une chemise pour l'anniversaire [birthday] de sa mère.** (Why?)

   Question: ______________________________

4. **Nous allons au village avec la voiture.** (How?)

   Question: ______________________________

Dialogue [06_01/Tr. 27]

The miller immediately sets off to start bargaining, leaving Jean, Aurélie, and Thibault to wander around the bustling streets of the market town. Before long, they stumble upon a strange sight.

THIBAULT. **Jean, Aurélie? Est-ce que vous regardez les deux rats là-bas? Qu'est-ce qu'ils font?**

JEAN. I have no idea . . . **mais ça a l'air bizarre**!

AURÉLIE. **Hé, ho! Les rats! Qu'est-ce que vous faites là? Qu'est-ce que vous avez?**

RAT #1, *quietly.* **Chut! C'est un œuf! Mais chut! Le renard arrive! Il aime manger nos œufs.**

AURÉLIE, *whispering.* **OK, mais pourquoi est-ce que tu es sur ton dos avec l'œuf dans les pattes?**

JEAN, *to the other rat.* **Oui! Et, pourquoi est-ce que tu tires ton ami par la queue?**

RAT #1, *in a hushed voice.* **Chuuuuut! Nous n'avons pas envie de casser notre œuf . . .**

RAT #2. **Mais nous avons besoin de cacher notre œuf parce que le renard arrive.**

THIBAULT, *speaking normally.* **C'est *votre* œuf?**

RAT #2. **CHUUUT! S'IL VOUS PLAÎT!! . . . Mais oui! Les gentilles dames ici au marché laissent toujours des œufs pour nous . . .**

JEAN. Hmm . . . I've heard that kind of story before . . .

RAT #1. **C'est vrai! Elles font toujours ça, les vieilles dames du marché.**

THIBAULT. **C'est bizarre, votre manière de porter un œuf.** But I guess so is *eating* raw egg . . .

RAT #2, *forgetting his fear, his pride now wounded.* **Ah mais, nous ne mangeons pas les œufs comme ça! Nous faisons des omelettes.**

RAT #1. **Oh là là, nous faisons des omelettes délicieuses.**

RAT #2. **Et mon ami fait des gâteaux supers!**

RAT #1. **Ça va, ça va, ils ne sont pas si bons . . .**

RAT #2, *turning to his friend.* **Tu fais des gâteaux magnifiques!**

RAT #1. **Ah, ben, merci . . . c'est gentil.**

RAT #2. **Non, mais vraiment, je trouve tes gâteaux très, très bien. Quand tu fais le gâteau au vieux fromage—OH! Ça, j'aime beaucoup. Ah, et ton gâteau aux têtes de poissons—super!**

AURÉLIE, JEAN, AND THIBAULT, *under their breath.* **Dégoûtant!**

AURÉLIE. Mmmm.

CHANT [06_02/TR. 28]

Faire (to do/make)

Person	Singular	Plural
1st Person	**je fais** (I do/I make)	**nous faisons** (we do/we make)
2nd Person	**tu fais** (you do/you make)	**vous faites** (you do/you make)
3rd Person	**il/elle fait** (he/she/it does; he/she/it makes)	**ils/elles font** (they do/they make)

VOCABULAIRE [06_03/TR. 29]

Français	Anglais
faire, je fais	to do/to make, I do/I make
arriver, j'arrive	to arrive, I arrive
cacher, je cache	to hide (something), I hide (something)
casser, je casse	to break, I break
tirer, je tire	to pull, I pull
dégoûtant	disgusting
l'œuf	the egg
l'omelette	the omelet
le rat	the rat
la dame	the lady

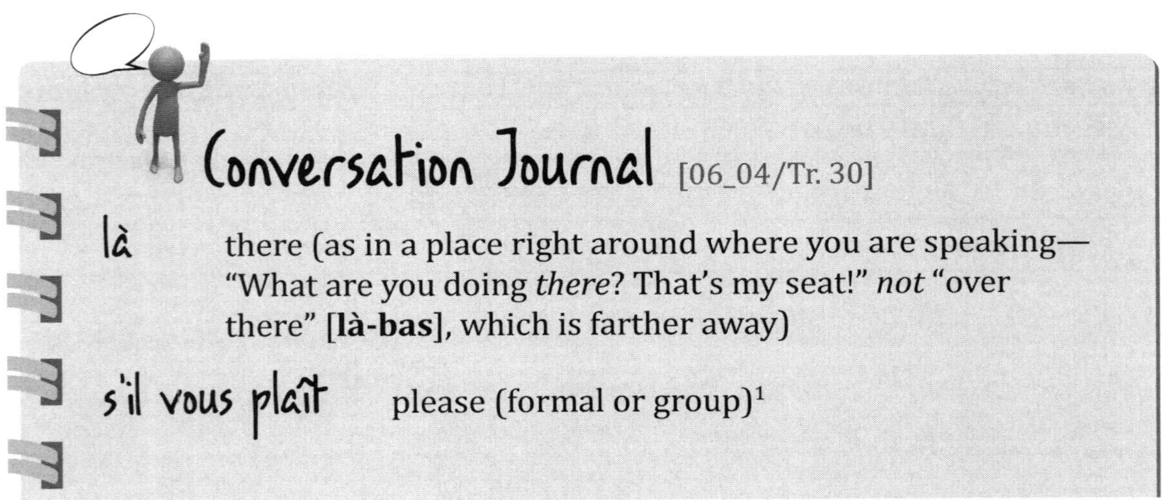

Conversation Journal [06_04/Tr. 30]

là there (as in a place right around where you are speaking—"What are you doing *there*? That's my seat!" *not* "over there" [**là-bas**], which is farther away)

s'il vous plaît please (formal or group)[1]

1. This is an identical expression to **s'il te plaît**, which you learned in *FFCA* **chapitre** 8. The only difference is that you use **s'il te plaît** in an *informal* situation with *one* other person (for example, your good friend), and you use **s'il vous plaît** in a formal situation (with a teacher, for instance—see *FFCA* **chapitre** 5) or with a group of people (the **vous** plural, from *FFCA* **chapitre** 4). Why do you think the rats used it in this **chapitre**'s dialogue?

Irregular Verbs, Part 4: Faire

The irregular verb you learn in this chapter—**faire**—is quite handy. It can mean two different things in English: to do or to make. So, for example, **Il fait un sandwich** means, "He is making a sandwich." However, **Il fait ses devoirs** means, "He is doing his homework."

For French speakers, the meaning is clear from the context: Is some physical object being created, such as a sandwich, a cake, or an electric car? If that's the action, then French speakers think of **faire** in the sense of "to make." But if the context is one of just accomplishing an action, such as doing the dishes, doing your homework, or doing your best, and nothing new is being made, well, French speakers still use the verb **faire**, but they have in mind the sense of "to do" rather than "to make."

Here are some examples:

Je fais une omelette.	I'm making an omelette.
Vous faites des gateaux.	You're making cakes.
Elle fait les devoirs.	She's doing the homework.

Asking Questions with Question Words, Part 2: Qui and Quoi

In **chapitre** 4, you learned how to ask questions using question words in two ways: First, you used just **Est-ce que . . . ?** in yes or no questions such as, "Do rats like eggs?" or "Are you tired?" Second, you learned a way to ask questions using question words combined with **est-ce que** for questions such as, "*How* do you go to the city?" or "*Where* is he working?" or "*When* does your school finish?" For example:

question word	+	**est-ce que**	+	normal sentence
Quand	+	**est-ce que**	+	**tu travailles?**

"When do you work?"

Now let's explore some exceptions to this "traditional" rule by looking at the question words **qui** (who) and **quoi** (what).

The Keys to *Qui*

You've actually already seen the word **qui** in action in this book. If you look back at *FFCA* **chapitre** 13, you will come across Jean asking M. L'oiseau, "**Qui habite là-bas?**" after the bird tells him about the green house where he steals all his cheese. If you translated word for word using the Conversation Journal, this question should have been no problem: "Who lives there?" So, **voilà**! You already know one way to use **qui**: Just plop it down at the beginning of a sentence as you would the word "who" in English:

***Qui* marche vers la forêt?**
Who is walking to the forest?

***Qui* reste dans la maison?**
Who is staying in the house?

***Qui* mange beaucoup de fromage?**
Who eats a lot of cheese?

Now, there is an even fancier way to use **qui**, which, honestly, does the same job as the way you've just seen, but is still something you should know about. There is no hard-and-fast rule about which of the two forms of the question is more appropriate, though the "fancy" way is perhaps a smidge more formal sounding. In any event, it looks like this:

***Qui est-ce qui* marche vers la forêt?**
Who is walking to the forest?

***Qui est-ce qui* reste dans la maison?**
Who is staying in the house?

***Qui est-ce qui* mange beaucoup de fromage?**
Who eats a lot of cheese?

Huh? *Quoi?*

When you want to use the question word **quoi** (what), things are not so simple. A question such as the **gardien**'s question in **chapitre** 4 (**"Mais, vous avez l'intention d'acheter quoi ici?"**) is grammatically correct, but not very polite. In fact, usually you'll only hear **quoi** in a question when it's either totally by itself, such as **"Quoi? Je ne chante pas bien!?"** ("*What*? I don't sing well!?"), or when it comes after a preposition, such as **"Avec *quoi*?"** ("With *what*?"), or **"Près de *quoi*?"** ("Near *what*?"), or **"Dans *quoi*?"** ("In *what*?") and so on.

Normally, if you want to ask "What are you doing?" or "What is he looking for?" or "What are they singing?" the word **quoi** does not even appear! Instead, we get the following form, with our old friend **est-ce que** (this time with the question word **que** stuck on the front as **qu'**):

Qu'est-ce que tu fais?	What are you doing?
Qu'est-ce qu'il cherche?	What is he looking for?
Qu'est-ce qu'ils chantent?	What are they singing?

You've already learned **que** in *FFCA* **chapitre** 3 as meaning "that," but here you see that this little word can also function as an additional question word on top of the previous seven you've learned so far. Context makes it pretty clear when **que** is being used as a question word vs. the word "that."

Chant-Confused Conjugation

Go back to the beginning of this chapter and study the chant of the verb **faire** for a few minutes before you try to do this exercise. Then, do your best to put this chart of conjugations of the verb **faire** back in the correct order by crossing out the incorrect forms and replacing them with the correct ones. If any of the forms are correct, you can leave them that way.

Person	Singular	Plural
1st Person	**je faisons** ____________ (I do/I make)	**nous fais** ____________ (we do/we make)
2nd Person	**tu fait** ____________ (you do/you make)	**vous font** ____________ (you do/you make
3rd Person	**il/elle fais** ____________ (he/she/it does; he/she/it makes)	**ils/elles faites** ____________ (they do/they make)

A Conversation with the Fox

After slipping away from the gourmet rats, Jean, Aurélie, and Thibault cross paths with the fox, who is on the hunt for something. Imagine that the questions to the left are what the fox asks the three travelers. Match the appropriate response on the right to each question on the left by drawing a line between them:

______ 1. **"Qui êtes-vous?"**

______ 2. **"Qu'est-ce que vous faites ici?"**

______ 3. **"Qu'est-ce que vous achetez au marché?"**

______ 4. **"Qui cache mon œuf?!"**

______ 5. **"Où sont les rats!?"**

A. "We're just here to do some shopping."

B. "Not sure. Probably somewhere around here. . . . Excuse us . . . gotta go!"

C. "I'm Jean, and this is Aurélie and Thibault."

D. "I haven't seen any *people* around here with it . . . "

E. "Oh, uh, nothing—fruits, vegetables . . . no eggs, though!"

Ask It Aloud!

Translate the following questions into French, and then try asking them out loud. Compare your pronunciation to the audio file (06_05/Tr. 31).

1. When is the fox arriving?

    ____

2. What are they doing with the egg?

    ____

3. Why are you (**vous**) hiding an egg?

    ____

4. What is he doing with his tail?

    ____

5. Who eats a cake with fish heads?

    ____

Grammaire

Circle the correct answer.

1. In French, the verb **faire** can mean:
    a. to do and to finish.
    b. to make and to finish.
    c. to do and to make.
    d. to have and to hold.

2. Identify one question below that would *never* happen using the question word "what" in French:
    a. **Quoi est-ce que tu fais?**
    b. **Qu'est-ce qu'il mange?**
    c. **Vous parlez de quoi?**
    d. **Qu'est-ce que tu cherches?**

3. What is the difference between the question **"Qui nage dans le lac?"** and the question **"Qui est-ce qui nage dans le lac?"**
    a. The first question asks, "Who is swimming in the lake?" and the second asks, "Who does swim in the lake?"
    b. The first question asks, "What is swimming in the lake?" and the second asks, "Who is swimming in the lake?"
    c. There is no difference in meaning.
    d. The first question asks, "Who is swimming in the lake?" and the second asks, "What is swimming in the lake?"

Nouveau Vocabulaire

Fill in the blank with the correct translation for each word.

Français	Anglais
1. **faire, je fais**	______________
2. **arriver, j'arrive**	______________
3. **cacher, je cache**	______________
4. **casser, je casse**	______________
5. **tirer, je tire**	______________
6. **dégoûtant**	______________
7. **l'œuf**	______________
8. **l'omelette**	______________
9. **le rat**	______________
10. **la dame**	______________

Ancien Vocabulaire

Fill in the blank with the correct translation for each word.

Français	Anglais
1. **l'arbre**	______________
2. **une sœur**	______________
3. **une fille**	______________
4. **espérer [que], j'espère [que]**	______________
5. **rester, je reste**	______________
6. **avoir peur de, j'ai peur de**	______________
7. **une femme**	______________
8. **une mère**	______________
9. **entrer, j'entre**	______________
10. **être d'accord, je suis d'accord**	______________

Lost Questions

In the left-hand column, you will see questions—or at least, the beginnings of questions—whose ends have been smudged and faded so that we will never know exactly what they're asking. In the right-hand column, though, you will see possible answers to all of the different questions. Using just your knowledge of question words, draw a line to the answer on the right that *could* be connected to the question on the left.

________	1. **Quand est-ce que je . . .**	A. **Dans la grange.**
________	2. **Qui est-ce qui va . . .**	B. **Parce que nous allons à la ville.**
________	3. **Où est la . . .**	C. **Deux.**
________	4. **Pourquoi est-ce que vous . . .**	D. **Tu travailles aujourd'hui.**
________	5. **Qu'est-ce qu'il . . .**	E. **Il fait une omelette.**
________	6. **Comment est-ce que tu . . .**	F. **Jean.**
________	7. **Combien de rats . . .**	G. **Je réussis parce que j'étudie!**

Traduction

In this **chapitre**'s dialogue with Jean, Aurélie, and Thibault, there are six (and only six) questions containing our famous question expression **est-ce que**. Take a glance back at the dialogue and do the following:

1. Rewrite the questions, in French, on the lines provided.
2. Then, translate each sentence.

1. Question: ______________________________________

____

Translation: ______________________________________

____

Rappel

As you write the French versions down, think about all you've learned about questions. What is **est-ce que**? How is it used? What is the correct order of the words in a question?

2. Question: ______________________________

   Translation: ______________________________

3. Question: ______________________________

   Translation: ______________________________

4. Question: ______________________________

   Translation: ______________________________

5. Question: ______________________________

   Translation: ______________________________

6. Question: ______________________________

   Translation: ______________________________

Dictée!

Listen to the audio file [06_06/Tr. 32] of the **dictée** for this **chapitre**. On the lines provided, write down the three sentences you hear. You do not need to write translations for them, though it's good practice to think through what the English translation would be. You may stop and repeat the audio file several times as you're writing down the sentences.

1. ______________________________

   ____

2. ______________________________

   ____

3. ______________________________

   ____

CHAPITRE 7 SEPT

DIALOGUE [07_01/TR. 33]

Slowly, the three travelers continue on through the fair, taking their leave of the rats, who remain busy complimenting each other. A fox passes, sniffing the air, but they steer clear of him and press on to the far end of the village where the last few merchants have their stands.

THIBAULT. **Alors, je veux aller à la ville avec vous, mais je dois parler avec mon père.** If he thinks it's all right, then we can leave right from here—this gate leads right out to the city.

AURÉLIE. **Est-ce qu'il est près d'ici, ton père?**

THIBAULT, *pointing at the stand of one of last merchants before the gate.* **Oui! Il est là-bas.** I think he's trying to trade our donkey. *They approach from behind and begin to pick up snippets of the conversation.*

LE MEUNIER. . . . un sac de pommes, cinq sacs de fraises, cinq sacs de pêches, et trois bons fromages?

LA DAME. Non monsieur! Je ne peux pas! C'est trop.

LE MEUNIER, *getting frustrated.* **Alors, je veux un sac de pommes, un de pommes de terre, un de tomates et trois fromages . . . ça, ça va?**

LA DAME. **Ben non, monsieur.**

LE MEUNIER. **S'il vous plaît!**

LA DAME. **Vous ne pouvez pas avoir les fruits, les légumes, *et* le fromage tout pour votre petit âne . . .** This cheese costs more than your donkey alone! **Il est de la ville, mon fromage. C'est très cher!**

LE MEUNIER. And you think my donkey isn't expensive? Just look at him! **Regarde sa tête! Regarde ses pattes! Sa queue! Son dos!** He's worth a fortune!

THIBAULT, *interrupting.* **Papa, Aurélie et Jean veulent aller à la ville maintenant. Est-ce que nous pouvons aller ensemble?**

LE MEUNIER. **Hmmm . . . vous voulez aller ensemble? Je ne suis pas sûr . . . la ville est loin. Ben . . .** , *seeing the woman scowling at him from behind her cheeses.* If you can bring back **trois bons fromages de la ville . . . oui, tu peux aller avec Jean et Aurélie.** You'd make your mother quite happy, too, seeing as I won't be bringing any home . . . **puisque le fromage ici est si cher . . .** , *he scowls back at the woman.*

THIBAULT. **Génial! Merci, Papa!**

JEAN and AURÉLIE. **Merci, monsieur!**

JEAN. **Nous pouvons trouver les fromages, pas de problème. Allons-y!**

Chant [07_02/Tr. 34]

Pouvoir (to be able to/can)

This **chapitre**, a "boot" verb:

Pouvoir (to be able to/can)

Person	Singular	Plural
1st Person	**je peux** (I can)	**nous pouvons** (we can)
2nd Person	**tu peux** (you can)	**vous pouvez** (you can)
3rd Person	**il/elle peut** (he/she/it can)	**ils/elles peuvent** (they can)

Vocabulaire [07_03/Tr. 35]

Français	Anglais
devoir, je dois	to have to, should; I have to, I should
pouvoir, je peux	to be able to, I can[1]
vouloir, je veux	to want, I want
cher	expensive
genial	great
une pomme	an apple
une fraise	a strawberry
une pêche	a peach
une pomme de terre	a potato
une tomate	a tomato

Conversation Journal [07_04/Tr. 36]

je suis sûr — I'm sure

Pas de problème. — No problem.

1. While it is possible to translate **pouvoir** as "to be able to," this is often not the most natural translation. More frequently, translating **pouvoir** as "can" makes the most sense. For example, in everyday conversation, which question would you usually ask someone: 1. "Are you able to swim?" or 2. "Can you swim?" You'd probably ask the second question, right? There is, of course, nothing grammatically wrong with the first question, but under normal circumstances, it just sounds a little funny to our ears. It seems like a more serious question somehow, one in which the speaker is perhaps assuming that there might be some reason (an injury? a rule

Boot Verbs

In this **chapitre** we run into what are called "boot verbs"—a special kind of verb that is irregular compared to what we have already seen with most **-er** and **-ir** verbs. But these boot verbs still have some hint of a pattern to them. What kind of pattern, you ask? It's all in the name: When you write out the conjugations as we usually do, these verbs take the shape of a boot!

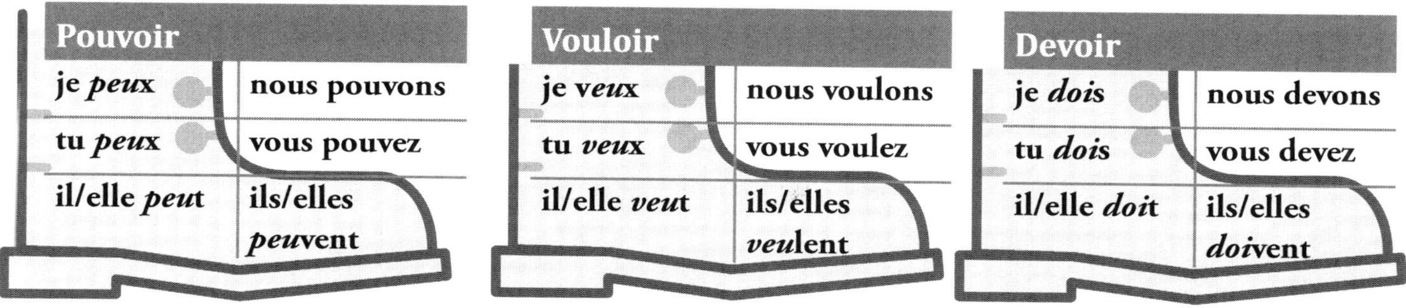

Pouvoir	
je *peux*	**nous pouvons**
tu *peux*	**vous pouvez**
il/elle *peut*	**ils/elles *peuvent***

Vouloir	
je *veux*	**nous voulons**
tu *veux*	**vous voulez**
il/elle *veut*	**ils/elles *veulent***

Devoir	
je *dois*	**nous devons**
tu *dois*	**vous devez**
il/elle *doit*	**ils/elles *doivent***

If you try to imagine using "to be able to," "to want," or "to have to" in a sentence, often you will stick them with another verb, as in these examples in English:

> I <u>can</u> *eat* a whole pizza.
> She <u>wants</u> to *get* a new frog.
> They <u>have to</u> *wear* more sunscreen.

Remarque

Notice how different the infinitive forms look from the "boot" part of each conjugation.

---

against swimming?) that might prevent the person from swimming. Similarly, the statement "I am able to walk there" sounds a bit different from "I can walk there." In the first statement it sounds as if the speaker were really intent on focusing on his or her ability to walk, again giving us the feeling that somehow, in the past, perhaps this ability was lacking (maybe the street was too dangerous?). Obviously, a lot depends on *how* you say each sentence—what word you put emphasis on, etc.—but our point is simply that these two expressions—"to be able to" and "can"—are not exactly synonymous much of the time.

Indeed, in many cases, our three boot verbs are often just ***helping verbs****—verbs that lead up to, or pave the way for, other verbs*. Notice that we put the other verbs in the *infinitive* when they are being helped by **pouvoir**, **vouloir**, or **devoir**:

Je peux *faire* un bon gâteau aux pommes!
I can make a good apple cake!

Nous voulons *acheter* une nouvelle maison.
We want to buy a new house.

Elles doivent *marcher* vers le village.
They have to walk to the village.

RENVOI

If you're popping brain cells trying to remember what "infinitive" means, check back in *FFCA* **chapitre** 3.

To make these kinds of sentences negative, **c'est facile**! We only need to put our **ne** and **pas** "spectacles" around the boot verb itself.

Nous ne voulons pas acheter une nouvelle maison.
We do not want to buy a new house.

Je ne peux pas faire un bon gâteau aux pommes.
I am not able to make a good apple cake.

One more thing: Just as **pouvoir** is not always translatable as "to be able to," so **devoir** is not always translated "to have to" or "should." For example, if we're talking about an important rule, it would be better to translate **devoir** with the stronger English word "must":

Vous devez porter des chaussettes.
You must wear socks.

Tu ne dois pas porter cette chemise!
You must not wear that shirt!

As you can see, when you use verbs such as **devoir** you must pay close attention to the context of the sentence in order to translate or use them properly. As another example, in this **chapitre**'s dialogue, Thibault explains to Jean and Aurélie that he needs to speak to his father before leaving with them for the city. Should we translate Thibault's sentence, "**Je dois parler avec mon père**" as "*I should* speak with my father," or "*I must* speak with my father," or "*I have to* speak with my father"? Either choice two or three would probably be best. Since Thibault needs permission from his father regarding his trip to the city, it is not simply a "good idea" for him to talk to his father—it is essential. There isn't a clear rule for which of the two translations is best, but the more important point is ruling out the weaker form "should," since the situation was more serious than that. In your exercises in this **chapitre**, again, multiple translations will be possible, so the key point is for you to be able to *imagine* what kind of situation matches the translation you provide for any given sentence.

Signs

Below are messages on five different signs. Your job is to draw a line linking the sign with the appropriate place in the right-hand column where you would expect to find it. Then, translate the sign in the space provided.

1. **Vous ne devez pas jouer avec les serpents.**

   Translation: ______________________________

   ____

2. **Vous pouvez acheter des légumes ici.**

   Translation: ______________________________

   ____

3. **Vous ne devez pas parler.**

   Translation: ______________________________

   ____

4. **Attention! Vous pouvez tomber!**

   Translation: ______________________________

   ____

5. **Vous ne devez pas marcher ici.**

   Translation: ______________________________

   ____

A. the library

B. a major highway

C. a mountain trail

D. the zoo

E. the market

Interpreting at the Market

Below are bits of conversations that you might have heard at the market when Jean, Aurélie, Thibault, and his dad were there. If the sentence is in French, first read it out loud, and compare your pronunciation to the audio file (07_05/Tr. 37). If the sentence is in English, don't bother reading it aloud; just translate it right into French![2]

1. **Qu'est-ce que vous voulez, Monsieur!?**

   Translation: ______________________________

2. **Est-ce que je peux regarder vos fromages?**

   Translation: ______________________________

3. Can I have a peach?

   Translation: ______________________________

4. **Je dois acheter trois sacs de pommes de terre; je n'ai pas assez de pommes de terre à la maison.**

   Translation: ______________________________

5. Does he want two tomatoes or three?

   Translation: ______________________________

6. **Est-que vous pouvez laisser un sac de fraises pour moi?**

   Translation: ______________________________

7. We want two pigs, please!

   Translation: ______________________________

2. Of course, we won't stop you if you really want to read them out loud, but you won't find any English answers on the audio file!

Grammaire

Circle the correct answer.

1. The verbs **devoir**, **pouvoir**, and **vouloir** are called "boot verbs" because:
   a. their meanings are all similar.
   b. they are all used in the same situations.
   c. if you write out their conjugations, they follow the same boot-shaped pattern.
   d. all boot verbs end in **-oir**, just as *all* non-boot verbs end in **-er**.
   e. they all come from Italy.

2. **Il peut . . .** is always translated as "He is able to . . . "
   a. true
   b. false, it can also be translated "he must"
   c. false, it can also be translated "he is willing to"
   d. false, it can also be translated "he can"

3. **Devoir**, **pouvoir**, and **vouloir** are often used as helping verbs. What do we call the form of the *other* verb that is "helped" by them? For example, what is the form of the underlined verb being helped by **pouvoir** in this sentence: **Est-ce que tu peux <u>chanter</u>?**
   a. the present tense
   b. the infinitive
   c. the helped verb
   d. the boot verb

4. Which of the following sentences correctly uses a boot verb *negatively*?
   a. **Il ne pas peut nager.**
   b. **Il ne peut nager pas.**
   c. **Il peut ne nager pas.**
   d. **Il ne peut pas nager.**

Nouveau Vocabulaire

Fill in the blank with the correct translation(s) for each word.

Français	Anglais
1. **devoir, je dois**	____________
2. **pouvoir, je peux**	____________
3. **vouloir, je veux**	____________
4. **cher**	____________
5. **si**	____________
6. **une pomme**	____________
7. **une fraise**	____________
8. **une pêche**	____________
9. **une pomme de terre**	____________
10. **une tomate**	____________

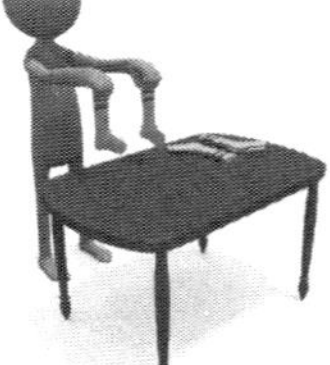

Ancien Vocabulaire

Fill in the blank with the correct translation(s) for each word.

Français	Anglais
1. **un cochon**	____________
2. **un renard**	____________
3. **un serpent**	____________
4. **un oiseau**	____________
5. **un cheval**	____________
6. **un mouton**	____________
7. **un loup**	____________
8. **un rat**	____________

Français	Anglais
9. **cacher, je cache**	______________________
10. **casser, je casse**	______________________

Fais Tes Devoirs (Do Your Homework)

Remember, in *FFCA* **chapitre 2** you learned that **les devoirs** means "homework." **Devoir**, you learned in this **chapitre**, simply means "to have to" or "must." So you see, **les devoirs** are just things you *must* do, like this verb chart! We've filled in the first box for you.

Person	Singular	Plural
1st Person	**je dois** (I must)	______________ (we must)
2nd Person	______________ (you must)	______________ (you must)
3rd Person	______________ (he/she/it must)	______________ (they must)

Which Helper?

To complete the following sentences, circle the correct helping verb from the choices underneath each blank.

1. What!? You haven't done your assignment yet? **Le cours** (**un cours** = a class) **commence dans quinze (15) minutes—tu ______________ faire tes devoirs!**
   (**dois / peux / veux**)

2. That was the best movie I've seen all summer! I can't wait for it to be out of the theaters—**je ______________ acheter le DVD**.
   (**dois / peux / veux**)

3. I think we're going to miss the bus, but don't worry—the shop isn't far.
   Nous ______________ marcher là-bas.
   (**devons / pouvons / voulons**)

4. Hey! We've got an emergency over here!
   Est-ce que vous __________________ chercher la police!?
   (**devez** / **pouvez** / **voulez**)

5. I can't go out tonight because my little brother is home, and I'm babysitting.
   Je __________________ être à la maison!
   (**dois** / **peux** / **veux**)

6. Most of the girls want to go surfing, so they'd rather not stay in town.
   Elles __________________ aller à la plage.
   (**doivent** / **peuvent** / **veulent**)

7. Huh? We have a test *tomorrow*!? **Nous __________________ étudier!**
   (**devons** / **pouvons** / **voulons**)

8. Sorry, lady, if your kids want to see giraffes and tigers, they're not going to get any of that here at our farm. **Ils __________________ aller au zoo.**
   (**doivent** / **peuvent** / **veulent**)

9. We seem to be lost. **Est-ce que je __________________ regarder la carte, s'il te plaît?**
   (**dois** / **peux** / **veux**)

10. Is your **grand-père** (grandfather) hungry now? We can find a restaurant whenever he wants. I'm afraid of him when he hasn't had enough to eat.
    Quand est-ce qu'il __________________ manger?
    (**doit** / **peut** / **veut**)

Dictée!

Listen to the audio file [07_06/Tr. 38] of the **dictée** for this **chapitre**. On the lines provided, write down the three sentences you hear. You do not need to write translations for them, though it's good practice to think through what the English translation would be. You may stop and repeat the audio file several times as you're writing down the sentences.

1. ____

2. ____

3. ____

CHAPITRE 8 HUIT

DIALOGUE [08_01/TR. 39]

Striking out on the road again, the travelers swap stories about zoo life and village life, the city and the country, people and animals alike. The long, flat road takes a straight course to the city, and eventually the fields begin to give way to more and more trees. It is under one of these that the travelers meet our next curious—but probably familiar—character.

LE LAPIN. Excusez-moi, les amis. Quelle heure est-il?

THIBAULT. **Bonjour petit lapin! Il est onze heures. Mais, qu'est-ce que tu fais là?**

LE LAPIN. Pas grand-chose. Just relaxing, catching a few winks. You should try it. **Vous marchez trop vite! D'où est-ce que vous venez?**

THIBAULT. **Nous venons du village. Et toi?**

LE LAPIN. Je viens aussi du village! J'attends mon amie, la tortue. Elle arrive, je suis sûr. Nous faisons une course à pied.

AURÉLIE. **Vous faites une course à pied . . . et tu dors?**

LE LAPIN. Bien sûr, je dors! Il est onze heures! It's still early! How am I supposed to run so fast without a few *zzzzs* every so often?

AURÉLIE. **Tu dois courir! Pourquoi est-ce que tu attends ton amie?**

LE LAPIN. Oh, je n'ai pas peur de mon amie, la tortue. Je cours très vite. Mais les tortues? Elles sont très lentes!

JEAN. **Aurélie, il a raison.** Turtles are pretty slow. But I'm sure that you will be on your way soon, right?

LE LAPIN. Ben, non. After my nap I was going to pick some fruit around here. **Les arbres ici sont magnifiques, n'est-ce pas? C'est délicieux, toutes les poires, les cerises! Alors, aujourd'hui, je dors et je mange.** Maybe I'll run tomorrow.

AURÉLIE. **Mais tu es fou!**

THIBAULT, *also dumbfounded*. **Bon, ben . . . bonne chance.** We need to be continuing on!

LE LAPIN. Au revoir!

JEAN. **Bon appétit!**

REMARQUE

Toi is another word meaning "you," and **moi** is a pronoun meaning "me" (check out the introduction to *FFCA* **chapitre** 12, where you saw **moi** in action by itself for the first time). You'll see more of this form in **chapitre** 13! Also, on an unrelated note, instead of using the French word for "hare" (as the rabbit is referred to in the traditional story of the Tortoise and the Hare), we've used a more common word in this dialogue: the word **lapin**, which means "rabbit." On the other hand, **tortue** can be either "turtle" or a "tortoise."

Chant [08_02/Tr. 40]

Il est sept heures. (It is seven o'clock.)

Il est sept heures, déjà, alors, il est sept heures, et toi tu dors.
Il est huit heures, déjà, alors, il est huit heures et toi tu dors.
Il est neuf heures, déjà, alors! Il est neuf heures, et toi tu dors.
Il est dix heures, déjà! Alors! Il est dix heures, tu dors encore!
Tout ça n'est pas très amusant: toi tu dors, et moi j'attends!

Vocabulaire [08_03/Tr. 41]

Français	Anglais
attendre, j'attends	to wait, I wait
courir, je cours	to run, I run
dormir, je dors	to sleep, I sleep
avoir raison/tort, j'ai raison/tort	to be right/wrong, I am right/wrong
venir, je viens	to come, I come
une course	a race
une cerise	a cherry
une poire	a pear
fou	crazy
vite[1]/lent	fast/slow

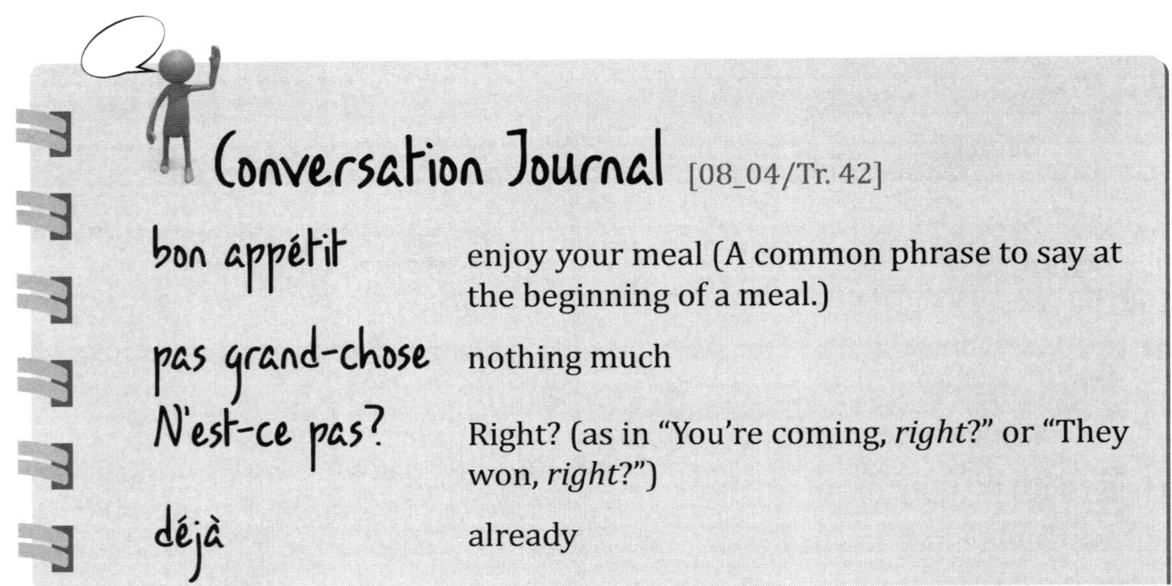

Conversation Journal [08_04/Tr. 42]

bon appétit	enjoy your meal (A common phrase to say at the beginning of a meal.)
pas grand-chose	nothing much
N'est-ce pas?	Right? (as in "You're coming, *right*?" or "They won, *right*?")
déjà	already

1. We've translated the word **vite** as "fast" in English, as in "He runs fast" or "You talk really fast!" This is true when "fast" describes an action. However, when we want to talk about a person (or an animal, or something else)—and *not* about an action—we need the French word **rapide**: **il est rapide** (he is fast) or **Son chat est très rapide!** (Her cat is really fast!). **Vite** is an *adverb*, a word describing actions—verbs—and **rapide** is an *adjective*, used to describe nouns. **Lent** (slow) is an adjective as well, so be careful because **vite** and **lent** are not exactly opposites (**lentement**, "slowly," would be the opposite of **vite**).

Quelle Heure Est-Il?

Quelle heure est-il? Five o'clock? Six o'clock? **Quelle heure est-il?** Are we on time? Did we miss the show? **Quelle heure est-il?** Aren't they open yet? When will everyone get here? **Quelle heure est-il?** Hmmm . . . maybe you've cracked this question by now—thanks to the **chant**, plus the different (but related!) questions in this paragraph. Did you guess that it means "What time is it?"

The question **Quelle heure est-il?** does not actually contain the word "time," as in our English expression, "What *time* is it?" Instead, in French we use the word **heure**, or "hour" in English, to ask, literally, "Which hour is it?"[2] And so the logical response includes the word **heure** as well!

Il est une heure.	It is one o'clock.
Il est huit heures.	It is eight o'clock.
Il est onze heures.	It is eleven o'clock.

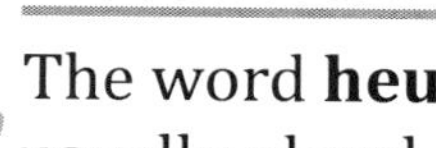

ATTENTION

The word **heure** is usually plural (**heures**) since we're usually talking about a number larger than one. However, when it's one o'clock, we use the singular **heure** as you can see to the left. Either way, it all sounds the same, since the **s** in **heures** is not pronounced. So don't say too much!

If you want to say that you're doing something *at* five o'clock, or you're going somewhere *at* seven o'clock, all you need to do is throw in the little preposition **à** ("to" or "at") like this:

Je fais mes devoirs à cinq heures.
I do my homework at five o'clock.

Ta sœur arrive à deux heures.
Your sister is arriving at two o'clock.

Twelve O'Clock Rock

If you want to talk about something happening in the middle of the *day* (12:00 p.m.), you'd say **midi** in French: **Je mange à midi.**

On the other hand, if you're describing something in the middle of the *night* (12:00 a.m.), you'd say **minuit**: **Je ne mange pas à minuit! Je dors!**

2. Again, as with some other expressions we've learned—for example, the Curious Haves—the French way of speaking (saying "Which hour is it?" instead of "What time is it?") may seem bizarre to us who speak English; but, to a French speaker, asking "What time is it?" will seem bizarre, too!

More Irregular Verbs

There's no way around it: We've got to tackle some more irregular verbs this **chapitre**. Note that three of this **chapitre**'s four irregular verbs end in **-ir**. However, they do not follow our familiar pattern of **-ir** verbs such as **finir** (to finish) or **réussir** (to succeed), as you will see. We recommend repeating the conjugations out loud to yourself as you commit them to memory. Also, check out the cool cognates that we have in English to help you remember each French verb:

Courir (to run)

RENVOI

For a review of cognates, see *FFCA* **chapitre** 3!

Cognates

Courier—A courier is a messenger; and messengers are always running, **n'est-ce pas**?

Current—Think of a river's current, always flowing, or running, along its path.

In French, **courant** can be used to talk about someone who is running, a river's current, or a current trend or fashion!

Person	Singular	Plural
1st Person	**je cours** (I run)	**nous courons** (we run)
2nd Person	**tu cours** (you run)	**vous courez** (you run)
3rd Person	**il/elle court** (he/she/it runs)	**ils/elles courent** (they run)

Dormir (to sleep)

Cognates

Dormitory—This is a place where you sleep at camp, boarding school, or university/college (often just called a "dorm").

Dormant—This is an adjective describing something that is inactive, or in a state of rest.

Person	Singular	Plural
1st Person	**je dors** (I sleep)	**nous dormons** (we sleep)
2nd Person	**tu dors** (you sleep)	**vous dormez** (you sleep)
3rd Person	**il/elle dort** (he/she/it sleeps)	**ils/elles dorment** (they sleep)

Venir (to come)

Cognates

Advent—The advent of something is the moment when it *comes* along, the instant it first *comes* into the world, or its introduction.

Adventure—An adventure is an exciting or dangerous experience. Believe it or not, this noun is actually built from Latin words that describe something that *comes* to you!

Person	Singular	Plural
1st Person	**je viens** (I come)	**nous venons** (we come)
2nd Person	**tu viens** (you come)	**vous venez** (you come)
3rd Person	**il/elle vient** (he/she/it comes)	**ils/elles viennent** (they come)

Attendre (to wait)

Cognates

Attendant—This is someone who *waits on* you.

Person	Singular	Plural
1st Person	**j'attends** (I wait)	**nous attendons** (we wait)
2nd Person	**tu attends** (you wait)	**vous attendez** (you wait)
3rd Person	**il/elle attend** (he/she/it waits)	**ils/elles attendent** (they wait)

The Curious Haves, Part 6

This **chapitre**'s installment of the Curious Haves features two different and opposite expressions using the verb **avoir**: The first is **avoir raison**, which means "to be right" and the second is **avoir tort**, which means "to be wrong." And now you can see why this is quite curious: In French, we say "to have right (or reason)" and "to have wrong"! For example, consider the two conversations below:

> "The capital of the United States is New York City."
>
> **"Comment? Non! Tu as tort. La capitale est Washington, DC!"**
> "Excuse me? No! You're wrong. The capital is Washington, DC!"

"My friends are afraid of your snake. They think he's dangerous."

"Ils ont raison. Il est très dangereux! C'est un cobra."
"They are right. It's very dangerous. It's a cobra."

Finally, as a refresher, try your hand at filling in the **avoir** chart below. It is like a normal verb chart, but you have to factor in whether or not you should add **raison** or **tort** to the form of **avoir**. We've filled in one box for you, and the answers are upside down at the bottom of the page.

Avoir Raison ou Tort?

Person	Singular	Plural
1st Person	____________________ (I am right)[A]	____________________ (we are wrong)[B]
2nd Person	**tu as tort** (you are wrong)	____________________ (you are right)[C]
3rd Person	____________________ (he is right)[D] ____________________ (she is wrong)[E]	____________________ (they are wrong)[F]

[A]j'ai raison [B]nous avons tort [C]vous avez raison [D]il a raison [E]elle a tort [F]ils ont raison

Quelle Heure Est-Il?

Look at the five clocks below. Say what time it is out loud in French and check your pronunciation against the audio file (08_05/Tr. 43). Then, write the sentences out in French in the space provided underneath the clocks.

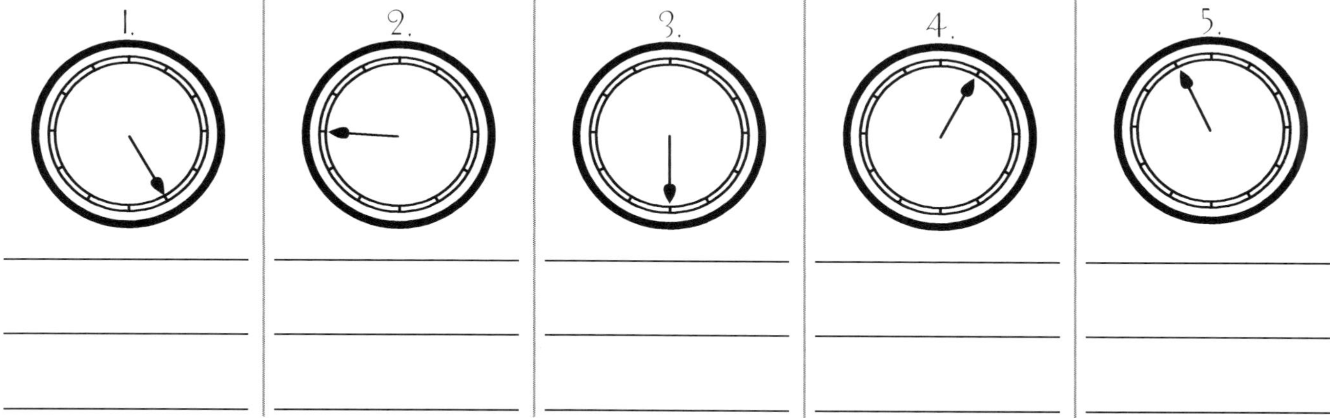

Quelle Heure Est-Il Vraiment?

Imagine you're teaching your little brother or sister how to tell time. For each clock below, you ask him/her: "**Quelle heure est-il?**" Read the different responses provided, and either say, "You're right!" (**Tu as raison!** or **Vous avez raison!** if you imagine you are teaching more than one sibling) or "You're wrong!" (**Tu as tort!** or **Vous avez tort!**). If the response is wrong, write the correct time on the line below the image of the clock face. Here is an **exemple**:

"Quelle heure est-il?"
Response: **"Hmmm . . . Il est six heures."**
Your Response: "Tu as tort!"
Correct Time: "Il est trois heures."

1.
"Quelle heure est-il?"
Response: **"Il est deux heures."**
Your Response: ____________________
Correct Time: ____________________

2. **"Quelle heure est-il?"**
Response: "**Hmmm . . . Je ne suis pas sûr. Il est cinq heures, peut-être?**"

Your Response: ______________________________

Correct Time: ______________________________

---

3. 

"Quelle heure est-il?"
Response: "**Je pense qu'il est trois heures.**"

Your Response: ______________________________

Correct Time: ______________________________

---

4. 

"Quelle heure est-il?"
Response: "**Euh . . . il est une heure, je pense.**"

Your Response: ______________________________

Correct Time: ______________________________

---

5. 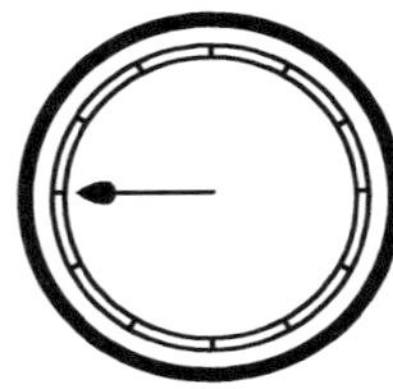

"Quelle heure est-il?"
Response: "**Il est onze heures, je suis sûr!**"

Your Response: ______________________________

Correct Time: ______________________________

Traduction

If you look back in this **chapitre**'s dialogue, you will see the question that the rabbit asks our three travelers: **"D'où est-ce que vous venez?"** (**de** + **où** + **est-ce que**). As you might have guessed from their answer (**Nous venons du village.** "We're coming from the village."), this question means, "Where are you coming from?" However, it also means, "Where do you come from?" in general, as in, what part of the world or what part of a certain country are you from?

Translate into French just the underlined questions below using your new knowledge of the verb **venir**. The beginnings of the sentences may give you clues about how to translate the sentences.

1. Those girls, where do they come from?

   Translation: ______________________________

2. How about you guys? Where do you come from?

   Translation: ______________________________

3. I feel like I've seen you before at school. Where do you come from?

   Translation: ______________________________

4. He looks foreign. Where does he come from?

   Translation: ______________________________

5. I've never seen so many families camp here. Where do they come from?

   Translation: ______________________________

6. I've heard that some of our ancestors were from a different continent. Is that true?

   Where do we come from?

   Translation: ______________________________

Grammaire

Circle the correct answer.

1. When you ask "What time is it?" in French, you are actually asking:
   a. Which hour is it? c. What is the time?
   b. Which time is it? d. What is time, anyway?

2. Which of the following sentences about time is phrased *correctly*?
   a. Il est trois heure. c. Il est une heure.
   b. Il est une heures. d. Il est six heure.

3. What is the difference in pronunciation between the two underlined words:
   Trois heures and **Une heure**?
   a. There is no difference in pronunciation.
   b. You can hear a *z* sound at the end of **heures**, but not at the end of **heure**.
   c. You can hear an *s* sound at the end of **heures**, but not at the end of **heure**.
   d. The first word is pronounced *HERS* and the second is just ER.

4. Among the following possibilities, which is the only way to translate the sentence "I am right" into French?
   a. **Je suis raison.** c. **J'ai raison.**
   b. **Je suis tort.** d. **J'ai tort.**

Nouveau Vocabulaire

Fill in the blank with the correct translation(s) for each word.

Français	Anglais
1. **attendre, j'attends**	______________________
2. **courir, je cours**	______________________
3. **dormir, je dors**	______________________
4. **avoir raison/tort, j'ai raison/tort**	______________________
5. **venir, je viens**	______________________
6. **une course**	______________________
7. **une cerise**	______________________
8. **une poire**	______________________
9. **fou**	______________________
10. **vite/lent**	______________________

Ancien Vocabulaire

Fill in the blank with the correct translation(s) for each word.

Français	Anglais
1. **devoir, je dois**	______________________
2. **pouvoir, je peux**	______________________
3. **vouloir, je veux**	______________________
4. **avoir l'air (de), j'ai l'air (de)**	______________________
5. **un berger**	______________________
6. **très**	______________________
7. **tout**	______________________

Français	Anglais
8. **ensemble**	______________
9. **une idée**	______________
10. **un endroit**	______________

Résumé

Résumé is the French word for "summary." In this section, your job is to complete the summary of what happened in this **chapitre**'s Jean and Aurélie episode. In each sentence, there are *three* blanks. Start by completing the middle blank, which asks you for the appropriate form of the verb (you'll find the choices for the verb below the blank). After that, the verb you just chose will be *sandwiched* between two other blanks. What structure have we learned in French that *sandwiches* a verb? **Ne** and **pas**, of course! We left you two extra spaces for **ne** and **pas** because some of the sentences need to be made *negative* in order to be an accurate **résumé**, or summary, of our story!

For example:

Jean ________ __est__ ________ **une souris.**
(**est** / **es** / **sont**)

Aurélie __n'__ __est__ __pas__ **une souris.**
(**est** / **es** / **sont**)

1. **Le lapin** __________ __________ __________ **du village.**
(**vient** / **viens** / **venez**)

2. **Il** __________ __________ __________ beaucoup.
(**cours** / **court** / **courons**)

3. **Il** __________ __________ __________ **la tortue.**
(**attendez** / **attends** / **attend**)

4. **Aurélie** __________ __________ __________ **que le lapin est fou.**
(**pense** / **penses** / **pensent**)

5. **Le lapin aime** __________ __________ __________ .
(**dort** / **dormons** / **dormir**)

6. **Jean, Aurélie, et Thibault** __________ __________ __________ **. Ils marchent.**
(**dormons** / **dorment** / **dormir**)

Traduction

Translate from English to French the following sentences about different characters you've met so far in the story of Jean and Aurélie's journey.

1. The rats are making an omelet at five o'clock.

   Translation: ______________________________

2. The wolf thinks that he looks like a shepherd. But he is wrong. He looks crazy.

   Translation: ______________________________

3. The guard's dog likes to sleep. He is very cute.

   Translation: ______________________________

4. The rabbit wants to sleep. He does not want to run.

   Translation: ______________________________

5. The turtle cannot run very fast. But the turtle doesn't sleep.

   Translation: ______________________________

Dictée!

Listen to the audio file [08_06/Tr. 44] of the **dictée** for this **chapitre**. On the lines provided, write down the three sentences you hear. You do not need to write translations for them, though it's good practice to think through what the English translation would be. You may stop and repeat the audio file several times as you're writing down the sentences.

1. ______________________________

   ____

2. ______________________________

   ____

3. ______________________________

   ____

CHAPITRE 9 NEUF

DIALOGUE [09_01/Tr. 45]

The travelers' path dips and bends through stretches of orchards and gardens with small houses set back from the road. Before long, they can't resist the temptation to stray from the road and explore the fruit trees and vines.

THIBAULT. **Ouah, nous n'avons pas de fruit comme ça chez moi.**

JEAN. **Nous non plus. Est-ce que vous voyez tous les pommiers et les cerisiers?!**

AURÉLIE. **Et les vignes avec tous les raisins! Ils ont l'air délicieux!**

LE RENARD BOUDEUR (THE MOPEY FOX), *surprising the three friends from behind.* **Oh, vous allez manger les raisins?**

AURÉLIE. **Ouah! Encore un renard!**

THIBAULT. **Bonjour, mon ami. Oui, oui. Nous allons manger les raisins—pourquoi?** They don't belong to you, do they? They're just growing wild here, it seems.

LE RENARD BOUDEUR. Non, non, ce ne sont pas mes raisins. Mais ce n'est pas une bonne idée. Vous n'allez pas aimer les raisins.

JEAN. **Ah, est-ce que les raisins ne sont pas bons?**

LE RENARD BOUDEUR. Non.

THIBAULT. **D'accord, je comprends maintenant. Est-ce que tu viens d'ici?**

LE RENARD BOUDEUR. Non.

THIBAULT. **Mais tu manges souvent les raisins ici, alors?**

LE RENARD BOUDEUR. Non.

THIBAULT. **Euh . . . alors, je ne comprends pas. Comment est-ce que tu sais que les raisins sont mauvais?** Have you ever tried them?

LE RENARD BOUDEUR. Je ne peux pas. They are too high for me to pick them.

THIBAULT. You mean you can't reach the grapes, **mais tu sais qu'ils sont mauvais**?

LE RENARD BOUDEUR. Si je ne peux pas manger les raisins, ils ne peuvent pas être très bons. I'm just warning you. **Mais j'ai faim. Je vais chercher les œufs de la ferme . . . vous pouvez manger les raisins si vous voulez. Moi, je pars.**

JEAN, *as **LE RENARD BOUDEUR** shuffles away.* That fox had some strange ideas about grapes, I dare say.

THIBAULT. I agree. I'm not quite sure what to make of all this, but I bet I know what Aurélie is thinking. **Tu vas manger les raisins, n'est-ce pas?**

AURÉLIE. **Bien sûr!**

Chant [09_02/Tr. 46]

The Future Tense—Starring the Verb *Manger* (to eat)

Person	Singular	Plural
1st Person	**je vais manger** (I will eat)	**nous allons manger** (we will eat)
2nd Person	**tu vas manger** (you will eat)	**vous allez manger** (you will eat)
3rd Person	**il/elle va manger** (he/she/it will eat)	**ils/elles vont manger** (they will eat)

Vocabulaire [09_03/Tr. 47]

Français	Anglais
comprendre, je comprends	to understand, I understand
prendre, je prends	to take, I take
voir, je vois	to see, I see
partir, je pars	to leave, I leave (location)[1]
savoir, je sais	to know, I know (facts or abilities)
un raisin	a grape
une région	a region
souvent	often
le pommier	the apple tree
le cerisier	the cherry tree
la vigne	the vine

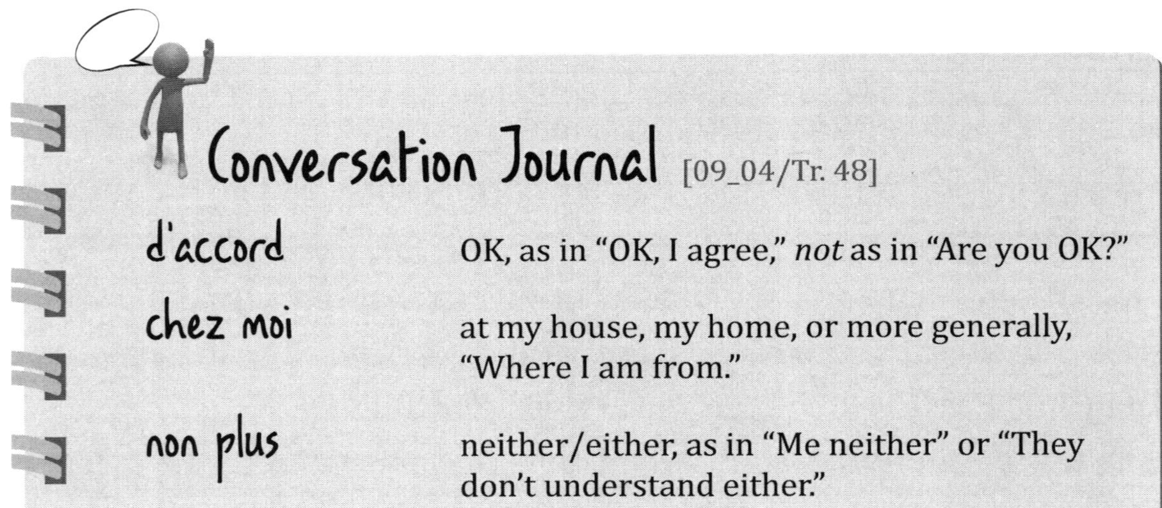

Conversation Journal [09_04/Tr. 48]

d'accord	OK, as in "OK, I agree," *not* as in "Are you OK?"
chez moi	at my house, my home, or more generally, "Where I am from."
non plus	neither/either, as in "Me neither" or "They don't understand either."

1. In *FFCA* **chapitre** 13 you learned the verb **laisser**, which also means "to leave." However, **laisser** means "to leave *something* behind" (such as your wallet, or your friend), whereas **partir** only means to move from a location and travel to another location. You cannot **partir** something—you can only **partir** *to* or *from* somewhere.

Verbs: Tense

Ages ago, in *FFCA* **chapitre** 2, we said that to analyze a verb properly you needed to talk about its three ingredients: person, number, and tense. Well, it's been quite a while, but we've now arrived at **ingrédient numéro trois**: *tense*.[2]

When we speak of verbs and tense, the word "tense" is just a synonym for the word "time." In fact, it comes to us from a Latin word meaning "time" (*tempus*) and then French (**temps**). So the "tense" ingredient is telling us at what *time* the action of the verb takes place. Up until now, all of the verbs in this book have been in the *present tense. Verbs in the present tense describe actions happening now, in the present.* In this **chapitre** you are going to learn about the *future tense*: *Verbs in the future tense describe actions that will happen in the future.* In **chapitre** 11, you'll learn about the *past tense*, the purpose of which we're sure you can figure out by now.

The Future Tense

Describing actions that will happen in the future is not very difficult, as this **chapitre**'s chant reveals. In fact, talking about the future in French is fairly similar to talking about the future in English—we just use the verb "to go" (**aller**) + the infinitive:

Je	**vais**	**manger.**
I	am going	to eat.

Tu	**vas**	**dormir.**
You	are going	to sleep.

These two examples remind us that, in French, the infinitive form of the verb (**manger** and **dormir**, above) already includes the word "to," so we don't need to add anything extra. Indeed, if those sentences included the preposition **à** ("to" or "at"), they would be wrong.

On the other hand, if we're not using the verb **aller** to make the future tense, but just using it to talk about going *to* a place, then we can keep the preposition **à** as we always have:

Je	**vais**	**à**	**la ville.**
I	am going	to	the city.

2. "Tense" is not a word you probably use very often—or hear very often for that matter, other than someone saying "Ow! My muscles are really *tense*!" But that's not really the same word that we're talking about now.

And to make the future tense negative, we only need to put our good old **ne** and **pas** spectacles around the verb **aller**, like this:

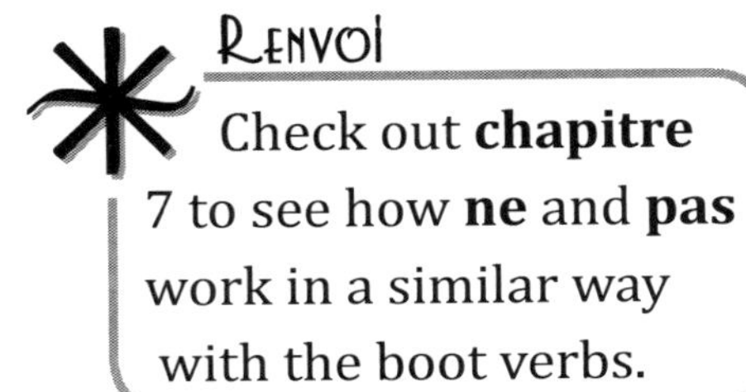

Je ne vais pas manger. — I am not going to eat.

Tu ne vas pas dormir. — You are not going to sleep.

Where There's a Will, There's Aller

One final note about the future tense with **aller**: Up until now we have been translating sentences such as **Je vais manger** as "I *am going* to eat." There is a different, but equally acceptable translation, however. **Je vais manger** can be translated as "I *will* eat." Here are some other examples:

Nous allons dormir dans la forêt.
We are going to sleep in the forest. *or* We will sleep in the forest.

Il ne va pas étudier aujourd'hui.
He is not going to study today. *or* He will not study today.

More Irregular Verbs

In addition to learning about tense in this **chapitre**, we're going to tackle some other important irregular verbs. Let's begin with two very closely related ones: **prendre** (to take) and **comprendre** (to understand). If you can remember one of these conjugations, then you can remember both: They're the same!

To hear how to conjugate the following irregular verbs, be sure to check out the audio files.

Prendre (to take) [09_05/Tr. 49]; ***Comprendre*** (to understand)

Person	Singular	Plural
1st Person	**je prends** (I take)	**nous prenons** (we take)
2nd Person	**tu prends** (you take)	**vous prenez** (you take)
3rd Person	**il/elle prend** (he/she/it takes)	**ils/elles prennent** (they take)

To conjugate **comprendre**, all you need to do is add the prefix **com-** to the beginning of the forms of **prendre**: **je (com)prends**, **tu comprends**, **il comprend**, **nous comprenons**, etc.

Partir (to leave) [09_06/Tr. 50]

Person	Singular	Plural
1st Person	**je pars** (I leave)	**nous partons** (we leave)
2nd Person	**tu pars** (you leave)	**vous partez** (you leave)
3rd Person	**il/elle part** (he/she/it leaves)	**ils/elles partent** (they leave)

Savoir (to know) [09_07/Tr. 51]

Person	Singular	Plural
1st Person	**je sais** (I know)	**nous savons** (we know)
2nd Person	**tu sais** (you know)	**vous savez** (you know)
3rd Person	**il/elle sait** (he/she/it knows)	**ils/elles savent** (they know)

The phrase **Je sais** means "I know." You can add the word **que** ("that") just after it to introduce an idea (which represents the thing that you know): **Je sais *que* tu aimes les chats.** (I know *that* you like cats.) Or try this tricky one: **Je sais *que* tu sais *que* mon chien est méchant!** (I know *that* you know *that* my dog is mean!)

Voir (to see) [09_08/Tr. 52]

Person	Singular	Plural
1st Person	**je vois** (I see)	**nous voyons** (we see)
2nd Person	**tu vois** (you see)	**vous voyez** (you see)
3rd Person	**il/elle voit** (he/she/it sees)	**ils/elles voient** (they see)

While you simply need to memorize irregular forms like those explained here, know that these are actually the building blocks of other verbs that you will be able to conjugate easily once you've mastered these "base" forms. For instance, **surprendre** (to surprise) is conjugated just like **prendre** and **comprendre**, just with the **sur-** prefix. **Prévoir** (to predict or foretell) is conjugated just like **voir**, simply adding the **pré-** prefix.

Say It Aloud!

This exercise has two parts. First, translate each sentence from English into French. Then, say each French sentence aloud, comparing your pronunciation to the audio file (09_09/Tr. 53).

1. Aurélie is eating the grapes.
   Translation: ______________________________
2. The fox is not eating the grapes.
   Translation: ______________________________
3. "The grapes will be bad!"
   Translation: ______________________________
4. The fox is going to look for the apple trees.
   Translation: ______________________________
5. "We will stay near the vines."
   Translation: ______________________________
6. "You are not going to like the grapes!"
   Translation: ______________________________

Changing Tenses

Go back to the previous exercise and look only at your French translations. Rewrite the French sentences below, changing the present-tense sentences to future tense and the future-tense sentences to present tense.

1. ______________________________
   ____
2. ______________________________
   ____
3. ______________________________
   ____
4. ______________________________
   ____

5. ____

____

6. ____

____

I Know That You Know . . . Or Do You?

Below might be one of the most confusing sentences you've ever seen. Translate it into English on the lines provided!

Je sais que tu sais que nous savons qu'elle sait que vous savez que j'aime la grammaire.

____

Grammaire

1. Grammatically speaking, the word "tense" means:
   a. time
   b. tight
   c. verb
   d. ingredient
2. Which sentence below is in the *future tense*?
   a. **Jean veut partir.**
   b. **Le lapin ne doit pas attendre.**
   c. **Nous allons marcher.**
   d. **Aurélie ne veut pas rester.**
3. One sentence has *one* extra word that shouldn't be there. Which sentence is it?
   a. **Vous allez courir?**
   b. **Ils vont à aimer mon gâteau.**
   c. **Thibault ne va pas rester dans le village.**
   d. **Les chiens ne vont pas manger le chat.**
4. Which negative sentence is *correct*?
   a. **Vous ne pas allez dormir dans la maison.**
   b. **Vous n'allez dormir pas dans la maison.**
   c. **Vous allez ne pas dormir dans la maison.**
   d. **Vous n'allez pas dormir dans la maison.**

Nouveau Vocabulaire

Fill in the blank with the correct translation for each word.

Français	Anglais
1. **comprendre, je comprends**	______
2. **prendre, je prends**	______
3. **voir, je vois**	______
4. **partir, je pars**	______
5. **savoir, je sais**	______
6. **un raisin**	______
7. **une région**	______
8. **souvent**	______
9. **le pommier**	______
10. **le cerisier**	______
11. **la vigne**	______

Ancien Vocabulaire

Fill in the blank with the correct translation for each word.

Français	Anglais
1. **courir, je cours**	______
2. **une course**	______
3. **vite/lent**	______
4. **la jambe**	______
5. **la main/les mains**	______

Français	Anglais
6. **le bras**	______________
7. **une bouche**	______________
8. **le pied**	______________
9. **un œil/des yeux**	______________
10. **le dos**	______________

The Body in Action

Draw lines to match the actions on the left with the different parts of the body used in those actions on the right.

1. **je comprends** — A. **avec la bouche**
2. **je pars** — B. **avec les yeux**
3. **je vois** — C. **avec les pieds**
4. **je prends** — D. **avec la tête**
5. **je parle** — E. **avec les mains**

Missing Letters

In the two conjugation charts below, many of the verb forms are missing letters. Your job is to fill them in so that they're complete! We've done the first box of the first chart as an example for you.

Voir (to see)

Person	Singular	Plural
1st Person	**je v o i s** (I see)	**nous v o y o ____ s** (we see)
2nd Person	**tu v o ____ s** (you see)	**vous v o ____ e z** (you see)
3rd Person	**il/elle v o i ____** (he/she/it sees)	**ils/elles v o ____ e n t** (they see)

Partir (to leave)

Person	Singular	Plural
1st Person	**je p a ____ s** (I leave)	**nous p a r t ____ n s** (we leave)
2nd Person	**tu p a ____ s** (you leave)	**vous p a r t ____ z** (you leave)
3rd Person	**il/elle p a r ____** (he/she/it leaves)	**ils/elles p a r ____ e n t** (they leave)

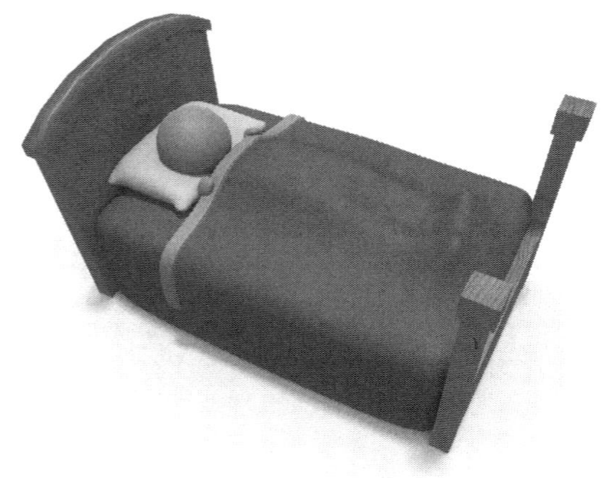

Traduction

Though the following episodes are not exactly from the dialogues of the last few **chapitres**, you will recognize the situations easily. Translate the sentences and conversations into English.

1. **Thibault, Aurélie, et Jean ne comprennent pas les rats.**
   "Est-ce que vous voyez les rats?"
   "Oui! Nous voyons les rats! Les rats prennent un œuf. Mais qu'est-ce qu'ils vont faire avec ça?!"

   Translation: ______________________________

   ____

   ____

   ____

2. **Le lapin attend la tortue. Elle va arriver. Le lapin ne va pas partir avant.**
   "Pourquoi est-ce que vous partez? Vous ne voulez pas rester ici pour manger les fruits et dormir?"

   Translation: ______________________________

   ____

   ____

   ____

   ____

3. **Le renard voit les raisins, mais il ne peut pas manger les raisins. "Je sais que ces raisins ne vont pas être délicieux!"**
   Aurélie whispers to Jean, **"Comment est-ce qu'il sait?"**
   Jean replies, **"Je ne sais pas!"**

   Translation: ______________________________

   ____

   ____

   ____

   ____

Dictée!

Listen to the audio file [09_10/Tr. 54] of the **dictée** for this **chapitre**. On the lines provided, write down the three sentences you hear. You do not need to write translations for them, though it's good practice to think through what the English translation would be. You may stop and repeat the audio file several times as you're writing down the sentences.

1. ______________________________

   ____

2. ______________________________

   ____

3. ______________________________

   ____

CHAPITRE 10 CINQ

In this unit, we picked up where we had left off with the special question words **qui** and **quoi**, and we added a major new verb to our list: **faire**. We then dug our heels into the *boot verbs* of **chapitre** 7 (**devoir**, **pouvoir**, **vouloir**). We followed that up with a triple whammy in **chapitre** 8: **Quelle heure est-il?** and telling time, part 6 of the Curious Haves—**avoir raison/tort**—and a whole bunch of new irregular verbs, such as **venir** and **attendre**. Finally, in **chapitre** 9, we discovered another **paquet** (bunch) of irregular verbs, as well as the *future tense* (**aller** + an infinitive verb), which lets us say "I *will* do something" or "You *are going to* do something." Take a look back over the vocabulary from the preceding four chapters and note any words with which you're still having trouble. We'll meet you on the other side for some rocking review exercises!

	French	English
☐	**faire, je fais**	
☐	**arriver, j'arrive**	
☐	**cacher, je cache**	
☐	**casser, je casse**	
☐	**tirer, je tire**	
☐	**dégoûtant**	
☐	**l'œuf**	
☐	**l'omelette**	
☐	**le rat**	
☐	**la dame**	
☐	**devoir, je dois**	
☐	**pouvoir, je peux**	
☐	**vouloir, je veux**	

	French	English
☐	**cher**	
☐	**si**	
☐	**une pomme**	
☐	**une fraise**	
☐	**une pêche**	
☐	**une pomme de terre**	
☐	**une tomate**	
☐	**attendre, j'attends**	
☐	**courir, je cours**	
☐	**dormir, je dors**	
☐	**avoir raison/tort, j'ai raison/tort**	
☐	**venir, je viens**	

	French	English
☐	**une course**	______
☐	**une cerise**	______
☐	**une poire**	______
☐	**fou**	______
☐	**vite/lent**	______
☐	**comprendre, je comprends**	______
☐	**prendre, je prends**	______
☐	**voir, je vois**	______

	French	English
☐	**partir, je pars**	______
☐	**savoir, je sais**	______
☐	**un raisin**	______
☐	**une région**	______
☐	**souvent**	______
☐	**le pommier**	______
☐	**le cerisier**	______
☐	**une vigne**	______

My List of Words to Master

So that you can easily review the words you are having difficulty remembering, write them down on the lines provided below.

Sentences

Write five sentences using words you have put on your list of words to master.

1. ____

____

____

2. ____

____

____

3. ____

____

____

4. ____

____

____

5. ____

____

____

GRAMMAIRE

The Verb *Faire* ("to do/make," **Chapitre** 6)

Write the correct form of the verb **faire** in the following blanks, and then translate each sentence into English.

1. **Les oiseaux ____________________ leurs maisons dans les arbres.**

   Translation: ____

   ____

2. **Son frère a cinq ans aujourd'hui. Elle ____________________ un cadeau pour son anniversaire** (birthday)**.**

   Translation: ____

   ____

3. **Nous avons faim! Alors, nous ____________________ un gâteau aux fraises.**

   Translation: ____

   ____

4. **"Madame, pourquoi est-ce que vous ____________________ une omelette avec des cerises!?"**

   Translation: ____

   ____

5. **"Ah! Ce n'est pas une omelette: je ____________________ un clafoutis.**[1] **Quand tu ____________________ un clafoutis, tu as besoin d'œufs et de cerises!"**

   Translation: ____

   ____

---

1. A **clafoutis** is a traditional French dessert. It is like a thin, spongy, cake that usually contains cherries or other fruit. Photo courtesy of Rotem Danzig, https://commons.wikimedia.org/w/index.php?curid=2354473

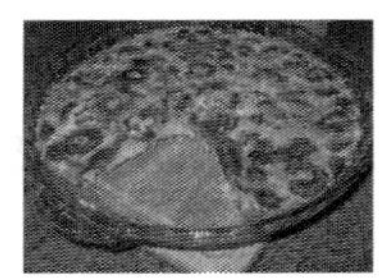

What Are They Doing?

Below there are five pictures of different people engaged in different activities. In each case, you must do two things: First, ask what the subject (in parentheses below the image) is doing by writing the question **Qu'est-ce que + faire**. Second, answer the question you formulated, still using the subject pronoun you see below the image. An example is below. By the way, to help you out with the second step, we've put the possible actions in the *infinitive* form to the right—you'll have to conjugate them, of course.

Example:

(il)

Question: **Qu'est-ce qu'il fait?** (What is he doing?)

Answer: **Il chante!** (He's singing!)

dormir

courir

jouer

étudier

manger

1.

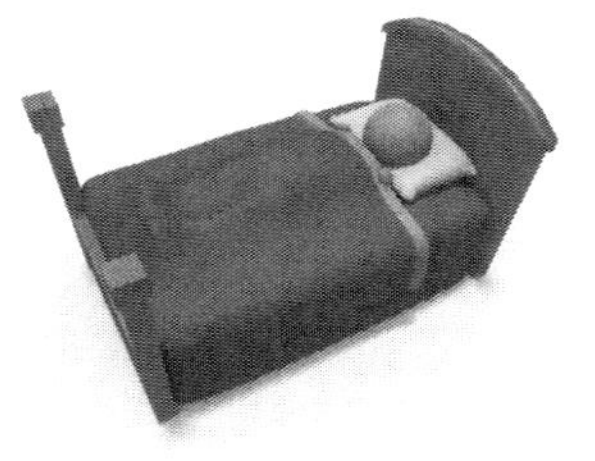

(il)

Question: ______________________________

____

Answer: ______________________________

____

2.

(vous)

Question: ______________________________

____

Answer: ______________________________

____

3.

(elles)

Question: ______________________________

____

Answer: ______________________________

____

4. 

(nous)

Question: ______________________________

____

Answer: ______________________________

____

5. 

(il)

Question: ______________________________

____

Answer: ______________________________

____

Boot Verbs (Chapitre 7)

Which Boot Fits?

Three of the four conjugation charts below are trying to trick you into thinking that they're the correct one for the boot verb **pouvoir**. It's your job to decide which one of the four is correct. Circle it and ignore the others once you've identified the correct one!

A.

je peut (I can)	**nous pouvons** (we can)
tu peut (you can)	**vous pouvez** (you can)
il/elle peut (he/she/it can)	**ils/elles peuvent** (they can)

B.

je peux (I can)	**nous peuvons** (we can)
tu peux (you can)	**vous peuvez** (you can)
il/elle peut (he/she/it can)	**ils/elles peuvent** (they can)

C.

je pue (I can)	**nous puons** (we can)
tu pues (you can)	**vous puez** (you can)
il/elle pue (he/she/it can)	**ils/elles puent** (they can)

D.

je peux (I can)	**nous pouvons** (we can)
tu peux (you can)	**vous pouvez** (you can)
il/elle peut (he/she/it can)	**ils/elles peuvent** (they can)

Give 'Em the Boot

Translate the following questions into French using the boot verbs you learned in **chapitre** 7. (Hint: You may recognize these situations from Jean and Aurélie's adventures.)

1. **Qu'est-ce qu'ils veulent faire avec l'œuf?**

   Translation: ______________________________

2. **Comment est-ce que vous pouvez trouver des fromages dans la forêt?**

   Translation: ______________________________

3. **Qui veut aller à la ville?**

   Translation: ______________________________

4. **Où est-ce que nous pouvons acheter des légumes?**

   Translation: ______________________________

5. **Comment est-ce que nous pouvons dormir dans la grange avec tous les animaux?**

   Translation: ______________________________

6. **Pourquoi est-ce que vous devez partir?**

   Translation: ______________________________

Telling Time, Irregular Verbs (Chapitre 8)

1. In French, how do you ask, "What time is it?"

   ____

2. Write down, in French, what time each clock is showing.

   a. ______________________________

   b. ______________________________

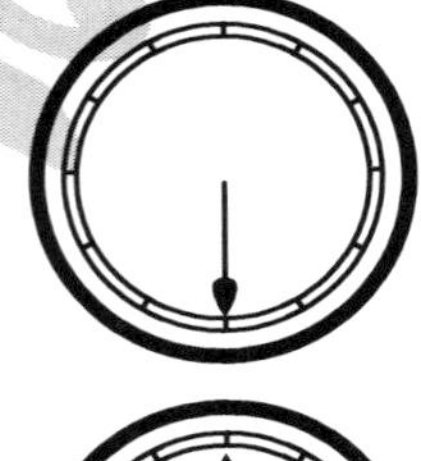

c. ______________________________

d. ______________________________

e. ______________________________

3. Some Irregulars: Help sort out the confused conjugation. Cross out the incorrect verb forms and fill in the blank with the correct one. We've taken care of one box for you.

Venir (to come)

Person	Singular	Plural
1st Person	**je vient** ________	**nous viennent** ________
2nd Person	**tu ~~venons~~** viens	**vous viennent** ________
3rd Person	**il/elle viens** ________	**ils/elles vient** ________

4. Circle the correct conjugation of each verb.
   a. **Jean et Aurélie ne ____________ pas vers la ville.**
   (court / courons / courent)

   b. **La mère de Thibault ____________ le fromage dans son village.**
   (attendent / attends / attend)

   c. **Les animaux dans le zoo ____________ Jean et Aurélie.**
   (attendent / attends / attend)

d. **"Nous ne _______________ pas de la forêt. Nous _______________ du zoo!"**
(viennent / venons / vient) (est / sont / sommes)

e. **Thibault _______________ du village.**
(vient / viens / viennent)

f. **Le lapin ne _______________ pas. Il veut _______________ la tortue.**
(cours / courons / court) (attend / attendre / attends)

The Future Tense, More Irregular Verbs (Chapitre 9)

1. **Traduction:** Translate the following conversation. If a sentence is in French, translate it into English; if it is in English, translate it into French.

A: "What are you doing?"
Translation: ____

B: **"J'attends mes amis."**
Translation: ____

A: **"Où sont tes amis?"**
Translation: ____

B: "I don't know."
Translation: ____

A: **"Est-ce qu'ils vont venir?"**
Translation: ____

B: "Maybe."
Translation: ____

A: "I don't see your friends."
Translation: ____

B: **"Moi non plus."**
Translation: ____

A: "Well, then, when are you going to leave?"
Translation: ____

B: **"Je ne sais pas."**
Translation: ____

A: "OK, well, I'm leaving now."

Translation: ______________________________

B: "You're right! I'll go with you!"[2]

Translation: ______________________________

2. **Ifs Only + Say It Aloud!** Translate the following sentences, which all begin with the word "if" (**si**). Then go back and pronounce the French sentences, comparing your pronunciation with the audio file (10_01/Tr. 55).

a. **Si tu ne manges pas, tu vas avoir faim.**

Translation: ______________________________

b. **Si je ne cours pas, je ne vais pas arriver avant neuf heures.**

Translation: ______________________________

c. **Si vous n'étudiez pas, vous n'allez pas réussir à l'école.**

Translation: ______________________________

d. **Si elles ne prennent pas la voiture, elles vont devoir marcher.**

Translation: ______________________________

e. **S'il ne voit pas ses amis au village, il va partir.**

Translation: ______________________________

2. Note: "You" = **toi** at the end of this sentence (see **chapitre** 13).

DIALOGUE [11_01/TR. 56]

Full of fresh fruit, our travelers spend a pleasant night under the stars. The distant lights of the city appear faintly on the horizon. The next morning, traffic on the road begins to pick up, and among the many wagons and carts rolling along, the three companions happen upon a rather slow-moving voyager.

AURÉLIE. **Hé oh! Je vois une tortue, là-bas. C'est peut-être l'amie du lapin!**

THIBAULT. **Je pense que tu as raison, Aurélie.** Let's go talk to her—we can at least tell her that she's winning their race by a long shot. **Elle va être contente.**

They catch up to the tortoise.

JEAN. **Bonjour, Mademoiselle la Tortue!**

MADEMOISELLE LA TORTUE. Bonjour, bonjour! Comment allez-vous?

JEAN. **Ben, très bien, merci.**

AURÉLIE. **Est-ce que tu es l'amie du petit lapin du village?**

MLLE[1] LA TORTUE. Ah! Vous connaissez Monsieur le lapin!? Oui, bien sûr, je suis une de ses amis. Nous faisons une course cette semaine. Nous avons commencé dimanche.

JEAN. **Oui, oui, nous savons. Nous avons vu ton ami le lapin.** He's a few miles back. **Il dort, il mange—mais il ne court pas beaucoup.**

MLLE LA TORTUE. Ah bon? Ça c'est intéressant! *Très* intéressant!

JEAN. **Je pense que tu vas gagner, mademoiselle!**

MLLE LA TORTUE. Hmmm . . . tu as raison, peut-être. Even if he runs his fastest, I don't think he can catch me now. **Quand est-ce que vous avez parlé avec mon ami?**

THIBAULT. **Aujourd'hui, nous sommes mardi, n'est-ce pas?**

MLLE LA TORTUE. Oui.

THIBAULT. **Alors, nous avons vu le lapin hier, lundi. Oui, hier après-midi.** About seven miles behind.

MLLE LA TORTUE. Ah bon!? Alors, il ne va pas arriver à la ville avant le soir.

AURÉLIE. **Mais peut-être qu'il a fini de dormir! Peut-être qu'il a fini de manger! Peut-être qu'il va arriver demain matin . . . attention!**

MLLE LA TORTUE. Attention? Pourquoi est-ce que je dois faire attention? Je n'ai pas peur! Il va arriver trop tard.

AURÉLIE. **Ah bon? Trop tard? Comment?**

MLLE LA TORTUE. Vous marchez aussi vers la ville, n'est-ce pas?

JEAN. **Oui, et alors?**

MLLE LA TORTUE. Eh ben, nous allons arriver ce soir!

---

1. **Mlle** is the abbreviation for **Mademoiselle**, which means "Miss" in English (note that there is no period after the abbreviation). For **Monsieur** ("Mister"), we just use a capital **M.** (don't forget that period afterward), and for **Madame** it's **Mme** (no period after).

Chant [11_02/Tr. 57]

Le passé composé: avoir + the Past Participle

Person	Singular	Plural
1st Person	**j'ai chanté** (I sang)	**nous avons chanté** (we sang)
2nd Person	**tu as chanté** (you sang)	**vous avez chanté** (you sang)
3rd Person	**il/elle a chanté** (he/she/it sang)	**ils/elles ont chanté** (they sang)

Vocabulaire [11_03/Tr. 58]

Français	Anglais
connaître, je connais	to know, I know (personally)
gagner, je gagne	to win, I win
demain	tomorrow
avant	before
le soir	the evening
le matin	the morning
hier	yesterday
l'après-midi	the afternoon
la semaine	the week
tard	late

Faire attention — to pay attention (ex. **Je fais attention** = I pay attention)

mademoiselle — miss (as in "Excuse me, miss.")

cette — this, that (for feminine nouns; **ce**, from **chapitre** 3, is used for masculine nouns)

les jours de la semaine
the days of the week (Note that to say in French, "Today is Thursday"—or Friday, or Monday, etc.—we often say, "**Aujourd'hui, nous sommes jeudi,**"[2] which means "Today we are Thursday.")

Lundi, Mardi, Mercredi, Jeudi, Vendredi, Samedi, Dimanche
Monday, Tuesday, Wednesday, Thursday, Friday, Saturday, Sunday

Le Passé Composé (The Past Tense)

As promised, this **chapitre** introduces you to the past tense. Notice, however, what we've called this section: **le passé composé**. **Passé**, you might have guessed, means "past" in English, but what's with the **composé** part? Again, you can probably see the English cognate for this word: "compose" or, in this case, "composed." What does it mean when something is composed? It simply means that it is made up of different things that are put together. Well, that is exactly what the **passé composé**—the past tense in French—is: a composition of two different elements. Check out the two elements in action below—they are the two underlined words:

Nous avons parlé beaucoup aujourd'hui!	We talked a lot today!
Vous avez couru très loin.	You guys ran very far.
J'ai fini mes devoirs.	I finished my homework.

Do you see a pattern for the *first* element in the **passé composé** (i.e., the *first* underlined word in each sentence)? It is the verb **avoir** conjugated to match the subject of each sentence. Now, in this case, **avoir** does not mean "to have": It is simply the first element in making the past tense. Because **avoir** is not being used in its "normal" way (meaning "to have") but rather as a helping verb to form a tense (the past tense), we call it an *auxiliary* verb here. *Auxiliary verbs are verbs that help form different tenses.*

The second underlined word in each sentence may look bizarre to you, since you probably recognize the verbs, but have never seen them in this particular form. What you have in each case is called the *past participle* of the verb: **parlé** for **parler**, **couru** for **courir**, and **fini** for **finir**. *The past participle is the form of a verb that combines with the auxiliary to make the past tense.* Now, don't panic, you don't really need to learn a thousand new verb forms! Many past participles are very easy, and very similar: *All regular **-er** verbs form the past participle by replacing the final **-er** with the letter **é**.*

parler à **parlé**	**manger** à **mangé**
chercher à **cherché**	**chanter** à **chanté**

Another reliable rule is that *all regular **-ir** verbs form the past participle out of the infinitive form of the verb, minus the **-r**.*

réussir à **réussi**	**finir** à **fini**

2. In French, days of the week are not normally capitalized unless they are at the beginning of a sentence.

Still, it is true that many other verbs do not have a predictable past participle. Here are some irregulars:

courir à **couru**
voir à **vu**
être à **été**
devoir à **dû**
faire à **fait**
avoir (as in "to have/possess") à **eu**

ATTENTION

The word **eu** is pronounced simply like the letter **u** in French; see the Pronunciation Wizard in *FFCA* if you're not sure how it should sound.

These irregular exceptions, along with all of the other irregular and regular participles, are listed in the back of the book in appendix C. In the conjugation charts in that appendix, we call them "p.p." for "past participle." However, they also have their own appendix dedicated just to them (see appendix D). You'll want to spend some time soaking in the past participles in that section, and then flip back and forth to complete the exercises in this **chapitre**.

So, here's a quick diagram to review all of our new terms:

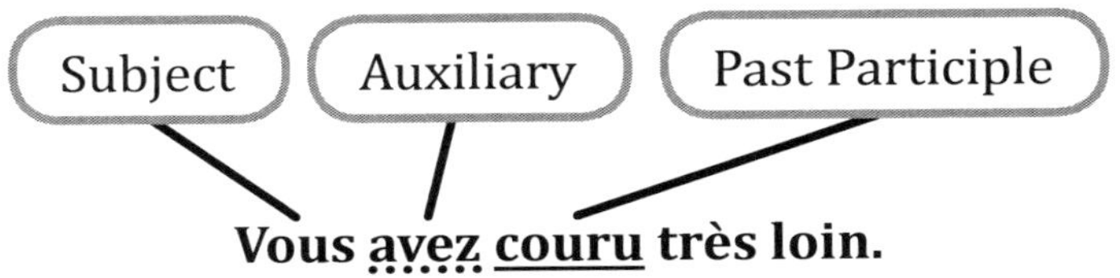

NEGATIVES AND THE PASSÉ COMPOSÉ

Making a past tense sentence negative is a piece of cake. In fact, it's just like making boot verbs and the future tense negative. That is, the spectacles (**ne** and **pas**) just surround the auxiliary verb **avoir** like this:

Vous n'avez pas nagé.
You didn't swim.

Je n'ai pas aimé ton chat.
I didn't like your cat.

CONNAÎTRE VS. SAVOIR

In **chapitre** 9, you learned the verb **savoir**, which means "to know." So, you might be a little curious as to just what the difference is between **savoir** and the verb you're learning this week, **connaître**, especially since we translated them both as "to know." It all comes down to how these verbs are used. **Connaître** is used to talk about knowing things "personally"—people, places, or other things that are *familiar* to us. The following are some examples:

Je connais ton frère.
I know your brother.

Il ne connaît pas New York City.
He doesn't know New York City.

Est-ce que vous connaissez la musique de Beethoven?
Do you know Beethoven's music?

On the other hand, to talk about *facts* or *abilities*, we use **savoir** (and notice that when we're talking about abilities, we use the *infinitive* form of the action):

Elle sait que les loups sont dangereux.
She knows that wolves are dangerous.

Ils ne savent pas chanter.
They don't know how to sing.

Est-ce que vous savez faire des gâteaux?
Do you know how to make cakes?

Finally, you've already learned how to conjugate **savoir**, so here's the conjugation of **connaître**. It is somewhat irregular, so **fais attention**!

Person	Singular	Plural
1st Person	**je connais** (I know)	**nous connaissons** (we know)
2nd Person	**tu connais** (you know)	**vous connaissez** (you know)
3rd Person	**il/elle connaît** (he/she/it knows)	**ils/elles connaissent** (they know)
—	Past Participle: **connu**	

W

Tense

Below are several sentences from this **chapitre**'s Jean and Aurélie episode. Your job is to say whether they are in the **passé composé**, the *present tense*, or the *future tense*. Write your answers in the blanks provided.

1. **Je vois une tortue là-bas.**

    ____

2. **Elle va être contente.**

    ____

3. **Vous connaissez Monsieur le lapin!?**

    ____

4. **Nous avons vu ton ami le lapin.**

    ____

5. **Nous avons commencé dimanche.**

    ____

6. **Mais peut-être qu'il a fini de dormir!**

    ____

7. **Il va arriver trop tard.**

    ____

8. **Eh ben, nous allons arriver ce soir!**

    ____

Messy Calendar

Fix the calendar below by crossing out the incorrect French words for the days of the week and writing the correct ones below the English words. We've done the first one for you as an example.

Monday	Tuesday	Wednesday	Thursday	Friday	Saturday	Sunday
~~Jeudi~~	Lundi	Vendredi	Samedi	Dimanche	Mardi	Mercredi
Lundi	______	______	______	______	______	______

Traduction + Say It Aloud!

Translate the following sentences from French into English. Then, go back and say the French sentences aloud, comparing your pronunciation to the audio file (11_05/Tr. 60).

1. **Hier, j'ai vu ma famille.**
   Translation: ______________________________
2. **Ils ont été très contents.**
   Translation: ______________________________
3. **Ma mère a fait un gâteau.**
   Translation: ______________________________
4. **Je n'ai pas fait attention.**
   Translation: ______________________________
5. **J'ai mangé tout le gâteau.**
   Translation: ______________________________
6. **Mon frère et mes sœurs n'ont pas aimé ça.**
   Translation: ______________________________
7. **"Qu'est-ce que tu as fait!?"**
   Translation: ______________________________
8. **J'ai dû partir.**
   Translation: ______________________________

Grammaire

1. In French, the past tense is made up of:
   a. one part.
   b. two parts.
   c. five parts.
   d. thirty-seven-and-a-half parts, not counting subparts.

2. The verb **avoir** is an auxiliary verb when:
   a. it means "to have or to possess," as in the sentence "**J'ai un chien.**"
   b. it is used as a part of the present tense.
   c. it is helping form the past tense.
   d. it is used in delicate conversations.

3. To say "I didn't sing yesterday" in French, we say:
   a. "**Je n'ai pas chanté hier.**"
   b. "**Je n'ai chanté pas hier.**"
   c. "**Je n'ai chanté hier.**"
   d. "**Je ne ai chanté pas hier.**"

4. If a verb is regular, and ends in **-er**, the way you can figure out its past participle is by:
   a. adding an **é** to the end of the infinitive.
   b. replacing the **-er** of the infinitive with the ending **é**.
   c. taking off the last **r** from the infinitive.
   d. It is impossible to figure this out, since past participles are irregular.

Nouveau Vocabulaire

Fill in the blank with the correct translation for each word.

Français	Anglais
1. **connaître, je connais**	________________
2. **gagner, je gagne**	________________
3. **demain**	________________
4. **avant**	________________
5. **le soir**	________________
6. **le matin**	________________
7. **hier**	________________
8. **l'après-midi**	________________
9. **la semaine**	________________
10. **tard**	________________

Ancien Vocabulaire

Fill in the blank with the correct translation for each word.

Français	Anglais
1. **regarder, je regarde**	________________
2. **comprendre, je comprends**	________________
3. **finir, je finis**	________________
4. **travailler, je travaille**	________________
5. **courir, je cours**	________________
6. **trouver, je trouve**	________________

Français	Anglais
7. dormir, je dors	____________
8. acheter, j'achète	____________
9. cacher, je cache	____________
10. vouloir, je veux	____________

Jean and Aurélie's Adventures

Describe what happened on each day of this *past* week in Jean and Aurélie's lives by looking at the descriptions written in each block of the calendar. Write your description in French, using the subject(s) (underlined) and the action(s) provided (in the past tense, of course![3]). Some days have two different events. We've completed one of the descriptions for you.

Lundi
- **Jean et Aurélie**
  - **dormir dans la forêt**

Mardi
- **Jean et Aurélie**
  - **parler avec Thibault**

Mercredi
- **Thibault, Jean, Aurélie**
  - **marcher au marché avec le père de Thibault**

Jeudi
- **Aurélie**
  - **voir le loup**
- **Le loup**
  - **avoir faim**

Vendredi
- **Jean, Aurélie, Thibault**
  - **trouver le village**
- **Le gardien**
  - **étre méchant**

Samedi
- **Les rats**
  - **cacher l'œuf**

Dimanche
- **Le lapin**
  - **commencer la course avec la tortue**

Lundi: ______________________________

____

Mardi: **Jean et Aurélie ont parlé avec Thibault.**

3. Remember, if you cannot figure out what the past participle of a verb is, you can look in the conjugation charts in appendix C, or in appendix D, which covers past participles.

Mercredi: ____

____

Jeudi: ____

____

Vendredi: ____

____

Samedi: ____

____

Dimanche: ____

____

Connaître vs. Savoir

Circle the correct form of either **connaître** or **savoir**. Remember, **connaître** is used to talk about knowing things "personally" and **savoir** is used to talk about facts or abilities.

1. **Nous ne ________________ pas nager.**
   (savons / connaissons)
2. **Ah oui! Je ________________ ton père!**
   (connais / sais)
3. **Jean ________________ parler en anglais et en français.**
   (sait / connaît)
4. **Aurélie ne ________________ pas parler en anglais.**
   (connaît / sait)
5. **Le lapin ne ________________ pas où est la tortue.**
   (sait / connaît)
6. **Jean, Aurélie, et Thibault ________________ que la ville est loin.**
   (savent / connaissent)
7. **Jean et Aurélie ________________ la ville parce qu'ils ont habité là-bas.**
   (saven / connaissent)

Confused Trios

The following sentences come in groups of three, but each trio looks almost as though it's the same sentence. Translate the trio so that it's clear what the different sentences mean. We've done the first one for you as an example.

Exemple:

J'ai un chien. I have a dog.
J'ai eu un chien. I had a dog.
Je vais avoir un chien. I will have a dog.

1. **Elle veut chanter.** ______________________

   Elle va chanter. ______________________

   Elle a chanté. ______________________

2. **Ils ont une voiture.** ______________________

   Ils vont avec la voiture. ______________________

   Ils ont eu une voiture. ______________________

3. **Il est content.** ______________________

   Il a été content. ______________________

   Il va être content. ______________________

4. **Tu veux manger le fromage.** ______________________

   Tu vas manger le fromage. ______________________

   Tu as mangé le fromage. ______________________

Dictée!

Listen to the audio file [11_06/Tr. 61] of the **dictée** for this **chapitre**. On the lines provided, write down the three sentences you hear. You do not need to write translations for them, though it's good practice to think through what the English translation would be. You may stop and repeat the audio file several times as you're writing down the sentences.

1. ______________________
2. ______________________
3. ______________________

CHAPITRE 12 DOUZE

DIALOGUE [12_01/TR. 62]

The road is getting busier with each passing hour, so the four travelers shift toward the shoulder of the road. ***Mademoiselle la Tortue*** *peppers Jean, Aurélie, and Thibault with questions about their trip to the city . . .*

MLLE LA TORTUE. So, exactly how far have you all come? Are you just on your way up from the orchards?

JEAN. **Pas du tout! Nous avons commencé dans la forêt. Nous avons marché de la forêt aux montagnes. Ensuite, nous avons marché des montagnes au fleuve. Du fleuve, nous sommes entrés au village.**

THIBAULT. That's when I first saw them. **J'ai rencontré Aurélie et Jean dans le village.**

AURÉLIE. **Et finalement, nous sommes partis pour la ville.**

MLLE LA TORTUE. Ouah! Incroyable! Vous avez fait un grand voyage! Vous marchez très, très vite!

JEAN. **Oui, et nous n'avons pas fini. Nous retournons chez nous—au zoo.**

MLLE LA TORTUE, *turning to Thibault.* You . . . you don't look like you live in the zoo.

THIBAULT. **Oui, tu as raison. J'habite dans mon village. Mais je ne suis jamais parti du village, alors j'ai voulu voir la ville.** When Aurélie and Jean told me about their plans to go back, **j'ai eu envie de venir**!

MLLE LA TORTUE. Ah! Tu n'as jamais vu la ville? Tu vas beaucoup aimer la ville. C'est chouette!

THIBAULT. **Tout le monde dit ça!**

MLLE LA TORTUE. Qu'est-ce que vous allez faire là-bas? Seulement visiter le zoo?

THIBAULT. Well, aside from Aurélie and Jean getting back home, **nous avons une chose très importante à faire**.

MLLE LA TORTUE. Hmmm . . . voir les musées?

THIBAULT. **Non. Nous n'allons pas voir les musées . . .**

MLLE LA TORTUE. Aller au restaurant?

JEAN. **Non. Les vaches ne peuvent pas manger dans les restaurants.**

AURÉLIE, *hurt.* **Et les souris!?**

MLLE LA TORTUE. Hmmm . . . alors, faire du shopping?

THIBAULT. **Pas vraiment . . .**

MLLE LA TORTUE. Ben, je ne sais pas, alors. Quoi?

THIBAULT. **Nous allons acheter du fromage.**

Chant [12_02/Tr. 63]

Mini Tour de France

Paris, c'est beau, Paris—je suis retourné.
L'Alsace est belle, très belle—il est retourné.
La Provence est superbe, ah oui, superbe—elle est retournée.
Et la Bretagne, la Normandie? Magnifique, magnifique—ils sont retournés . . .
elles sont retournées, nous sommes retournés, vous êtes retournés!
Et toi, tu es retourné?

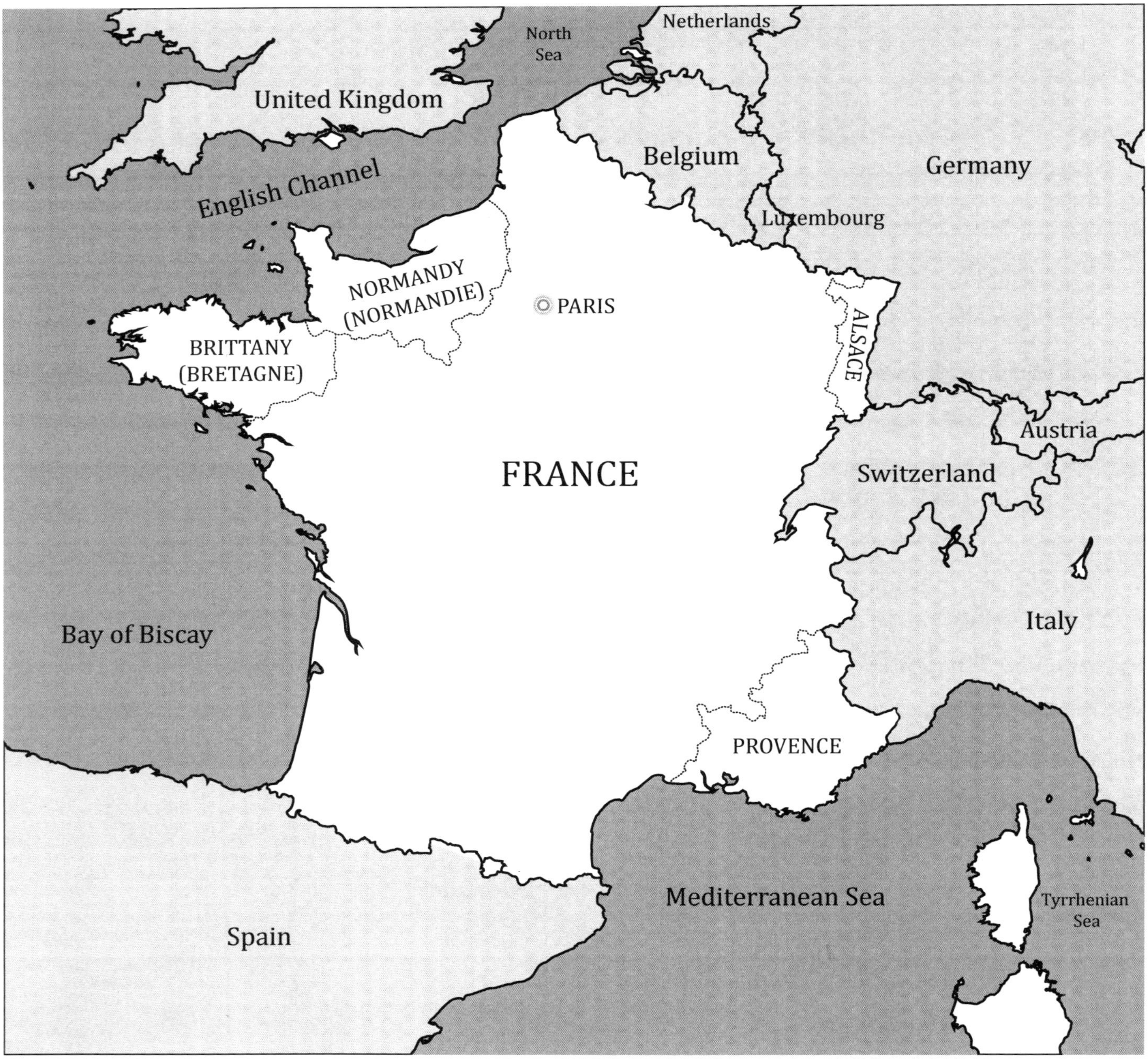

Netherlands
North Sea
United Kingdom
Belgium
Germany
English Channel
Luxembourg
NORMANDY (NORMANDIE)
PARIS
ALSACE
BRITTANY (BRETAGNE)
Austria
FRANCE
Switzerland
Italy
Bay of Biscay
PROVENCE
Mediterranean Sea
Tyrrhenian Sea
Spain

Le passé composé II: être + the past participle [12_03/Tr. 64]

Person	Singular	Plural
1st Person	**je suis retourné**[1] (I returned)	**nous sommes retournés** (we returned)
2nd Person	**tu es retourné** (you returned)	**vous êtes retournés** (you returned)
3rd Person	**il est retourné** (he returned) **elle est retournée** (she returned)	**ils sont retournés** (they returned) **elles sont retournées** (they, [f.] returned)

Vocabulaire [12_04/Tr. 65]

Français	Anglais
rencontrer, je rencontre	to meet, I meet
dire, je dis	to say, I say
retourner, je retourne	to return, I return
un musée	a museum
un restaurant	a restaurant
ensuite	then, next
finalement	finally
seulement	only
jamais	never[2]
après	after

Conversation Journal [12_05/Tr. 66]

Incroyable! Unbelievable!

Chouette! Awesome!

Laisse tomber! Forget it! (The literal translation is "Let it fall!")

1. One interesting difference between the French **retourner** and the English "to return" is that the French verb means more "to go back *somewhere*," as in "I'd love to return to Japan after spending the summer there last year." In English we use "to return" in that way, but just as often we use it to mean "to come back," as in: "When the waiter returns, he will bring you extra cheese." In French, this action is better translated with the verb **revenir** (to come back) rather than **retourner**.
2. When used as part of a negative sentence, **jamais** replaces the word **pas** (from the **ne** and **pas** "spectacles"—see chapter 3). For example: "I never liked cheese" translates as **Je n'ai *jamais* aimé le fromage**.

Le Passé Composé with Être

The **passé composé** has another trick up its sleeve that we did not see in our last **chapitre**. That is, the **passé composé** does not always use the verb **avoir** as its auxiliary, or helping, verb. Sometimes it uses **être**, the verb "to be." For example, check out these sentences, which are all in the past tense—**le passé composé**—thanks to different forms of **être**:

Je suis allé à l'école.
I went to (the) school.

Vous êtes venus du village?
You came from the village?

Il est retourné à la plage.
He returned to the beach.

RAPPEL

If you're rusty on your **être** conjugation, flip back to **chapitre** 1 for a few minutes and make sure you've got it down pat.

You can see that the **passé composé** is still *composed* of two parts—an auxiliary (above, we have: **suis**, **êtes**, and **est**) and the past participle (**allé**, **venus**, and **retourné**).

To Be or Not to Be?

But when does the auxiliary need to be **être** instead of **avoir**? There is a special set of verbs—some of which you haven't yet seen in this book—that take **être** as the auxiliary. Here is a short list of verbs that you have seen that need **être** to change into the past tense. Included is the base form[3] of the past participle (in parentheses):

aller (**allé**) – to go
entrer (**entré**) – to enter
partir (**parti**) – to leave
rester (**resté**) – to stay
retourner (**retourné**) – to return
tomber (**tombé**) – to fall
venir (**venu**) – to come

Though not a rule that works 100 percent of the time, it is helpful to notice that many of these verbs that use **être** communicate *movement* (going, coming, falling, leaving, etc.). **Rester** appears to be an exception to this, but actually you could think of **rester** (to stay, *not to rest!*—it's a **faux ami**!) as related to the others because it is the *exact opposite* of movement—the absence of movement.

We've indicated in appendix C whether or not the past tense of a certain verb uses **avoir** (as is the case most of the time) or **être**, so if you ever have any doubts, just check the back of the book.

3. By using the expression "base form," we are anticipating that the past participle may change, but always as a variation on the forms we've provided in parentheses here. We explain more in the next section of this **chapitre** ("Agreement with Past Participles").

Agreement with Past Participles

You might remember that we've used the word "agreement" before, back when we talked about *adjectives* that must agree with the nouns they describe (see **chapitre** 13 of *FFCA*). Basically, that meant that adjectives must reflect certain qualities of the nouns they modify—to match those qualities by either adding an **e** (for feminine nouns), an **s** (for plural nouns), or both:

le	**chat** (masculine singular noun)	**mignon** (masculine singular adjective)
les	**filles** (feminine plural noun)	**mignonnes**[4] (feminine plural adjective)

Well, the same thing is true of past participles *when the auxiliary is* ***être***. They also must add an **e** for feminine subjects and an **s** for plural subjects. Sometimes they must add an **e** *and* an **s** when the subject is feminine and plural.

Elles sont retournées.	They returned.
Ils sont partis.	They left.

Are you starting to see why the past tense with **être** actually changes from subject to subject (for examples see this **chapitre**'s verb chart)? Here are some more examples:

Elle est tombée. She fell.
(feminine, singular subject = extra **e** on the past participle)

Ils sont entréS dans la maison. They entered the house.
(masculine, plural subject = extra **s** on the past participle)

Il est venu du village. He came from the village.
(masculine, singular subject = "base" form of the past participle)

Elle est venue du village. She came from the village.
(feminine, singular subject = extra **e** on the past participle)

Elles sont alléeS au lac. They went to the lake.
(feminine, plural subject = extra **e** and extra **s** on the past participle)

> **ATTENTION**
> None of these additions—the extra **e** or the extra **s**—change the pronunciation at all. They really only show up when you're reading and writing.

4. Sometimes we even double the last consonant, as here for **mignon+n+es**.

Now, see if you can crack one last mystery before the Worksheet section. Without looking at the next paragraph, try to figure out what's going on in the following sentences. **Hint:** They are all grammatically correct!

Je suis venu.	I came.
Je suis venue.	I came.
Nous sommes partis.	We left.
Nous sommes parties.	We left.
Est-ce que tu es tombé?	Did you fall?
Est-ce que tu es tombée?	Did you fall?
Vous êtes très gentils!	You are really nice!
Vous êtes très gentilles!	You are really nice!

Did you guess that **je**, **tu**, **nous**, and **vous** depend on the gender of people being described? That is exactly what is happening in those sentences. For example, if I were a girl, I would say, "**Je suis venue**" (I came), but if I were a boy, I would say, "**Je suis venu**"—without the extra **e** since I don't need to make the past participle feminine. Or, let's say my mother is telling a story about something that happened to her and her sisters. She might begin by saying, "**Nous sommes parties de la maison à sept heures**" (We left the house at seven o'clock), and in that case, **parties** reflects the fact that the subject—**nous**—happens to be all *female* (extra **e**) and *plural* (extra **s**). Bottom line? Don't believe this **chapitre**'s verb chart (at least 100 percent!). **Je**, **tu**, **nous**, and **vous** change the past participle according to who is being described when you're using **être**!

One More Irregular!

In this **chapitre** you encounter the verb **dire** (to say), which is used quite frequently, as you might suspect. Its conjugation is a little strange, so pay close attention to the chart below!

Person	Singular	Plural
1st Person	**je dis** (I say)	**nous disons** (we say)
2nd Person	**tu dis** (you say)	**vous dites** (you say)
3rd Person	**il/elle dit** (he/she/it says)	**ils/elles disent** (they say)
—	past participle: **dit** with **avoir**	

Sentences That Just Can't Seem to Agree

In the following sentences, the past participles do not agree with the subjects. Fix the sentences by rewriting them with the correct agreement between the past participles and subjects. Then, translate each corrected sentence into English. If the subject is **je**, **tu**, **nous**, or **vous**, we have put the gender in parentheses: either masculine (m) or feminine (f).

1. **Isabelle est parti ce matin.**

   Fixed: ______________________________

   Translation: ______________________________

2. **Nous** (m) **sommes arrivé hier. Nous** (m) **sommes venu de la ville.**

   Fixed: ______________________________

   Translation: ______________________________

3. **Ils sont retourné au village.**

   Fixed: ______________________________

   Translation: ______________________________

4. **Je** (f) **suis venu à six heures.**

   Fixed: ______________________________

   Translation: ______________________________

5. **Jean est entrée dans le village.**

   Fixed: ______________________________

   Translation: ______________________________

6. **Elles sont tombé de l'arbre!**

   Fixed: ______________________________

   Translation: ______________________________

7. **Je** (m) **suis allées à la plage à dix heures.**

   Fixed: ______________________________

   Translation: ______________________________

Sniff Out the Imposters!

Remember, only the **passé composé** with **être** requires the past participle to agree with the subject. The **passé composé** with **avoir** doesn't change one bit. However, among the sentences below, several past-tense constructions with **avoir** are trying to act like the past tense with **être**. Locate these constructions and change them back by writing the corrected sentence in the blank provided. If the construction of the past tense is correct, then just write "correct" on the correction blank. Then, translate all of the sentences (the correct ones and the impostors you had to fix) into English.

1. **Finalement, nous avons trouvés le restaurant.**

   Correction: ______________________________

   Translation: ______________________________

2. **Aurélie est partie du village.**

   Correction: ______________________________

   Translation: ______________________________

3. **Elles ont rencontrées un loup.**

   Correction: ______________________________

   Translation: ______________________________

4. **Je n'ai jamais vue le musée.**

   Correction: ______________________________

   Translation: ______________________________

5. **Ils ont achetés trois pommes, et ensuite ils ont mangés dans les champs.**

   Correction: ______________________________

   Translation: ______________________________

6. **Après le village, elles sont allées à la ville.**

   Correction: ______________________________

   Translation: ______________________________

Grammaire

Circle the correct answer.

1. The past tense in French can be formed with two different helping verbs: _________ and _________.
   a. **être** and **savoir**
   b. **avoir** and **être**
   c. **faire** and **avoir**
   d. **être** and **faire**

2. Grammatically, those two verbs are called _____________ when used to form the past tense.
   a. auxiliaries
   b. infinitives
   c. conjugations
   d. **passé composé**

3. What's wrong with the following sentence? **Mes chiens sont parti!** (My dogs left!)
   a. It is missing the word **ne**, because it is negative.
   b. The word **chien** should not have an **s** because it is singular.
   c. The word **parti** should have an **s** because it is the past participle being used with **être**.
   d. The word **sont** should be **ont** because **partir** doesn't use **être** in the **passé composé**.

4. What's wrong with the following sentence? **Je ne veux pas jamais retourner là-bas.** (I never want to go back there.)
   a. **Je** might be describing a feminine subject, so **retourner** should be **retournée**.
   b. **Là-bas** should come before **retourner**.
   c. The sentence is in the past tense, so **retourner** should be **retourné**.
   d. The word **jamais** (never) replaces the word **pas**, so **pas** shouldn't be in the sentence.

Nouveau Vocabulaire

Fill in the blank with the correct translation for each word.

Français	Anglais
1. rencontrer, je rencontre	________________
2. dire, je dis	________________
3. retourner, je retourne	________________
4. un musée	________________
5. un restaurant	________________
6. ensuite	________________
7. finalement	________________
8. seulement	________________
9. jamais	________________
10. après	________________

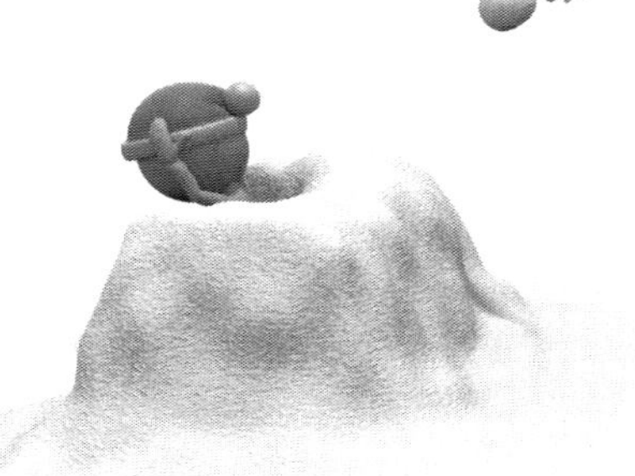

Ancien Vocabulaire

Fill in the blank with the correct translation of each word.

Français	Anglais
1. **un endroit**	______________
2. **la ferme**	______________
3. **la grange**	______________
4. **la montagne**	______________
5. **le champ**	______________
6. **le fleuve**	______________
7. **le lac**	______________
8. **la plage**	______________
9. **l'eau**	______________
10. **la mer**	______________

Dites-Le À Haute Voix! (Say It Aloud!)

Fill in the following sentences using the correct form of the *past tense* of the verb indicated next to each blank in parentheses. Then, translate the sentences into English. Finally, go back and say each of the French sentences aloud, checking your answers with the audio file (12_06/Tr. 67).

1. **Hier nous __________ __________ (rester) dans les montagnes pour seulement deux heures.**

   Translation: ____________________

   ____

2. **Elle __________ __________ (manger) mon gâteau!**

   Translation: ____________________

   ____

3. **"Hé hoh! Vous __________ __________ (laisser) vos chaussures à côté du fleuve!"**

   Translation: ____________________

   ____

4. **À six heures aujourd'hui, je __________ __________ (partir) pour la plage.**

   Translation: ____________________

   ____

5. **Hier, quand tu** (f) __________ __________ **(partir), ils __________ __________ (être) tristes.**

   Translation: ____________________

   ____

6. **J'________________ ________________ (voir) les animaux dans la ferme. Ils ________________ (venir) près de moi.**

   Translation: ____

   ____

Now try some negative sentences.

7. **Ils ____________ ____________ ____________ (ne pas vouloir) venir au lac, alors je (ne pas aller) ____________ ____________ ____________ ____________.**

   Translation: ____

   ____

8. **Les visiteurs ____________ ____________ ____________ (ne pas pouvoir) comprendre les enfants à l'école. Ils ____________ ____________ (parler) trop vite.**

   Translation: ____

   ____

9. **Je ____________ ____________ ____________ (ne pas dire) ça!**

   Translation: ____

   ____

10. **Nous ____________ ____________ ____________ (ne pas trouver) notre chat.**

   Translation: ____

   ____

11. **"Vous** (m) **____________ ____________ ____________ (ne jamais aller) aux États-Unis!?"** (**États-Unis** = United States).

   Translation: ____

   ____

He Said That She Said . . .

Figure out what happened in this ridiculous case of "whisper down the lane." Translate each step on your way down to the conclusion!

Il dit que ________________________________

tu dis qu'elle dit que ________________________________

nous disons que ________________________________

vous dites que ________________________________

je dis qu'ils disent que . . . laisse tomber!

____

Dictée!

Listen to the audio file [12_07/Tr. 68] of the **dictée** for this **chapitre**. On the lines provided, write down the three sentences you hear. You do not need to write translations for them, though it's good practice to think through what the English translation would be. You may stop and repeat the audio file several times as you're writing down the sentences.

1. ____

____

2. ____

____

3. ____

____

CHAPITRE 13 TREIZE

DIALOGUE [13_01/TR. 69]

The travelers finally reach the city's gate and enter triumphantly.

THIBAULT. **Nous sommes arrivés! Après deux jours!**

MLLE LA TORTUE. Oui, félicitations! Vous avez réussi votre voyage.

AURÉLIE. **Et félicitations à toi aussi, mademoiselle la Tortue: tu as gagné la course avec ton ami le lapin. Sans courir!**

MLLE LA TORTUE. Oui, mais aussi je suis venue à la ville sans faire de pause—that's what counts. **Vous voyez**, I didn't really dilly-dally **comme mon ami: je ne suis pas restée sous les arbres à côté de la route comme lui, je n'ai pas mangé de fruits comme lui**. And above all, **je n'ai jamais dormi au milieu de l'après-midi comme lui**!

JEAN. **Très bien!** So. Where to now, **mes amis**?

MLLE LA TORTUE. Moi, je vais attendre mon ami ici, donc, je pense que je vais dire "au revoir" maintenant. J'ai été contente de marcher avec vous!

THIBAULT. **Nous aussi! Merci . . . et à bientôt, nous espérons.**

JEAN, AURÉLIE. **Bonne soirée!**

Thibault, Aurélie, and Jean wander into the city, where shops and businesses are closing down for the night.

JEAN. **Hmm . . . Quelle heure est-il?**

THIBAULT. **Je ne sais pas—il est six heures, ou sept heures peut-être. Les magasins ferment.**

AURÉLIE. **Mince! Nous devons aller vite, alors. Le zoo ferme à huit heures. Thibault, est-ce que nous pouvons acheter ton fromage demain?**

THIBAULT. **Pas de problème.**

JEAN. **Et est-ce que ça va pour toi de dormir avec tous les animaux?**

THIBAULT. **Oui, oui, je peux dormir avec eux.** Honestly, I'm so tired I could sleep anywhere at this point!

AURÉLIE. **Moi aussi.**

JEAN. **Je suis d'accord.** *The three head off down the street. After a short distance, Jean pauses and whispers to Aurélie . . .* **Mais, entre nous, est-ce que tu sais pourquoi je suis vraiment content de retourner chez nous?**

AURÉLIE. **Non, pourquoi?**

JEAN. **Parce que finalement, après notre grand voyage, nous allons être avec des animaux normaux!**

Chant [13_02/Tr. 70]

Stressed Pronouns: *Moi, je suis beau!* (I'm handsome!)

Moi, je suis beau!
Moi, je suis intelligent!
Moi, je suis magnifique!
Moi, je suis sympathique!
Hmmm . . . toi, tu es orgueilleux!!![1]

Person	Singular	Plural
1st Person	**moi (me)**	**nous (us)**
2nd Person	**toi (you)**	**vous (you)**
3rd Person	**lui/elle (him/her)**	**eux/elles (them [m.]/them [f.])**

Vocabulaire [13_03/Tr. 71]

Français	Anglais
fermer, je ferme	to close, I close
faire une pause, je fais une pause	to take a break, I take a break
un voyage	a trip, a voyage
un magasin	a store
la route	the road
au milieu de	in the middle of
sans	without
sous	under
normal	normal
la fin	the end

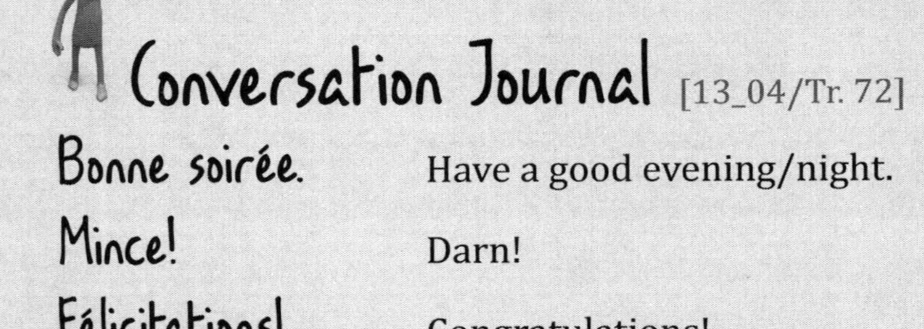

Conversation Journal [13_04/Tr. 72]

Bonne soirée.	Have a good evening/night.
Mince!	Darn!
Félicitations!	Congratulations!
entre nous	between us *or* just between us (Note the preposition **entre**, which means "between.")

1. **Orgueilleux** means "proud" or "self-centered" in English.

Stressed Pronouns

Je, **tu**, **il**, **elle**, **nous**, **vous**, **ils**, and **elles**—you've got these *pronouns* down pat by now. They correspond to the English words "I," "you," "he," "she," and so on. These are our *subject pronouns*, which means they can serve as the *subject*, or the "doer," of any action (verb) in a sentence. This **chapitre** introduces another set of pronouns used in different circumstances. They rarely take the place of the subject, or actor, in a sentence, but these *stressed pronouns*, as we shall see, play some pretty important roles just the same. As you read and repeat this **chapitre**'s chant, think of the following relationships between these new stressed pronouns and their English equivalents:

Person	Singular	Plural
1st Person	me à **moi**	us à **nous**
2nd Person	you à **toi**	you à **vous**
3rd Person	him à **lui** her à **elle**	them (m) à **eux** them (f) à **elles**

Renvoi

You've already seen stressed pronouns in action in this book. Check back in the Jean and Aurélie dialogues in **chapitre** 12 of *FFCA* and **chapitre** 8 of this book!

A word of caution: We cannot *always* translate our new stressed pronouns with these English words, but for the most part, they are good matchups. (We'll let you know if a translation trap is looming!) So, when do we use these guys? Here's a list of some of the instances in which they are used:

1. *When we want to give emphasis* to part of a sentence, we use a stressed pronoun (notice that in each case we stick the stressed pronoun right in front of the regular subject pronoun):

   Toi, tu es très intelligente!
   You're very smart! *or* You, you're very smart! (compared to other people)

   Lui, il connaît tous les animaux dans la forêt.
   He knows all the animals in the forest. *or* As for him, he knows all the animals in the forest. *or* This guy, he knows all the animals in the forest. (unlike other people who are not experts)

   Moi, je pense que la carte n'est pas bonne.
   I think that the map is not good. *or* Me, I think that the map is not good. *or* As for me, I think the map is not good. (Other people may trust the map, but this is my opinion).

Do you remember this scene when Jean and Aurélie met **Monsieur l'Oiseau** (**chapitre** 12 of *FFCA*)?

JEAN. **Bonjour, monsieur. Je m'appelle Jean.**
Hello, sir. My name is Jean.

AURÉLIE. **Et moi, je m'appelle Aurélie.**

Here, Aurélie chimes in with something that could be translated as "And me, my name is Aurélie."

2. The second kind of situation in which we use stressed pronouns is less about how important the word is. This rule is really easy, in fact. We use stressed pronouns *after a preposition* (by the way, if you want to review a quick list of all the prepositions you've seen so far, check out appendix E):

Tes frères sont méchants. Je ne veux pas jouer avec eux.
Your brothers are mean. I don't want to play with them.

Est-ce que tu as peur de moi?
Are you scared of me?

Regarde! Le loup marche à côté de nous!
Look! The wolf is walking next to us!

Let's look at this comment from when Jean and Aurélie met Thibault (**chapitre** 1):

JEAN. I'll be glad to see the city **avec toi**, Thibault!
I'll be glad to see the city with you, Thibault!

ATTENTION

Notice that we cannot always translate **lui** as "him" or **moi** as "me." That's because "him" and "me" cannot be the subjects (or part of the subjects) of a sentence—we cannot say "Him would like to go back to the city" or "Me have the same eyes as my Dad"!! We must use "he" and "I." So, in proper English, even though you may hear it sometimes, we cannot say *"my sister and me did it." Because both people are subjects, we have to say "my sister and I." French speakers, however, consider it a multiperson subject, and therefore make an exception here. They do actually say, "my sister and me": **ma sœur et moi**.

3. The third way in which we use stressed pronouns is *as part of a multiperson subject*:

    Aurélie et lui, ils ont envie de retourner à la ville, n'est-ce pas?
    Aurélie and he, they'd like to return to the city, right?

    Mon père, ma sœur, et moi, nous avons tous des cheveux noirs.
    My dad, my sister, and I, we all have black hair.

4. Finally, we use stressed pronouns as part of various short expressions that are not full sentences, but in which a subject appears. For the examples here, we'll provide some context with a line in English that, one could imagine, might precede the bolded French expression in a conversation.

    "Who likes cuddling with large, carnivorous cats?"
    Pas moi! "Not I!" *or* "Not me!"

    "I think I'm going to get the chocolate shake."
    Et toi? "And you?"

    "Who do you want to be like when you grow up?"
    Comme elle. "Like her."

    "Our team made it to the second round, but I'm not sure about our rivals."
    Eux aussi! "They as well!" *or, informally,* "Them, too!"

Of course, you could substitute any of the stressed pronouns in these expressions, depending on the context.

Pickin' Pronouns

In some of the following sentences, you will need to circle the correct pronoun to fill in the blank. In other sentences, you will need to circle whether the pronoun used in the sentence (underlined) is a stressed pronoun or a subject pronoun. In still other sentences, you'll need to do both. We've provided two examples for you.

Exemple:

Nous ne voulons pas aller au musée sans __________ (tu / toi).

Jean aime parler avec Aurélie. Il aime aussi marcher avec elle. (stressed / subject)

1. **Il n'a pas voulu jouer avec** __________ **(eux / ils).**
2. **Vous, vous devez faire attention!** (stressed / subject)
3. __________ **(Moi / Je) pense que le marché va fermer.**
4. **Je ne parle pas à** __________ **(lui / il), je parle à** __________ **(toi / tu).**
5. __________ **(Lui / Il) n'est jamais retourné.**
6. **Nous, nous savons comment aller à la ville.** (stressed / subject)
7. **Pourquoi est-ce que tu étudies à côté d'elle? Elle parle toujours.** (stressed / subject)
8. **Regarde! Les chats marchent très près de** __________ **(moi / je).**
9. __________ **(Eux / Ils), ils ne connaissent pas ma famille.**
10. **Oh!?...** __________ **(Tu / Toi) as acheté un cadeau pour** __________ **(moi / je)?**

Say It Aloud!

Translate the following sentences from French into English. Then, go back and say each original French sentence out loud, comparing your pronunciation to the audio file (13_05/Tr. 73).

1. **Quand est-ce que tu as parlé avec lui?**
   Translation: ______________________________

2. **Toi, tu as fait un voyage magnifique!** (**faire un voyage** = go on a trip)
   Translation: ______________________________

3. **Je vais jouer avec eux.**
   Translation: ______________________________

4. **Est-ce que vous allez partir sans moi?**
   Translation: ______________________________

5. **Elles, elles sont arrivées ce matin.**
   Translation: ______________________________

6. **Je pense que son chat a peur de toi.**
   Translation: ______________________________

7. **Il est méchant. Vous devez faire attention à lui.**
   Translation: ______________________________

Grammaire

Circle or fill in the correct answer.

1. Fix the following chart by crossing out the incorrect French translations and writing the correct translations in the blanks provided. We've done the first cell for you.

Person	Singular	Plural
1st Person	me à ~~**eux**~~ **moi**	us à **vous** __________
2nd Person	you à **moi** __________	you à **elles** __________
3rd Person	him à **elle** __________	them (m) à **toi** __________
	her à **nous** __________	them (f) à **lui** __________

2. Circle the correct answer. The chart that you just corrected shows the *only possible ways* to translate the words **moi**, **toi**, **lui**, **elle**, **nous**, **vous**, **eux**, and **elles** into English. (True / False)

3. A stressed pronoun, such as **moi**, **toi**, **lui**, etc., is always used after a/an:
   a. verb.
   b. adjective.
   c. conjugation.
   d. preposition.

4. Why would you repeat the pronoun **elle** in the following sentence? **Elle, elle est intelligente.**
   a. to emphasize, or to underline, the idea that *she* is really smart
   b. because this sentence is actually a question
   c. because repeating the word is more polite, more formal
   d. because you're talking about two different girls, so you need two different pronouns

5. Which one of these words does not belong?
   a. **moi**
   b. **tu**
   c. **lui**
   d. **eux**

6. How could you say, "He and his friend know how to sing" in French?
   a. **"Il et son ami savent chanter."**
   b. **"Il et lui ami savent chanter."**
   c. **"Lui et son ami savent chanter."**
   d. **"Ils savent chanter."**

7. In which of the following cases would it be *incorrect* to translate **moi** as "me"?
   a. **Il ne veut pas parler avec <u>moi</u>.**
   b. **Elles ont peur de <u>moi</u>.**
   c. **Sans <u>moi</u>, vous n'allez jamais réussir.**
   d. **Ma sœur et <u>moi</u>, nous aimons courir dans notre maison.**

Nouveau Vocabulaire

Fill in the blank with the correct translation for each word.

Français	Anglais
1. **fermer, je ferme**	________________
2. **faire une pause, je fais une pause**	________________
3. **un voyage**	________________
4. **un magasin**	________________
5. **la route**	________________
6. **au milieu de**	________________
7. **sans**	________________
8. **sous**	________________
9. **normal**	________________
10. **la fin**	________________

Ancien Vocabulaire

Fill in the blank with the correct translation for each word.

Français	Anglais
1. **un père**	________________
2. **une mère**	________________
3. **un enfant**	________________
4. **un frère**	________________
5. **une sœur**	________________
6. **une famille**	________________
7. **une femme**	________________

Français	Anglais
8. **un homme**	____________
9. **une fille**	____________
10. **un fils**	____________

Stressed Pronouns

In each of the following questions there are two sentences. The speaker really wants to make it clear about whom he is talking, so the second sentence is a repetition of the first. The second sentence contains a stressed pronoun to emphasize to *whom* he/she is referring. In the first sentence there is an underlined word, or a group of underlined words, which you must replace in the second sentence, where there is a blank. In order to do so, choose the appropriate *stressed pronoun* that would take the place of the underlined words. We've provided an example:

Exemple:

J'ai peur de <u>Pierre</u>. J'ai peur de <u>lui</u>.

1. **La tortue a fait une course avec <u>son ami</u>. Elle a fait une course avec ____________**
2. **Aurélie marche avec <u>Thibault et Jean</u>. Elle marche à côté d'____________.**
3. **Les rats ont eu peur <u>du renard</u>. Ils ont eu peur de ____________.**
4. *Aurélie explains,* **"Thibault veut venir à la ville avec <u>Jean et moi</u>. Thibault veut venir avec ____________."**
5. **Thibault pense beaucoup <u>à sa mère et à ses sœurs</u>. Il pense beaucoup à ____________.**
6. *Thibault thinks,* **"Je vais acheter du fromage pour <u>ma mère</u>. Je vais acheter du fromage pour ____________."**

Emphasis with Stressed Pronouns + Say It Aloud!

Make the sentences below a little bit stronger by adding the correct stressed pronoun at the beginning. Follow the provided example. Then, translate the sentences into English. Finally, go back and say the sentences aloud, comparing your pronunciation to the audio file (13_06/Tr. 74).

Exemple:

<u>Nous</u>, nous savons faire des bons gâteaux.
Translation: **We know how to make good cakes.**

1. ________________, **ils veulent aller à la plage.**

   Translation: ____

2. ________________, **vous comprenez?**

   Translation: ____

3. ________________, **elle ne sait pas parler français.**

   Translation: ____

4. ________________, **il n'a pas pu venir à ma fête (fête =** party**) d'anniversaire (anniversaire** = birthday).

   Translation: ____

5. ________________, **je dois faire mes devoirs.**

   Translation: ____

6. ________________, **tu es tombée de l'arbre?**

   Translation: ____

7. ________________, **elles sont très gentilles.**

   Translation: ____

8. ________________, **nous sommes arrivés à sept heures.**

   Translation: ____

Dictée!

Listen to the audio file [13_07/Tr. 75] of the **dictée** for this **chapitre**. On the lines provided, write down the three sentences you hear. You do not need to write translations for them, though it's good practice to think through what the English translation would be. You may stop and repeat the audio file several times as you're writing down the sentences.

1. ____
____

2. ____
____

3. ____
____

CHAPITRE 14 QUATORZE

DIALOGUE [14_01/TR. 76]

Jean, Aurélie, and Thibault are searching for a place in the zoo to sleep for the night.

JEAN. **Alors, Aurélie, où est-ce que nous dormons ce soir?**

AURÉLIE. **Je vais me coucher avec mes amies, les vaches. Elles se trouvent pas loin d'ici. Vous pouvez venir si vous voulez!**

THIBAULT. **Parfait!**

JEAN. **Parfait!**

THIBAULT. I didn't plan to spend my first night in the city sleeping with cattle, but it's as good a place as any. Where can I brush my teeth?

AURÉLIE. **Eeeuuhhh . . . les vaches ne se brossent pas les dents.**

THIBAULT. **Ah bon? Ben . . . d'accord.** Where can I wash up, then?

AURÉLIE. **Eeeuuhh, désolée. Les vaches ne se lavent pas non plus.**

THIBAULT. **Ça alors!**

JEAN. Well, that simplifies things, I guess. **À quelle heure est-ce que nous nous levons demain?**

THIBAULT. Not terribly early, I say. I won't need time to wash up or brush my teeth, after all. Ahem! *Thibault looks jokingly at Aurélie.* **Je pense que ça va si nous nous levons à neuf heures. Nous nous couchons tôt ce soir, donc ça ne doit pas être un problème.**

> **RENVOI**
> Do you remember how to tell time in French? If not, take a look back at **chapitre** 8 to refresh your memory.

JEAN. **Parfait! Comme ça, nous allons avoir le temps d'acheter tes fromages, Thibault. Ensuite, nous pouvons nous promener dans la ville ensemble.** We'll see lots of beautiful sights.

THIBAULT. **Génial! Mais d'abord, j'ai *très* faim—est-ce qu'il y a quelque chose à manger dans le zoo?**

JEAN. **Mmm . . . j'ai eu la même idée, Thibault! Je veux manger avant de me coucher!**

AURÉLIE. **Eh ben, vous devez venir avec moi pour rencontrer les vaches! Nous ne nous brossons pas les dents, et nous ne nous lavons pas, mais *manger*! ça, nous savons faire.**

Chant [14_02/Tr. 77]

Pronominal Verbs—*Je me lève* (I get up)

Person	Singular	Plural
1st Person	**je me lève** (I get up)	**nous nous levons** (we get up)
2nd Person	**tu te lèves** (you get up)	**vous vous levez** (you get up)
3rd Person	**il/elle se lève** (he/she/it gets up)	**ils/elles se lèvent** (they get up)

Vocabulaire [14_03/Tr. 78]

Français	Anglais
s'habiller, je m'habille	to get dressed, I get dressed
se brosser (les dents), je me brosse (les dents)	to brush (your teeth), I brush (my teeth)
se coucher, je me couche	to go to bed, I go to bed
se laver, je me lave	to wash (oneself), I wash myself
se lever, je me lève	to get up, I get up
se promener, je me promène	to go for a walk, I go for a walk
se trouver, je me trouve	to be located, I am located
même	same
quelque chose	something/anything
il y a	there is/there are
une dent	a tooth

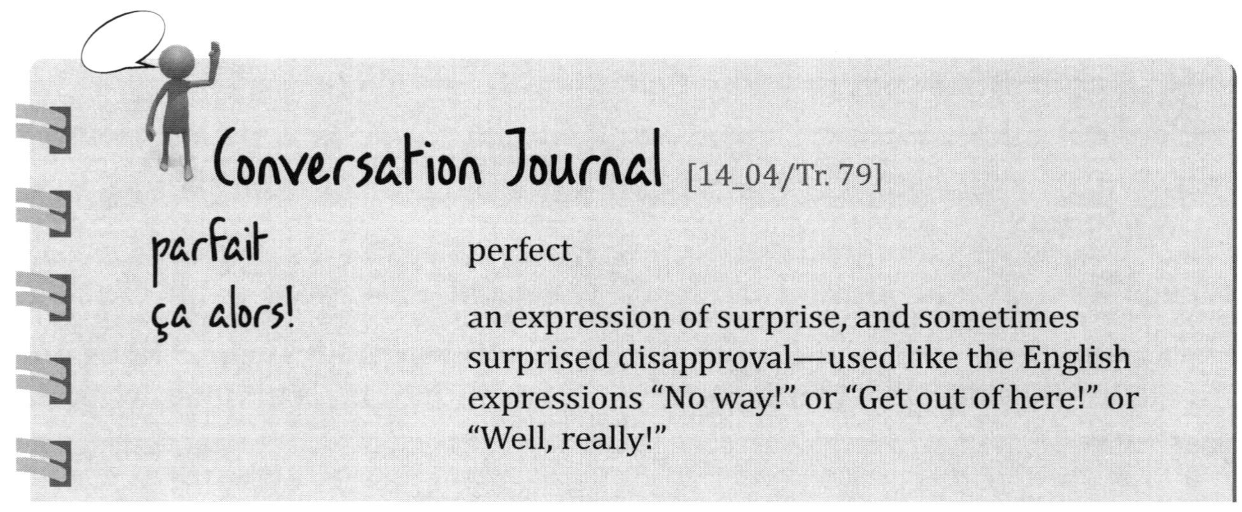

Conversation Journal [14_04/Tr. 79]

parfait — perfect

ça alors! — an expression of surprise, and sometimes surprised disapproval—used like the English expressions "No way!" or "Get out of here!" or "Well, really!"

Pronominal Verbs

In this **chapitre** we're tackling a new type of verb, one that uses a little "helper word" that comes before it. These verbs are called *pronominal verbs* ("pronominal" simply means "related to pronouns"). So, how do these verbs work, and what do pronouns have to do with them? Well, it turns out that the little helper word is itself a type of pronoun, but not a type that we've seen before. Let's take a closer look at how they work with two examples, one from the chant and the other from the Conversation Journal. Pay particular attention to the underlined words:

se lever

Person	Singular	Plural
1st Person	**je me lève** (I get up)	**nous nous levons** (we get up)
2nd Person	**tu te lèves** (you get up)	**vous vous levez** (you get up)
3rd Person	**il/elle se lève** (he/she/it gets up)	**ils/elles se lèvent** (they get up)

s'appeler

Person	Singular	Plural
1st Person	**je m'appelle** (My name is)	**nous nous appelons** (our name is)
2nd Person	**tu t'appelles** (Your name is)	**vous vous appelez** (your name is)
3rd Person	**il/elle s'appelle** (His/her/its name is)	**ils/elles s'appellent** (their name is)

The underlined words (that is, the helpers) are called *reflexive pronouns*. Here they are in a table:

Person	Singular	Plural
1st Person	**me**	**nous**
2nd Person	**te**	**vous**
3rd Person	**se**	**se**

As you look back at the chant (**se lever**), you'll notice that apart from these reflexive pronouns joining the verb forms, there is nothing else that changes about the way we conjugate the verb. In this case **lever** is a regular old **-er** verb, with the same conjugations we're used to (including the **accent grave** ` that occurs in the "boot" pattern).

Now, you might be wondering, why are there such things as pronominal verbs in the first place? Aren't the normal verbs we've been studying enough!? Well, it turns out that there are some cases in which these verbs are quite handy; you could even argue that they express certain ideas more easily than English does. There are three main categories for pronominal verbs: *reflexive*, *reciprocal*, and *idiomatic*. We'll explain the meanings of these fancy words over the next few sections. The most important thing, though, is that you understand that these are three different *uses* for pronominal verbs.

1. Reflexive Verbs

We've said before that verbs are action words, and these actions are performed by people, places, or things called *subjects*. Now, in many cases, the action being performed will somehow affect the subject doing the action. For instance, if you say, "I am brushing my teeth," you are the one doing the action and you are also the one affected by the action (hopefully, your teeth get cleaner). Or take the sentence "She is getting dressed"; in this case, "she" is the one doing the action, and "she" is the one who is affected by it (eventually she will have clothes on). For these kinds of actions, where the subject is the one doing *and* being affected by the action, French often uses one category of pronominal verb called a *reflexive verb*, since the action "reflects" back on the subject. So let's look at the two example sentences in French now:

I am brushing my teeth = **Je me brosse les dents.**

She is getting dressed = **Elle s'habille.**

In the present tense, all you need to do in order to use a reflexive verb (and, for that matter, any pronominal verb) is to stick the matching reflexive pronoun right *after* the subject. Matching, of course, means matching for person and number with the subject. In the first example, **Je me brosse les dents**, the subject is **je**, a first-person, singular subject pronoun. So, we match that subject with the first-person, singular reflexive pronoun **me** to get **je me**. (If needed, take a peek back at the table of our reflexive pronouns to see where we got the **me**.) From there we just conjugate the verb as we normally would—in this case, it's another plain, old **-er** verb: **je me brosse**. Finish it off with what you're brushing—teeth! **Je me brosse les dents.**

RAPPEL

Remember that for French speakers, it is obvious that when you brush your teeth, you are indeed brushing *your* teeth and not your neighbor's teeth! That's why this sentence just has **les dents** (literally "the teeth"), instead of "my teeth" as an English translation would have it.

The same thing happens with the second example: **elle** is a third-person, singular subject pronoun. So, looking at our reflexive pronoun table, we'll need to match that subject with **se**, the corresponding reflexive pronoun: **elle se**. Of course, when we go to make the full sentence, that word **se** winds up next to the verb form **habille**, which begins with a vowel sound, so we have to squeeze out the poor little **e** as so often happens!

Elle se habille → Elle s'habille.

It might sound a little funny when you use pronominal verbs with the subjects **nous** and **vous**, since the matching reflexive pronouns are the same words! But, fear not, it is perfectly acceptable to "repeat yourself" in these cases. In fact, you can't say it any other way! Here are some examples:

Nous nous habillons.	We're getting dressed.
Vous vous promenez.	You are going for a walk.

2. Reciprocal Verbs (a.k.a. "each other" actions)

"Reciprocate" is a fancy word meaning "to do something for or to someone who has done the same thing for or to you." ***Reciprocal verbs**, a second category of pronominal verbs, include actions in which two subjects are doing the same thing to each other: looking at each other, smelling each other, calling each other, loving each other, talking to each other, biting each other, and so on.* In French, the expression "each other" has no literal translation: The most common way to express this idea is simply to use a pronominal verb. Again, here are a few examples:

Ils parlent.	They are speaking.
Ils se parlent.	They are speaking with each other.
Est-ce que vous regardez?	Are you looking?
Est-ce que vous vous regardez?	Are you looking at each other?
Nous voyons.	We see.
Nous nous voyons.	We see each other.

3. Idiomatic Pronominal Verbs

*An **idiom** is an expression whose meaning cannot be guessed just by considering the meanings of the individual words.* For an example in English, think of what it means to "go bananas." It means to go crazy, right? But if you didn't *already* know that's what it meant, you couldn't figure it out just from the words "go" and "bananas," right? Compare that to a different expression, such as "Better late than never." If you've never heard that expression before, and someone says it to you after you show up at their house two hours late, you can still figure out what they mean based on the meanings of the words (i.e., it's better to be late than to never arrive).

Many pronominal verbs are neither reflexive (reflecting the action back on the subject) nor reciprocal (expressing an action done to or for each other). Instead, they simply mean something unique; something that cannot be guessed, or cannot be guessed very easily by trying to combine the meanings of the reflexive pronoun (**me**, **te**, **se**, **nous**, **vous**, **se**) and the main verb. Another way to think about this is that when you add the reflexive pronoun to these verbs, they actually mean something new: It's not simply the old meaning used in a reflexive or a reciprocal way. An example from this **chapitre**'s vocabulary section is the verb **se trouver**. We know that the verb **trouver** means "to find":

La souris trouve du pain dans la maison.
The mouse finds bread in the house.

But look what happens when we add the reflexive pronoun to **trouver**:

La maison se trouve dans la ville. The house is located in the city.

Le pain se trouve dans la maison. The bread is located in the house.

Other idiomatic pronominal verbs use verbs we've already learned as well: From **attendre** (to wait), we get **s'attendre (à)**, which means "to expect":

"Il s'attend à une bonne nouvelle." He's expecting good news.

In fact, the verb **s'appeler** (to be called or to be named), which you've seen so often, is actually built off the verb **appeler**, "to call":

"J'appelle la police!" I'm calling the police!

"Je m'appelle Sylvie." My name is Sylvie.

We should point out one last thing about pronominal verbs that makes them somewhat special, and that concerns their infinitive form. Remember, the infinitive form of a verb is the "original" form that has not been conjugated—forms such as **parler**, **réussir**, and **vouloir**. In our list of **vocabulaire** for this **chapitre**, we've always written the infinitive forms of pronominal verbs with the pronoun **se** (**se laver**, **se promener**, etc.). However, when used in different situations by different subjects, the infinitive forms of these verbs actually match their subjects by using the corresponding reflexive pronoun. So, for example, if you listen to what Aurélie says in her first line of the dialogue, you'll hear:

AURÉLIE. **Je vais me coucher avec mes amies, les vaches.** (I'm going to sleep with my friends, the cows).

She does *not* say:

***Je vais se coucher avec mes amies, les vaches.**

That is because she is the one speaking (she uses the word **je**, "I") and she is the one who will be doing the action expressed by the infinitive verb. One more example is the sentence "We want to go for a walk." The verb for "to go for a walk" is **se promener** in the infinitive form we've written in your **vocabulaire**. But, we do *not* say:

***Nous voulons se promener.**

Instead, we must change that little reflexive pronoun (**se**) to match the subject doing the action—or, in this case, the subject that *wants* to do the action:

Nous voulons nous promener.

This takes a little getting used to, but if you simply remember the rule that *infinitives must match* when using pronominal verbs, you'll have a good foundation.

Il y a

We'll close our grammar section with a quick look at another (idiomatic!) expression that is used a little bit differently in French than it is in English. The expression **il y a** means either "There is" or "There are":

Il y a une grande vache dans notre maison.
There is a large cow in our house.
Il y a cinq grandes vaches dans notre maison.
There are five large cows in our house.

Do you see how **il y a** works a bit differently from the English equivalent? There is no difference between singular and plural! **Il y a** works if you're talking about one thing or many things. In English, we need to use "There is" when we mean "There is one thing" and "There are" when we mean "There are many things."

Il y a is a very useful expression! It can be a statement, as the previous examples show, but also it can be used in different kinds of questions:

Est-ce qu'il y a une école dans ton village?
Is there a school in your town?
Pourquoi est-ce qu'il y a une grande vache dans notre maison?
Why is there a large cow in our house?

Swing Your (Pronominal) Partner Round and Round

Because one key to using pronominal verbs is getting the right pairing between the subject pronoun and the reflexive pronoun, we need practice in matching these "pronominal partners" together. In this exercise, draw a line that matches the subject to the correct reflexive pronoun. Remember that a certain reflexive pronoun will be used (much) more than once!

je	nous
tu	se
il	me
elle	te
nous	vous
vous	
ils	
elles	

Once you're finished, write out the pairings here, and practice saying each pair aloud a few times:

je ____________________

tu ____________________

il ____________________

elle ____________________

nous ____________________

vous ____________________

ils ____________________

elles ____________________

Night and Day

Using five verbs from our **vocabulaire** section (see the box below), describe your night-time, and then your morning routine in chronological order. We've provided the words **d'abord**, "first"; **ensuite**, "next"; and **finalement**, "finally". There is not a single "right" answer in terms of the order in which you do things (and, of course, we've left out a lot of other steps you take since we're only using five verbs!). You should use the first person singular pronoun **je** ("I") here, since you're speaking as yourself.

s'habiller   se brosser les dents   se coucher   se laver   se lever

We've provided a guide below that has enough blank spaces for each action to be used once. However, if you want to write out a longer routine in which you use certain verbs more than once, feel free!

D'abord ______________________________,

ensuite ______________________________,

ensuite ______________________________,

ensuite ______________________________,

et finalement ______________________________.

Traduction + Say it Aloud!

Translate the following sentences from French into English. Then, go back and say the French sentences aloud, comparing your pronunciation to the audio file [14_05/Tr. 80].

1. **Jean et Thibault vont se coucher avec les vaches.**

   Translation: ______________________________

2. **Mme la Tortue se lève tôt; le lapin se lève tard.**

   Translation: ______________________________

3. **Nous nous brossons les dents à neuf heures.**

   Translation: ______________________________

4. **Nous ne nous brossons pas les dents à trois heures!**[1]

   Translation: ______________________________

5. **Est-ce que tu te promènes dans la forêt?**

   Translation: ______________________________

6. **Non, je ne me promène pas dans la forêt. Les endroits intéressants se trouvent dans la ville!**

   Translation: ______________________________

Grammaire

1. Which list contains just the *reflexive* pronouns in French?

   a. **je, me, tu, te, il, se, elle, se, nous, nous, vous, vous, ils, se, elles, se**
   b. **je, tu, il, elle, nous, vous, ils, elles**
   c. **moi, toi, lui, elle, nous, vous, eux, elles**
   d. **me, te, se, nous, vous, se**

2. What does it mean that certain pronominal verbs are *reciprocal*?

   a. These verbs express actions that subjects want to do.
   b. These verbs express actions that two subjects are doing to each other or for each other.
   c. These verbs express actions that reflect back on or affect their subjects.
   d. These verbs express actions that are illegal.

3. Is there anything special about the *infinitive* forms of pronominal verbs?

   a. No.
   b. Yes. They all end in **-er**.
   c. Yes. They are always used with the reflexive pronoun **se**.
   d. Yes. They are always used with a reflexive pronoun that matches the subject.

4. What difference is there in the ways to say "there is" and "there are" in French?

   a. We use the expression **il y a** for "there is" and **il y ont** for "there are."
   b. There is no difference: Both ideas can be expressed by saying **il y a**.
   c. We do not have any way to say these things in French.
   d. We use **ils ont** for "there are" and **il a** for "there is."

---

1. Did you see where we put the little negative word **ne**? It comes in between the subject (in this case **nous**) and the reflexive pronoun (also **nous** here). The **ne . . . pas** structure still applies to pronominal verbs!

Nouveau Vocabulaire

Fill in the blank with the correct translation for each word.

Français	Anglais
1. **s'habiller, je m'habille**	________________
2. **se brosser (les dents), je me brosse (les dents)**	________________
3. **se coucher, je me couche**	________________
4. **se laver, je me lave**	________________
5. **se lever, je me lève**	________________
6. **se promener, je me promène**	________________
7. **se trouver, je me trouve**	________________
8. **même**	________________
9. **quelque chose**	________________
10. **il y a**	________________
11. **une dent**	________________

Ancien Vocabulaire

Fill in the blank with the correct translation for each word.

Français	Anglais
1. **magnifique**	________________
2. **délicieux**	________________
3. **facile**	________________
4. **sympathique (sympa)/gentil**	________________
5. **méchant**	________________

Français	Anglais
6. **amusant**	______________________
7. **moche**	______________________
8. **heureux**	______________________
9. **bizarre**	______________________
10. **mignon**	______________________

I Wash My Hands of It!

Here is a chart of the verb **se laver** (to wash up), which can also be used in the same way as **se brosser (les dents)**. That is, you can say **se laver les cheveux** (to wash one's hair) or **se laver les mains** (to wash one's hands). Complete the following chart using your new knowledge of pronominal verbs; the English translations are provided.

Se laver les mains (to wash one's hands)

Person	Singular	Plural
1st Person	______________________ (I wash my hands.)	______________________ (We wash our hands.)
2nd Person	______________________ (You wash your hands.)	______________________ (You wash your hands.)
3rd Person	______________________ (He washes his hands. She washes her hands.)	______________________ (They wash their hands.)

Question Formation

For each of the following statements, think of a *question* (**une question**—abbreviated as **Q**) that could have prompted that statement as an answer (in French, a **réponse**—abbreviated as **R**). Here are the steps you should take:

1. On the line provided, translate the **réponse** into English.
2. Come up with a good question that would produce that answer.
3. Write the question in French on the line provided.
4. Translate your French question into English on the line provided.

Before you start, check out the following example:

Q: Pourquoi est-ce que tu te laves les mains?
Translation: Why are you washing your hands?

R: Je me lave les mains parce que j'ai joué avec les cochons!
Translation: I'm washing my hands because I played with the pigs!

1. **Q:** ______________________________

   Translation: ______________________________

   R: Ils se brossent les dents à neuf heures.

   Translation: ______________________________

2. **Q:** ______________________________

   Translation: ______________________________

   R: Je m'habille dans ma chambre. (**une chambre** = a bedroom)

   Translation: ______________________________

3. **Q:** ______________________________

   Translation: ______________________________

   R: Elles se lavent les mains dans la salle de bain. (**une salle de bain** = a bathroom)

   Translation: ______________________________

4. **Q:** ______________________________

Translation: ______________________________

R: Nous nous levons tôt le matin. (**tôt le matin** = early in the morning)

Translation: ______________________________

5. **Q:** ______________________________

Translation: ______________________________

R: Ils se couchent tard parce qu'ils ne sont pas fatigués!

Translation: ______________________________

Dictée!

Listen to the audio file [14_06/Tr. 81] of the **dictée** for this **chapitre**. On the lines provided, write down the three sentences you hear. You do not need to write translations for them, though it's good practice to think through what the English translation would be. You may stop and repeat the audio file several times as you're writing down the sentences.

1. ______________________________

____

2. ______________________________

____

3. ______________________________

____

Dialogue [15_01/Tr. 82]

Following a good meal and a solid night's sleep, the three companions slip out of the zoo to see the city. After a full day of sightseeing, delicacy tasting, and memory making, Aurélie expresses concern.

Aurélie. **Allons-y les amis! Nous devons nous dépêcher si nous voulons acheter les fromages. Il est déjà huit heures!**

Jean. **Mince! Aurélie a raison!** They may have already sold out.

Thibault, *smiling*. **Pourquoi est-ce que vous vous inquiétez? Je me suis occupé de ça! J'ai appelé ce matin—**I reserved three big wheels. As soon as I woke up, **je me suis souvenu**!

Aurélie. **Oh purée, il est fort, Thibault!**

The three friends head to the shop to pick up Thibault's order. Upon leaving, Jean reflects.

Jean. **Tu sais, Thibault, nous ne rencontrons pas souvent des garçons comme toi au zoo. Nous allons nous souvenir de toi!**

Thibault. **Et moi, je vais me souvenir de vous. Nous nous sommes amusés ensemble!**

Aurélie. **Est-ce que tu vas te souvenir de comment retourner au zoo?**

Thibault. **Bien sûr! Et je vais venir avec toute ma famille.**

Jean. **Super. Je pense que Aurélie et moi, nous préférons rester dans la ville maintenant—la campagne, c'est bien, mais nous nous sentons mieux au zoo!**

Thibault. **Et moi, je me sens bien à la campagne.** But visiting friends is always worth a journey!

Jean. And so is a **bon fromage**!

Chant [15_02/Tr. 83]

Past-Tense Pronominals—*Je me suis amusé.* (I had fun.)

Person	Singular	Plural
1st Person	**je me suis amusé(e)** (I had fun)	**nous nous sommes amusé(e)s** (we had fun)
2nd Person	**tu t'es amusé(e)** (you had fun)	**vous vous êtes amusé(e)(s)** (you had fun)
3rd Person	**il s'est amusé/elle s'est amusée** (he had fun/she had fun)	**ils se sont amusés/elles se sont amusées** (they had fun)

Vocabulaire [15_03/Tr. 84]

Français	Anglais
s'amuser, je m'amuse	to have fun, I have fun
se dépêcher, je me dépêche	to hurry, I hurry
s'endormir, je m'endors	to fall asleep, I fall asleep
s'inquiéter (de), je m'inquiète (de)	to worry (about), I worry (about)
s'occuper de, je m'occupe de	to take care of, I take care of
se sentir, je me sens	to feel, I feel
se souvenir (de), je me souviens (de)	to remember (**de** + something), I remember (**de** + something)
fort	strong (can also mean "good" or "capable" as a more familiar, colloquial expression—see dialogue)
la campagne	the countryside
mieux	better

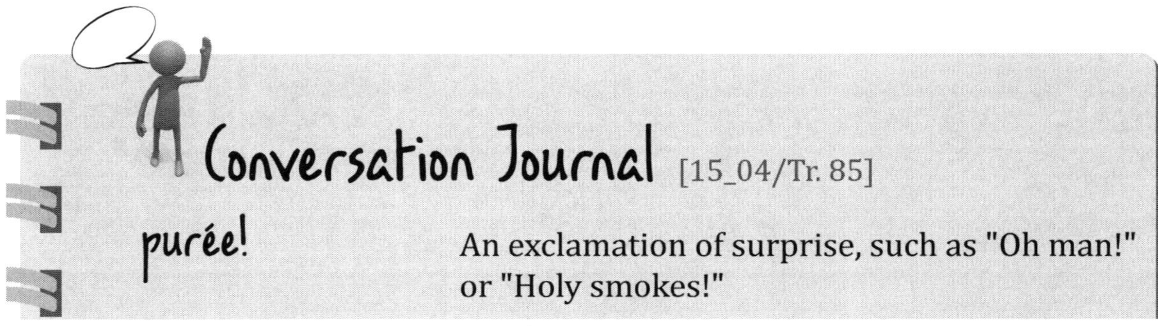

Conversation Journal [15_04/Tr. 85]

purée! — An exclamation of surprise, such as "Oh man!" or "Holy smokes!"

Pronominal Verbs, Part Two: The Past Tense

You already know how to use pronominal verbs to express actions happening in the present tense and the future tense:

Present **Je me couche.** = "I go to bed."
Future **Je vais me coucher.** = "I will go to bed."

Present **Tu te couches.** = "You go to bed."
Future **Tu vas te coucher.** = "You will go to bed."

And so on. The key for the present tense was to remember to match both the reflexive pronoun and the conjugation of the verb with the subject. For the future tense, we only needed to remember to change the reflexive pronoun to match the subject. Then we just tacked on the infinitive.

To use a pronominal verb in the past tense, things are a little bit more complicated. There are three main ingredients. The good news, though, is that you already know about all three: The trick is simply combining them! To figure out how it works, let's take one of the third-person plural forms from this **chapitre**'s chant as our example:

Elles se sont amusées. = "They had fun."
(1 = se, 2 = sont, 3 = es)

1. Reflexive pronoun: Well, OK, this one is a little obvious. If we're talking about putting a *pronominal* verb in the past tense, we need to use a reflexive pronoun! So, no big change here from the present tense or the future tense. Just choose one of the same old reflexive pronouns (**me**, **te**, **se**, **nous**, **vous**, **se**) to match the subject.

2. **Être**: The verb **être** is back! You may recall that many verbs we'd learned about previously, such as verbs of motion, use **être** as their helping verb in the past tense: **venir**, **aller**, **retourner**, etc. However, things are a little different here. The reason we use **être** with **s'amuser** is *not* because it is a verb of motion (you may stay in one place and still have fun!) but because **s'amuser** is a pronominal verb. *All pronominal verbs* are conjugated with **être**. The key here is making sure you stick the

> **Attention**
> You should notice that for some forms of **être** (**tu** and **il/elle**), the letter **e** gets squeezed out of the reflexive pronoun because the form of **être** begins with a vowel, giving us **tu t'es** and **il s'est** or **elle s'est**.

(matching) form of **être** *after* the reflexive pronoun. While we're on the subject of **être**, take a moment to glance back at the chant from this **chapitre**.

3. Agreement: Do you remember **chapitre** 12 and our discussion of agreement when using verbs that take **être** in the past tense? If so, agreement with pronominal verbs should be a familiar story, since the same basic rule applies: *The past participle agrees with the subject with respect to gender and number.*

In our example sentence—**Elles se sont amusées**—the participle (**amusées**) has an extra **e** as well as an extra **s** because the subject (**elles**) is feminine, which gives us the extra **e**, and plural, which gives us the extra **s**. Compare that to the following:

Il <u>s'</u> <u>est</u> amus<u>é</u>. = He had fun.
1 2 3

Again, we have (1) the reflexive pronoun (**se** becomes **s'** before a vowel), plus (2) the appropriate form of **être**. This time, though, for (3), there is no additional **s** (because the subject—**il**—is singular) and no additional **e** is needed (because **Il** is masculine). This also works, of course, when you swap in proper names for the subject:

Thibault s'est <u>amusé</u>. = Thibault had fun.

Aurélie s'est <u>amusée</u>. = Aurélie had fun.

Thibault is a masculine, singular subject, so no extra letters are added. Aurélie is feminine (but still singular), so the past participle gets an extra **e**. By the way, you may have already guessed this, but generally the extra **e** and extra **s** don't change the pronunciation of the past participle: **amusé** sounds the same as **amusée**, **amusés**, and **amusées**!

Now here is a question: When a person says "**Je m'amuse**" ("I'm having fun"), do we know what gender that person is just by looking at the subject pronoun **je**? No! A boy could say that sentence, or a girl, a man, or a woman! What about "**Tu t'amuses**" ("You're having fun")? Is **tu** a boy, girl, man, or woman? We don't know! The gender always changes depending upon *who* is speaking (or being spoken to, in the case of **tu** or **vous**). Therefore, we can't make a firm rule about whether or not to add an **e** to the past participle of certain pronominal verbs because the people to whom they refer could be masculine or feminine. Instead, *each time we use these verbs, we need to consider who is speaking or being spoken to.* That is why, in the chant, there are all of those **e**s in parentheses—you might need them, but you might not.

As an example, let's continue with Thibault and Aurélie. Look at the difference between each pair of sentences. Can you explain why each pair is different?

Thibault says, "**Je me suis amusé.**" = "I had fun."
Aurélie says, "**Je me suis amusée.**" = "I had fun."

Jean asks Thibault, "**Est-ce que tu t'es amusé?**" = "Did you have fun?"
Jean asks Aurélie, "**Est-ce que tu t'es amusée?**" = "Did you have fun?"

In each pair, the subject of the second sentence (**je/tu**) refers to Aurélie, who is a female: Therefore we add the extra **e** on the past participle.

Now, one major exception to this rule of having past participles agree with their subjects is when the subject is doing an action to another, separate thing. For example, to wash your *hands* or brush your *teeth*: In these cases, where there is a *thing* that a subject is acting on, or doing something to (brushing your *teeth*, washing your *hands*), we do not need to worry about making the past participle agree with the subject in the past tense:

Je me suis brossé les dents.
(I brushed my teeth.)

Tu t'es brossé les dents.
(You brushed your teeth.)

Il s'est brossé les dents.
(He brushed his teeth.)

Elle s'est brossé les dents.
(She brushed her teeth.)

Nous nous sommes brossé les dents.
(We brushed our teeth.)

Vous vous êtes brossé les dents.
(You brushed your teeth.)

Ils se sont brossé les dents.
(They brushed their teeth.)

Elles se sont brossé les dents.
(They brushed their teeth.)

Jean s'est brossé les dents.

Aurélie s'est brossé les dents. (OK, we know she didn't really, but just for the sake of the example . . .)

As you can see, **brossé**, the past participle, never changes!

We'll conclude on a somewhat negative note. That is, grammatically negative, of course: We still have not discussed how to make pronominal verbs negative! The big question is, Where does the **ne . . . pas . . .** sandwich go? Here are two sets of example sentences from the past, present, and future tenses so that you can see the differences. The first set of three uses Aurélie (a third-person, singular, feminine subject). The second set of three uses the subject **nous**—"we."

Past **Aurélie ne s'est pas brossé les dents.** (Aurélie did not brush her teeth.)
Present **Aurélie ne se brosse pas les dents.** (Aurélie does not brush her teeth.)
Future **Aurélie ne va pas se brosser les dents.** (Aurélie will not brush her teeth.)

Past **Nous ne nous sommes pas brossé les dents.** (We did not brush our teeth.)
Present **Nous ne nous brossons pas les dents.** (We do not brush our teeth.)
Future **Nous n'allons pas nous brosser les dents.** (We will not brush our teeth.)

As you can see, in every case the negative word **ne** always comes directly *after* the subject. That will never change. The word **pas**, however, does change positions a bit: *For both the past and the future, this word forms the sandwich around the helping verb* (some form of **être** for past, and **aller** for future). In fact, we can be even more specific about what kind of sandwich this is—not peanut butter and jelly, not tuna salad, not even a **jambon et fromage** (ham and cheese)—it is a *time sandwich*. That is, the negative marker, **ne . . . pas . . .** , makes a time sandwich by forming around the word that helps sentences get into the past or future tense—the helping verb. So, rule 1: Put **ne** right after the subject. Rule 2: Put **pas** right after the verb that "helps" sentences become past or future tense.

Don't be worried if this seems complicated to understand all at once: The best way to learn these patterns is to practice them. They may seem like a giant puzzle right now, but once you get used to the rhythm of how each tense sounds with the **ne . . . pas . . .** sandwich, using them will become second nature!

Être, the Multitasker

Do you know what a multitasker is? It's someone who can do many things at once. Well, the verb **être** is a bit of a multitasker, as you may have noticed in your study of French. It can function as its own verb (the verb "to be"), or it can help form the past tense—**le passé composé**—for both pronominal and non-pronominal verbs. In the following sentences, identify whether **être** is being used as its *own verb*, with a *pronominal verb*, or with a *non-pronominal* (normal) verb. In the blanks provided next to the word "code," you can identify these sentences as *O* (own verb), *PP* (pronominal past), or *NP* (normal past). (These are not official codes, of course—they're just to help us practice.) Then, translate the sentences. Here are a couple of examples:

Example 1: **Les pêches sont chères ici!**
Code: O
Translation: The peaches are expensive here.

Example 2: **Les rats se sont inquiétés du renard.**
Code: PP
Translation: The rats worried about the fox.

1. **Les fromages sont délicieux.**
   Code: ________
   Translation: ____
   ____

2. **Le lapin (rabbit) ne s'est pas dêpéché dans sa course avec la tortue (turtle/tortoise).**
   Code: ________
   Translation: ____
   ____

3. **Nous nous sommes endormis dans la voiture.**
   Code: ________
   Translation: ____
   ____

4. **Thibault est retourné à la campagne avec ses fromages.**
   Code: ________

   Translation: ____

   ____

5. **La mère de Thibault ne s'est pas inquiétée pendant** (**pendant** = during) **son voyage.**
   Code: ________

   Translation: ____

   ____

6. **Il est d'accord avec moi.** (Hint: Check out the vocabulary from **chapitre** 4!)
   Code: ________

   Translation: ____

   ____

7. **Ils sont arrivés au marché dans l'après-midi.**
   Code: ________

   Translation: ____

   ____

The Anti-Dialogue

Let's see what would happen if we made some of the positive sentences from this week's dialogue into *negative* sentences. To do this, first add your **ne . . . pas . . .** sandwich to the correct place in the sentence. Then, translate the sentences. Check out the following example before you get started:

Example: AURÉLIE. **Nous ^(ne) devons ^(pas) nous dépêcher si nous voulons acheter les fromages.**

Translation: We must not hurry if we want to buy the cheese.

1. JEAN. **Aurélie a raison!**

   Translation: ______________________________

   ____

2. THIBAULT. **Pourquoi est-ce que vous vous inquiétez ?**

   Translation: ______________________________

   ____

3. **Je me suis occupé de ça!**

   Translation: ______________________________

   ____

4. **Je me suis souvenu!** (Hint: The word **souvenu** is the past participle of a verb in this **chapitre**'s **vocabulaire**. I'll bet you can guess which one!)

   Translation: ______________________________

   ____

5. AURÉLIE. **Oh purée, il est très fort, Thibault!**

   Translation: ______________________________

   ____

L'EDITEUR EST EN VACANCES! (THE EDITOR IS ON VACATION!)

The tireless editor of *French for Children Primer B* finally decided enough was enough and took a small vacation as we were writing this book. While he was away, several sentences suffered various kinds of grammatical and vocabulary-related difficulties. Using the English sentences as a guide, fix the French sentences so that they are correct. Write each corrected French sentence on the line provided. Sometimes the mistake is a wrong word and sometimes the mistake has to do with the pronominal verb. Several sentences have multiple mistakes!

1. Incorrect: **Les animaux dans le zoo se couche tard.**
   English: The animals in the zoo go to bed late.

   Correct: ______________________________

   ____

2. Incorrect: **Le village se trouvent dans la ville.**
   English: The village is located in the countryside.

   Correct: ______________________________

   ____

3. Incorrect: **Le loup s'êtes dépêché pour aller aux champs.**
   English: The wolf hurried to go to the fields.

   Correct: ______________________________

   ____

4. Incorrect: **Nous ne nous sommes endormis pas à l'école!**
   English: We did not fall asleep at school!

   Correct: ______________________________

   ____

5. Incorrect: **Je veux se coucher tôt ce matin.**
   English: I want to go to bed early this evening.

   Correct: ____

   ____

6. Incorrect: **Est-ce que vous voulez se promener?**
   English: Do you want to go for a walk?

   Correct: ____

   ____

7. Incorrect: **Les amis ne se sommes pas parlé.**
   English: The friends did not talk to each other.

   Correct: ____

   ____

Grammaire

1. Which of the following verbs use some form of **être** as a helping verb in the past tense? Circle each verb.

   a. **aller**
   b. **venir**
   c. **se souvenir**
   d. **manger**
   e. **s'inquiéter**
   f. **vouloir**

2. How would you translate the words **se sont** in the following sentence: **"Les souris se sont amusées"**?
   a. Trick question! You cannot directly translate **se sont**: the word **se** is a part of the pronominal verb **s'amuser** (to have fun) and the word **sont** is just a helping verb making the sentence past tense. The sentence should be translated simply as, "The mice had fun."
   b. The word **se** means "himself" and **sont** means "are," so the correct translation of the sentence is "The mice himself are fun."
   c. The word **se** means "themselves" and **sont** means "are," so the correct translation of the sentence is, "The mice themselves are fun."
   d. The word **se** means "each other" and **sont** means "are," so the correct translation of the sentence is, "The mice are fun with each other."
3. Which of the following is the correct French translation of the sentence "I will not go to bed!"?
   a. **"Je ne vais se coucher pas!"**
   b. **"Je ne vais me coucher pas!"**
   c. **"Je ne vais pas se coucher!"**
   d. **"Je ne vais pas me coucher!"**
4. Which of the following is the correct French translation of the sentence: "He took care of his cat"?
   a. **"Il est occupé de son chat."**
   b. **"Il s'occupe est de son chat."**
   c. **"Il s'est occupé de son chat."**
   d. **"Ill s'occuper de son chat."**

Nouveau Vocabulaire

Fill in the blank with the correct translation for each word.

Français	Anglais
1. **s'amuser, je m'amuse**	______________
2. **se dépêcher, je me dépêche**	______________
3. **s'endormir, je m'endors**	______________
4. **s'inquiéter (de), je m'inquiète (de)**	______________
5. **s'occuper de, je m'occupe de**	______________
6. **se sentir, je me sens**	______________
7. **se souvenir (de), je me souviens (de)**	______________
8. **fort**	______________
9. **la campagne**	______________
10. **mieux**	______________

Ancien Vocabulaire

Fill in the blank with the correct translation for each word.

Français	Anglais
1. **faire une pause, je fais une pause**	______________
2. **le soir**	______________
3. **le matin**	______________
4. **hier**	______________
5. **l'après-midi**	______________

Français	Anglais
6. **la semaine**	______________________
7. **demain**	______________________
8. **tard**	______________________
9. **quelque chose**	______________________
10. **il y a**	______________________

Back to the Future

The following sentences are in the present tense. Your job is to:

a. **Say it Aloud!** Practice reading the sentence out loud, and compare your version to the audio file/track [15_05/Tr. 86].

b. Translate the sentence into English.

c. Change the sentence so that it is in either the future tense or the past tense. Out of the six sentences, choose three for the future tense and three for the past tense (it doesn't matter which three you choose for which tense).

1. **Je me brosse les dents très tôt le matin.**

Translation: ____

____

Change Tense: ____

____

2. **Vous vous amusez au musée!**

Translation: ____

____

Change Tense: ____

____

3. **Aurélie ne se souvient pas de comment aller au marché.**

   Translation: ____

   ____

   Change Tense: ____

   ____

4. **Je me sens bien au milieu de la forêt.**

   Translation: ____

   ____

   Change Tense: ____

   ____

5. **Les moutons s'inquiètent du nouveau berger.**

   Translation: ____

   ____

   Change Tense: ____

   ____

6. **Les garçons ne se regardent pas.**

   Translation: ____

   ____

   Change Tense: ____

   ____

Dictée!

Listen to the audio file [15_06/Tr. 87] of the **dictée** for this **chapitre**. On the lines provided, write down the three sentences you hear. You do not need to write translations for them, though it's good practice to think through what the English translation would be. You may stop and repeat the audio file several times as you're writing down the sentences.

1. ______________________________

   ____

2. ______________________________

   ____

3. ______________________________

   ____

CHAPITRE 16 SEIZE

It's time for a quick review of **chapitres** 11–15. In this **partie**, you learned about the past tense, or **passé composé**, starting in **chapitre** 11, where you saw how to form it with **avoir**. In **chapitre** 12, you learned that the verb **être** is sometimes—though not often—used to make the **passé composé**, too. Finally, in **chapitre** 13, you discovered the difference between *stressed pronouns* such as **moi**, **toi**, **lui**, etc., and the regular old *subject pronouns* you're used to: **je**, **tu**, **il**, **elle**, **nous**, etc.

Let's begin with a review of the vocabulary. Then, it's on to the review exercises!

	French	English
☐	**connaître, je connais**	________
☐	**gagner, je gagne**	________
☐	**demain**	________
☐	**avant**	________
☐	**le soir**	________
☐	**le matin**	________
☐	**hier**	________
☐	**l'après-midi**	________
☐	**la semaine**	________
☐	**tard**	________
☐	**rencontrer, je rencontre**	________ ________
☐	**dire, je dis**	________
☐	**retourner, je retourne**	________
☐	**un musée**	________

	French	English
☐	**un restaurant**	________
☐	**ensuite**	________
☐	**finalement**	________
☐	**seulement**	________
☐	**jamais**	________
☐	**après**	________
☐	**fermer, je ferme**	________
☐	**faire un pause, je fais une pause**	________ ________
☐	**un voyage**	________
☐	**un magasin**	________
☐	**la route**	________
☐	**au milieu de**	________
☐	**sans**	________
☐	**sous**	________

French	English
☐ normal(e)	
☐ la fin	
☐ s'habiller, je m'habille	
☐ se brosser (les dents), je me brosse (les dents)	
☐ se coucher, je me couche	
☐ se laver, je me lave	
☐ se lever, je me lève	
☐ se promener, je me promène	
☐ se trouver, je me trouve	
☐ même	
☐ quelque chose	
☐ il y a	

French	English
☐ s'amuser, je m'amuse	
☐ se dépêcher, je me dépêche	
☐ s'endormir, je m'endors	
☐ s'inquiéter (de/pour), je m'inquiète (de/pour)	
☐ s'occuper de, je m'occupe de	
☐ se sentir, je me sens	
☐ se souvenir (de), je me souviens (de)	
☐ fort	
☐ la campagne	
☐ mieux	

My List of Words to Master

So that you can easily review the words you are having difficulty remembering, write them down on the lines provided below.

Sentences

Write five sentences using words you have put on your list of words to master.

1.

2.

3.

4.

5.

GRAMMAIRE

The *Passé Composé* with *Avoir* (Chapitre 11)

Circle or fill in the correct answers.

1. What is wrong with all of the following sentences, which use the **passé composé**?
   Nous avons chante aujourd'hui.
   Vous n'avez pas mange vos cerises!
   J'ai rencontre un loup à côté de la route.
   Finalement, elle a gagne la course.

   a. The past participles of the sentences do not agree with the subjects. For example, **Nous avons chante** should be **Nous avons chantes**.

   b. These verbs need to use **être** to form the **passé composé**.

   c. The past participles do not have any accents on the final **e**.

   d. These sentences are actually in the future tense.

2. What is wrong with all of the following sentences, which use the **passé composé**?
   Ils ont cachés leur œuf sous l'arbre.
   Elles n'ont pas cassées la voiture.
   Elle a tirée son chat par la queue.
   Vous avez travaillés seulement sept heures?

   a. The forms of **avoir** are not correct.

   b. The past participles agree with the subjects, but they should not, since the helping verb is **avoir**, not **être**.

   c. There are too many accents on the past participles.

   d. You shouldn't use the **passé composé** unless you are a trained specialist.

3. Now that you've determined what's wrong with the sentences in the two previous exercises, correct the sentences and then translate them into English.

   a. **Nous avons chante aujourd'hui.**

   Correction: ______________________________

   ____

   Translation: ______________________________

   ____

b. **Vous n'avez pas mange vos cerises!**

Correction: ______________________________

____

Translation: ______________________________

____

c. **J'ai rencontre un loup à côté de la route.**

Correction: ______________________________

____

Translation: ______________________________

____

d. **Finalement, elle a gagne la course.**

Correction: ______________________________

____

Translation: ______________________________

____

e. **Ils ont cachés leur œuf sous l'arbre.**

Correction: ______________________________

____

Translation: ______________________________

____

f. **Elles n'ont pas cassées mon nez.**

Correction: ______________________________

____

Translation: ______________________________

____

g. **Elle a tirée son chat par la queue.**

Correction: ____

____

Translation: ____

____

h. **Vous avez travaillés seulement sept heures?**

Correction: ____

____

Translation: ____

____

The *Passé Composé* with *Être* (Chapitre 12)

1. Some verbs use **avoir** to form the **passé composé**, or past tense, while other verbs use **être**. When used as helping (auxiliary) verbs, we call **avoir** and **être**:

   a. infinitives.
   b. conjugations.
   c. irregular verbs.
   d. auxiliary verbs.

2. Why does the word **retournées** end in **e** and an **s** in the following sentence? **Les filles sont retournées!**

   a. If the past participle is used with **être**, it always receives extra letters.
   b. If the **passé composé** is formed with **être**, the past participle needs to agree with the subject.
   c. **Les filles** always requires an extra **e** and **s** in the past participle, no matter if it's with **avoir** or with **être**. For example: **Les filles ont chantées**.
   d. The author of this book must have been half asleep while writing that sentence.

3. One common feature of verbs that use **être** to form the **passé composé** is that:

   a. They are often verbs describing *movement*.
   b. They are usually verbs with *three or more syllables*.
   c. They are always *irregular verbs*.
   d. The past participles of these verbs *always have an extra* ***e***.

4. The verbs in the following box are all mixed up. Some of them use **avoir** to form the past tense (**passé composé**), but others use **être**. Your job is to assign each verb to the correct list beneath the box. We've done one as an example for you.

aller	~~**manger**~~	**tomber**
travailler	**partir**	**acheter**
casser	**étudier**	**entrer**
parler	**pouvoir**	**devoir**
rester	**vouloir**	**réussir**
retourner	**finir**	**comprendre**

Passé Composé with **Avoir**

manger ________ ________

________ ________

________ ________

________ ________

________ ________

____

____

Passé Composé with **Être**

____

____

____

____

____

____

Stressed Pronouns (Chapitre 13)

1. The following are some quotes that you could imagine hearing over the course of Jean and Aurélie's adventures. Draw lines to match the quotes on the left with the situation described on the right.

a. **"Nous avons peur d'eux!"**	i. Thibault talking to Jean and Aurélie
b. **"Je suis content de voyager avec vous."**	ii. Wolf talking about "his" sheep
c. **"Ils ont besoin de moi."**	iii. Miller talking to the town's guard
d. **"Lui, il est bizarre."**	iv. Heron explaining why he's ignoring all the fish around him
e. **"Qu'est-ce que vous voulez savoir de nous?"**	v. Hare inquiring about her friend, the tortoise
f. **"Vous avez parlé avec elle?"**	vi. Jean whispering to Aurélie about Thibault's father, the miller
g. **"Eux, ils ne sont pas délicieux!"**	vii. Jean and Aurélie talking about the hunting dogs

2. Now, translate the French sentences into English. There may be multiple ways to translate those sentences using stressed pronouns for emphasis.

   a. **"Nous avons peur d'eux!"** ______________________________

   ____

   b. **"Je suis content de voyager avec vous."** ______________________________

   ____

   c. **"Ils ont besoin de moi."** ______________________________

   ____

   d. **"Lui, il est bizarre."** ______________________________

   ____

   e. **"Qu'est-ce que vous voulez savoir de nous?"** ______________________________

   ____

f. **"Vous avez parlé avec elle?"** ______________________________

____

g. **"Eux, ils ne sont pas délicieux!"** ______________________________

____

Pronominal Verbs (Chapitre 14)

1. Look at the following English sentences. Circle the one which you could say using a *pronominal* verb in French (given the vocabulary you've learned in this book).
   a. The children left the school.
   b. I arrived late.
   c. She should take a break.
   d. We talked to each other this morning.
2. Again, which of the English sentences below could you say using a *pronominal* verb in French?
   a. They washed themselves in the river.
   b. I know your brother.
   c. They don't understand French.
   d. She's right. I run fast!
3. In each of the following conjugations, insert the correct reflexive pronoun.
   a. Je ________ couche.
   b. Tu ________ couches.
   c. Il ________ couche.
   d. Elle ________ couche.
   e. Nous ________ couchons.
   f. Vous ________ couchez.
   g. Ils ________ couchent.
   h. Elles ________ couchent.

Traduction

Translate the following English sentences into French, or vice versa.

1. **Il y a une forêt près de chez moi où j'aime me promener.**

   Translation: ____

   ____

2. Thibault, Jean, and Aurélie get up very late.

   Translation: ______________________________

   ____

3. I like to brush my teeth.

   Translation: ______________________________

   ____

4. His house is located near a big road.

   Translation: ______________________________

   ____

Past and Future Tenses + *ne . . . pas . . .* with Pronominal Verbs (Chapitre 15)

1. In French, the past tense (**passé composé**) is formed with a helping verb and a past participle. What is the helping verb with the past tense for *all* pronominal verbs?

   a. **avoir**

   b. **venir**

   c. **aller**

   d. **être**

2. The following sentences got jumbled around. Put the words of the French sentences in the correct order, and then translate each sentence into English.

   a. **la à enfants sont amusés se campagne les.**

      Correct Order: ______________________________

      ____

      Translation: ______________________________

      ____

b. **est souvenu il s' moi de.**

Correct Order: ______________________________

____

Translation: ______________________________

____

c. **pour à voyage 7 heures demain je me lever dois demain mon.**

Correct Order: ______________________________

____

Translation: ______________________________

____

CHAPITRE 17

DIX-SEPT

Félicitations! (Congratulations!) You've made it! Here we are at the last chapter, **le dernier chapitre**, to take some time to review all that you've learned. This end-of-book review **chapitre** is organized according to the three units, or **parties**, of this book:

- **Partie** 1: Irregular Verbs, Negatives, and Question Formation
- **Partie** 2: Question Formation Part 2, Boot Verbs, and Future-Tense Verbs
- **Partie** 3: Past-Tense Verbs, Stressed Pronouns, and Pronominal Verbs

Plus, we'll have a final vocabulary review at the end just to make sure all of those new words are properly tucked away in the French-speaking corner of your brain.

Partie 1: Irregular Verbs, Negatives, and Question Formation

1. **Confused Conjugations:** Below are the conjugation charts for **être** and **avoir**, two of our irregular verbs. Some of the French forms have accidentally been switched from one chart to the other—and not necessarily to the same spot. Your job is to find the mix-ups, cross them out, and write the correct forms in the boxes.

Être (to be)

Person	Singular	Plural
1st Person	**je suis** ________________ (I am)	**nous sommes** ________________ (we are)
2nd Person	**tu as** ________________ (you are)	**vous êtes** ________________ (you are)
3rd Person	**il/elle est** ________________ (he/she/it is)	**ils/elles ont** ________________ (they are)

Avoir (to have)[1]

Person	Singular	Plural
1st Person	**j'ai** ________________ (I have)	**nous avons** ________________ (we have)
2nd Person	**tu as** ________________ (you have)	**vous avez** ________________ (you are)
3rd Person	**il/elle est** ________________ (he/she/it has)	**ils/elles sont** ________________ (they have)

2. Switch the following sentences around by making the positive sentences negative and the negative sentences positive. Then, translate what you've written into English.

   a. **Je n'ai pas de serpent.**

   Positive/Negative: ____

   ____

   Translation: ____

   ____

   b. **Mon chat aime mon serpent.**

   Positive/Negative: ____

   ____

   Translation: ____

   ____

   c. **Le chat n'a pas peur de lui.**

   Positive/Negative: ____

   ____

   Translation: ____

   ____

1. You learned the conjugation of **avoir** in **chapitre** 8 of *FFCA*.

d. **Mon serpent ne veut pas manger mon chat.**

Positive/Negative: ____

____

Translation: ____

____

e. **Les animaux sont toujours très sympathiques.**

Positive/Negative: ____

____

Translation: ____

____

f. **Vraiment? Vous êtes d'accord?**

Positive/Negative: ____

____

Translation: ____

____

3. The following questions are not entirely complete. Help finish them off by adding any words—or parts of words—that might be missing. There will only be one missing item per sentence. Then, translate each corrected sentence into English. An example has been provided to start you off.

Exemple: Pourquoi est- ce que vous voulez rester à la maison?

Translation: Why do you want to stay at home?

a. **Pourquoi est-ce ____________ nous devons acheter douze sacs de pommes de terre?**

Translation: ____

____

b. ____________ **est-ce que nous allons manger douze sacs de pommes de terre?**

Translation: ____

____

c. **Comment est-ce que** ____________ **pouvons finir douze sacs?**

Translation: ____

____

d. **Est-**____________ **que tu connais une bonne recette pour les pommes de terre?** (**recette** = recipe)

Translation: ____

____

e. ____________**-ce que tes amis peuvent manger avec nous?**

Translation: ____

____

Partie 2: Question Formation Part 2, Boot Verbs, and Future-Tense Verbs

1. Circle the correct answer. What is the difference between these two questions: "Qui veut une cerise?" and "Qui est-ce qui veut une cerise?"
   a. The first question is asking, "Who wants a cherry?" while the second is asking, "Who is who, and who wants a cherry?"
   b. The first question is essentially asking the same thing as the second question.
   c. The first question is asking, "Who wants a cherry?" while the second question asks, "Who would like a cherry?"
   d. The first question is asking, "Who wants a cherry?" and the second question asks, "Who is a cherry?"

2. Circle the correct answer. Which question will you *never* see in French?
   a. **Quand est-ce que tu veux manger?**
   b. **Qu'est-ce que tu veux manger?**
   c. **Où est-ce que tu veux manger?**
   d. **Quoi est-ce que tu veux manger?**
3. Translate the following questions into French:
   a. "When can you (**tu**) come to my house?"

      Translation: ______________________________

      ____

   b. "What can we do at your house?"

      Translation: ______________________________

      ____

   c. "What do you want to do?"

      Translation: ______________________________

      ____

   d. "Can we play with the fish?"

      Translation: ______________________________

      ____

   e. "Do we have to play with fish?"

      Translation: ______________________________

      ____

   f. "Who *doesn't* like playing with fish?"

      Translation: ______________________________

      ____

   g. "Are you crazy?"

      Translation: ______________________________

      ____

4. On the left-hand side of the following chart there are French sentences followed by English translations. Using the left side of the chart as a guide, see if you can translate into French the English sentences on the right side of the chart.

Je ne vais pas manger mes légumes. I'm not going to eat my vegetables.	a. I'm not going to look at my vegetables. Translation: ______________________ ______________________ ______________________
Nous allons chercher des fruits dans la forêt. We're going to look for fruit in the woods.	b. We're going to find fruit in the forest. Translation: ______________________ ______________________ ______________________
Il ne va pas courir très loin. He will not run very far.	c. He will not swim very far. Translation: ______________________ ______________________ ______________________
Vous allez avoir faim. You will be hungry.	d. You won't be hungry. Translation: ______________________ ______________________ ______________________
Elles vont comprendre le musée. They will understand the museum.	e. They won't understand the museum. Translation: ______________________ ______________________ ______________________
Je ne vais pas avoir peur de toi. I will not be afraid of you.	f. You will be afraid of my cat. Translation: ______________________ ______________________ ______________________

Partie 3: Past-Tense Verbs and Stressed Pronouns

1. Fill in the blanks. In French, the past tense is called the ______________________. It is made up of two parts. Do you remember the names of those parts? Identify them in the boxes below:

Vous avez mangé beaucoup.

A _ _ i _ _ _ _ _ y	P _ _ _ P _ _ t _ c _ _ l _

2. Draw lines between the following two columns to match the infinitives with their past-tense forms. We've done the first one for you. Then, once you've checked your answers, cover up the list and see if you can memorize them in two or three tries.

Infinitive	**Past-Tense Form (or P_ _ _ P_ _ t_ c_ _ l _)**
chanter	**dit**
finir	**pu**
rencontrer	**eu**
devoir	**allé**
manger	**fini**
pouvoir	**chanté**
aller	**été**
être	**pensé**
faire	**dû**
dire	**fait**
penser	**rencontré**
avoir	**mangé**

3. We've given you a choice of two options for how to translate the first few words of each of the following sentences. Circle the correct option, and then translate the rest of the sentence into French. Be sure to write the entire French sentence on the blank provided. Use the example as a guide:

   Exemple: Our dog fell off the tree. (Notre chien est tombé / Notre chien a tombé)

   Translation: **Notre chien est tombé de l'arbre.**

   a. My mom left at eight o'clock with my brother.
   (**Ma mère a parti** / **Ma mère est partie**)

   Translation: ______________________________

   ____

   b. She went to the zoo with him. (**Elle est allée** / **Elle a allé**)

   Translation: ______________________________

   ____

   c. They looked at the snakes. (**Ils sont regardés** / **Ils ont regardé**)

   Translation: ______________________________

   ____

   d. My mom didn't like the snakes; she is afraid of them.
   (**Ma mère n'est pas aimée** / **Ma mère n'a pas aimé**)

   Translation: ______________________________

   ____

   e. Then they met a nice cow and, with her, a funny mouse.
   (**Ensuite, ils sont rencontrés** / **Ensuite, ils ont rencontré**)

   Translation: ______________________________

   ____

   f. But my mom and my brother thought that they were a little bizarre.
   (**Mais ma mère et mon frère ont pensé** / **Mais ma mère et mon frère sont pensés**)

   Translation: ______________________________

   ____

g. They spoke French! (**Elles sont parlés / Elles ont parlé**)

Translation: ______________________________

____

4. Consider the pronominal verb **se souvenir** ("to remember"). How should we translate the reflexive pronouns (**me**, **te**, **se**, **nous**, **vous**, etc.) that are associated with this verb? For example, how would one translate the **me** in **je me souviens** or the **te** in **tu te souviens**? Circle the correct answer.

   a. The reflexive pronoun means "myself" or "yourself," as in: "I remember myself" or "You remember yourself."

   b. The reflexive pronoun has no single-word translation in this case—it is simply a part of the verb, and does not mean anything "extra." The translation would be "I remember" or "You remember."

   c. The reflexive pronoun means "each other" in this case, giving us, "I remember each other" or "You remember each other."

   d. The reflexive pronoun means the sentence is automatically in the past tense: "I remembered" or "You remembered."

A-Tense-Tion!

1. In the following table there are three columns. On the left is the past tense, in the middle is the present tense, and on the right is the future tense. For each row, use the sentence already there as a guide and then change the sentence into the other two tenses where the blanks remain. We've done the first line for you as an example.

Le Passé Composé	Le Présent	Le Futur
Elles se sont inquiétées.	**Elles s'inquiètent.**	**Elles vont s'inquiéter.**
Nous nous sommes brossés les dents.	______ ______ ______	______ ______ ______
______ ______ ______	**Il s'amuse.**	______ ______ ______

Le Passé Composé	Le Présent	Le Futur
______________________ ______________________ ______________________	______________________ ______________________ ______________________	**Tu vas t'occuper de moi.**
Nous nous sommes habillés.	______________________ ______________________ ______________________	______________________ ______________________ ______________________
Elles se sont levées.	**Elles se lèvent.**	______________________ ______________________ ______________________

2. Now, translate the present-tense forms of the sentences from the table.

a. ____

____

b. ____

____

c. ____

____

d. ____

____

e. ____

____

Vocabulary Review

Try your hand at this final test of the vocabulary you've learned in this book. You should be able to score at least 75 percent on this test (though we hope it will be as close to 100 percent as possible!). If you don't score at least 75 percent, keep reviewing your vocabulary, and give it another try in a few days. The numbers after each word tell you from which chapter the word comes.

	French	English
☐	1. **avoir envie de, j'ai envie de (1)**	______ ______
☐	2. **ensemble (1)**	______
☐	3. **un manteau (2)**	______
☐	4. **un chapeau (2)**	______
☐	5. **une chemise (2)**	______
☐	6. **avoir l'air (de), j'ai l'air (de) (3)**	______ ______
☐	7. **ce (3)**	______
☐	8. **comme (3)**	______
☐	9. **être d'accord, je suis d'accord (4)**	______ ______
☐	10. **le marché (4)**	______
☐	11. **un légume (4)**	______
☐	12. **faire, je fais (6)**	______ ______
☐	13. **cacher, je cache (6)**	______ ______
☐	14. **devoir, je dois (7)**	______ ______
☐	15. **pouvoir, je peux (7)**	______ ______
☐	16. **vouloir, je veux (7)**	______ ______
☐	17. **une pomme de terre (7)**	______
☐	18. **venir, je viens (8)**	______ ______
☐	19. **avoir raison/tort, j'ai raison/tort (8)**	______ ______
☐	20. **dormir, je dors (8)**	______ ______

	French	English
☐	21. **savoir, je sais (9)**	______
☐	22. **le pommier (9)**	______
☐	23. **prendre, je prends (9)**	______
☐	24. **demain (11)**	______
☐	25. **hier (11)**	______
☐	26. **la semaine (11)**	______
☐	27. **dire, je dis (12)**	______
☐	28. **un musée (12)**	______
☐	29. **ensuite (12)**	______
☐	30. **sans (13)**	______
☐	31. **un magasin (13)**	______
☐	32. **s'habiller, je m'habille (14)**	______
☐	33. **se laver, je me lave (14)**	______
☐	34. **se trouver, je me trouve (14)**	______

	French	English
☐	35. **il y a (14)**	______
☐	36. **s'inquiéter (de), je m'inquiète (de) (15)**	______
☐	37. **s'occuper de, je m'occupe de (15)**	______
☐	38. **se souvenir (de), je me souviens (de) (15)**	______
☐	39. **la campagne (15)**	______
☐	40. **mieux (15)**	______

Vocabulaire by Chapter

Chapitre 1

Français	Anglais
être, je suis	to be, I am
voyager, je voyage	to travel, I travel
visiter, je visite	to visit, I visit
avoir envie de, j'ai envie de	to feel like/to want, I feel like/I want
un endroit	a place
une idée	an idea
ensemble	together
intelligent/bête	smart/dumb
content/triste	happy/sad
difficile/simple	difficult/simple

Conversation Journal

C'est dommage.	That's a shame. *or* That's too bad.
où?	where?
un peu	a little (For example: I know a *little* German.)
si	so (as in "*so* nice" or "*so* sad")

Chapitre 2

Français	Anglais
aller, je vais	to go, I go
un manteau	a coat
un chapeau	a hat
une chemise	a shirt
un pantalon	pants
une chaussure/chaussette	a shoe, a sock
un mouton	a sheep
un berger	a shepherd
une foire	a fair
un loup	a wolf
porter, je porte	to wear, I wear (Note: You've already learned that the verb **porter** means "to carry." It can also mean "to wear" as in "to wear clothing.")

Conversation Journal

Vas-y!/Allez-y!	Go ahead!/Go on!/Keep going! (a kind of encouragement)
aujourd'hui	today
très bien	very good
ça	that/it (**C'est ça!** = That's it!)

Chapitre 3

Français	Anglais
avoir l'air (de), j'ai l'air (de)	to seem (like), I seem (like)
commencer, je commence	to begin/to start, I begin/I start
des vêtements	clothes
un sac	a bag
une patte	a paw, hoof, foot
une queue	a tail
une manière	a way, a manner
le pain	bread
ce	this, that
comme	like (ex., "He looks *like* you.")

Conversation Journal

puisque	since (ex., "We're tired *since* we didn't sleep last night.")
pas du tout	not at all

Chapitre 4

Français	Anglais
acheter, j'achète	to buy, I buy
entrer, j'entre	to enter, I enter
être d'accord, je suis d'accord	to agree, I agree
terminer, je termine	to terminate/finish, I terminate/finish
le marché	the market
un fruit	a fruit
un légume	a vegetable
une chose	a thing
fatigué	tired
encore	again, more

Conversation Journal

Quand?	When?
Entrez!	Come in!, Enter!
Assez!	Enough!

Chapitre 6

Français	Anglais
faire, je fais	to do/to make, I do/I make
arriver, j'arrive	to arrive, I arrive
cacher, je cache	to hide (something), I hide (something)
casser, je casse	to break, I break
tirer, je tire	to pull, I pull
dégoûtant	disgusting
l'œuf	the egg
l'omelette	the omelet
le rat	the rat
la dame	the lady

Conversation Journal

là	there (as in a place right around where you are speaking—"What are you doing *there*? That's my seat!" *not* "over there" [**là-bas**], which is farther away)
s'il vous plaît	please (formal or group)

Chapitre 7

Français	Anglais
devoir, je dois	to have to, should; I have to, I should
pouvoir, je peux	to be able to, I can
vouloir, je veux	to want, I want
cher	expensive
une pomme	an apple
une fraise	a strawberry
une pêche	a peach
une pomme de terre	a potato
une tomate	a tomato

Conversation Journal

je suis sûr	I'm sure
Pas de problème.	No problem.

Chapitre 8

Français	Anglais
attendre, j'attends	to wait, I wait
courir, je cours	to run, I run
dormir, je dors	to sleep, I sleep
avoir raison/tort, j'ai raison/tort	to be right/wrong, I am right/wrong
venir, je viens	to come, I come
une course	a race
une cerise	a cherry
une poire	a pear
fou	crazy
vite/lent	fast/slow

Conversation Journal

bon appétit	enjoy your meal (A common phrase to say at the beginning of a meal.)
pas grand-chose	nothing much
N'est-ce pas?	Right? as in "You're coming, *right*?" or "They won, *right*?"
déjà	already

Chapitre 9

Français	Anglais
comprendre, je comprends	to understand, I understand
prendre, je prends	to take, I take
voir, je vois	to see, I see
partir, je pars	to leave, I leave (location)
savoir, je sais	to know, I know (facts or abilities)
un raisin	a grape
une région	a region
souvent	often
le pommier	the apple tree
le cerisier	the cherry tree
la vigne	the vine

Conversation Journal

d'accord	OK, as in "OK, I agree," *not* as in "Are you OK?"
chez moi	at my house, my home, or more generally, "Where I am from."
non plus	neither/either, as in "Me neither" or "They don't understand either."

Chapitre 11

Français	Anglais
connaître, je connais	to know, I know (personally)
gagner, je gagne	to win, I win
demain	tomorrow
avant	before
le soir	the evening
le matin	the morning
hier	yesterday
l'après-midi	the afternoon
la semaine	the week
tard	late

Conversation Journal

faire attention	to pay attention (ex. **Je fais attention** = I pay attention)
mademoiselle	miss (as in "Excuse me, Miss.")
cette	this, that (for feminine nouns; **ce**, from **chapitre** 3, is used for masculine nouns)
les jours de la semaine	the days of the week (Note that to say in French, "Today is Thursday"—or Friday, or Monday, etc.—we often say, "**Aujourd'hui, nous sommes jeudi**," which means "Today we are Thursday.")
Lundi, Mardi, Mercredi, Jeudi, Vendredi, Samedi, Dimanche	Monday, Tuesday, Wednesday, Thursday, Friday, Saturday, Sunday

Chapitre 12

Français	Anglais
rencontrer, je rencontre	to meet, I meet
dire, je dis	to say, I say
retourner, je retourne	to return, I return
un musée	a museum
un restaurant	a restaurant
ensuite	then, next
finalement	finally
seulement	only
jamais	never
après	after

Conversation Journal

Incroyable!	Unbelievable!
Chouette!	Awesome!
Laisse tomber!	Forget it! (The literal translation is "Let it fall!")

Chapitre 13

Français	Anglais
fermer, je ferme	to close, I close
faire une pause, je fais une pause	to take a break, I take a break
un voyage	a trip, a voyage
un magasin	a store
la route	the road
au milieu de	in the middle of
sans	without
sous	under
normal	normal
la fin	the end

Conversation Journal

Bonne soirée.	Have a good evening/night.
Mince!	Darn!
Félicitations!	Congratulations!
entre nous	between us *or* just between us (Note the preposition **entre**, which means "between.")

Chapitre 14

Français	Anglais
s'habiller, je m'habille	to get dressed, I get dressed
se brosser (les dents), je me brosse (les dents)	to brush (your teeth), I brush (my teeth)
se coucher, je me couche	to go to bed, I go to bed
se laver, je me lave	to wash (oneself), I wash myself
se lever, je me lève	to get up, I get up
se promener, je me promène	to go for a walk, I go for a walk
se trouver, je me trouve	to be located, I am located
même	same
quelque chose	something/anything
il y a	there is/there are
une dent	a tooth

Conversation Journal

parfait	perfect
ça alors!	an expression of surprise, and sometimes surprised disapproval—used like the English expressions "No way!" or "Get out of here!" or "Well, really!"

Chapitre 15

Français	Anglais
s'amuser, je m'amuse	to have fun, I have fun
se dépêcher, je me dépêche	to hurry, I hurry
s'endormir, je m'endors	to fall asleep, I fall asleep
s'inquiéter (de), je m'inquiète (de)	to worry (about), I worry (about)
s'occuper de, je m'occupe de	to take care of, I take care of
se sentir, je me sens	to feel, I feel
se souvenir (de), je me souviens (de)	to remember (**de** + something), I remember (**de** + something)
fort	strong (can also mean "good" or "capable" as a more familiar, colloquial expression—see dialogue)
la campagne	the countryside
mieux	better

Conversation Journal

purée!	An exclamation of surprise, such as "Oh man!" or "Holy smokes!"

Alphabetical Vocabulaire

Note: This glossary contains, in alphabetical order, all of the vocabulary words from *French for Children Primers A* and *B*. In this glossary, all nouns are designated as masculine *(m.)* or feminine *(f.)*. The abbreviation *CJ* applies to words that appear in the Conversation Journal section of the indicated chapter. Articles (**le**, **la**, etc.) have been omitted.

Français (French)	**Anglais** (English)	**Chapitre** (Chapter)	
		FFCA	***FFCB***
à	to, at	1	
à côté de	next to	6	
acheter, j'achète	to buy, I buy		4
adieu	farewell	15 (CJ)	
aimer, j'aime	to like/love, I like/love	2	
aller, je vais	to go, I go		2
Allons-y!	Let's go!	2 (CJ)	
alors	so (used very often in conversation, such as "*So*, you want to go fishing?")	1 (CJ)	
ami (m.)	friend	9	
amusant	funny	12	
s'amuser, je m'amuse[1]	to have fun, I have fun		15
âne (m.)	donkey	15	
animal (m.)	animal	9	
après	after		12
après-midi (m.)	afternoon		11
arbre (m.)	tree	4	
arriver, j'arrive	to arrive, I arrive		6
Assez!	Enough!		4 (CJ)
attendre, j'attends	to wait, I wait		8
Attention!	Careful!	11 (CJ)	
au milieu de	in the middle of		13
au revoir	good-bye	4 (CJ)	
aujourd'hui	today		2 (CJ)
aussi	too, also	8 (CJ)	
avant	before		11

1. It is common practice in French dictionaries to keep the se or s' in front of the verb, but to alphabetize the verb itself by the main root.

Français (French)	**Anglais** (English)	**Chapitre** (Chapter) *FFCA*	*FFCB*
avec	with	1	
avoir, j'ai	to have, I have	8	
avoir besoin de, j'ai besoin de	to need, I need	12	
avoir envie de, j'ai envie de	to feel like/to want, I feel like/I want		1
avoir faim, j'ai faim	to be hungry, I am hungry	9	
avoir l'air (de), j'ai l'air (de)	to seem (like), I seem (like)		3
avoir peur de, j'ai peur de	to be afraid of, I'm afraid of	11	
avoir raison/tort, j'ai raison/tort	to be right/wrong, I am right/wrong		8
beau	handsome	14	
beaucoup	a lot, many, very much	2	
belle	beautiful	14	
ben	This word is used in the same way we use the English word "well" when we don't know exactly what to say in a conversation. For example: "*Well*, I guess you can wear a bathing suit to the movies if you really want . . ." or "*Well*, I'm not sure what I'd do if my refrigerator exploded!"	2 (CJ)	
berger (m.)	shepherd		2
bien sûr	of course	2 (CJ)	
bientôt	soon	6 (CJ)	
bienvenue	welcome (as in "You are welcome here.")	7 (CJ)	
bizarre	bizarre	13	
blanc	white	12	
bleu	blue	12	
bon	good	14	
bon appétit	enjoy your meal (Used between friends/family much more often in French than in English!)		8 (CJ)
bonne chance	good luck	12 (CJ)	
Bonne soirée.	Have a good evening/night.		13 (CJ)
bonsoir	good evening	4 (CJ)	
bouche (f.)	mouth	14	
bras (m.)	arm	15	

Français (French)	**Anglais** (English)	**Chapitre** (Chapter) *FFCA*	*FFCB*
se brosser (les dents), je me brosse (les dents)	to brush (your teeth), I brush (my teeth)		14
c'est	that is, that's, this is	14 (CJ)	
C'est dommage.	That's a shame. *or* That's too bad.		1 (CJ)
ça	that/it (**C'est ça!** = That's it!)		2 (CJ)
ça alors!	an expression of surprise, and sometimes surprised disapproval—used like the English expressions "No way!" or "Get out of here!" or "Well, really!"		14 (CJ)
ça va	This phrase can be a question, such as "How are you?" "How are things going?" "How is it going?" or "Is everything OK?" It can also be an answer, such as "I'm doing fine" or "Things are going well." It all depends on how you say it—with a questioning tone of voice or with an answering tone of voice.	1 (CJ)	
cacher, je cache	to hide (something), I hide (something)		6
cadeau (m.)	present, gift	9	
campagne (f.)	countryside		15
carte (f.)	map	1	
casser, je casse	to break, I break		6
ce	this, that		3
cerise (f.)	cherry		8
cerisier (m.)	cherry tree		9
cette	this, that (for feminine nouns; **ce**, from **chapitre** 3, is used for masculine nouns)		11 (CJ)
champ (m.)	field	7	
chanter, je chante	to sing, I sing	4	
chapeau (m.)	hat		2
chat (m.)	cat	3	
chaussure/chaussette (f.)	shoe, sock		2
chemise (f.)	shirt		2
cher	expensive		7
chercher, je cherche	to look (for), I look (for)	3	
cheval (m.)	horse	9	
cheveux (m.)	hair	14	

Français (French)	**Anglais** (English)	**Chapitre** (Chapter) *FFCA*	*FFCB*
chez moi	at my house, my home, or more generally, "Where I am from."		9 (CJ)
chien (m.)	dog	3	
chose (f.)	thing		4
Chouette!	Awesome!		12 (CJ)
Chut!	Shhhh!, Be quiet!	1 (CJ)	
Ciao!	See you!/See you later! (pronounced CHOW)	7 (CJ)	
cinq	five	8	
cochon (m.)	pig	6	
combien	how many *or* how much (as in a question)	9 (CJ)	
comme	like (ex., "He looks *like* you.")		3
commencer, je commence	to begin/to start, I begin/I start		3
comment	This word can mean "how" as in the question, "How do you know?" but it can also mean, "Excuse me?"—a question one asks when one does not understand something.	3 (CJ)	
Comment t'appelles-tu?	What is your name?	4 (CJ)	
comprendre, je comprends	to understand, I understand		9
connaître, je connais	to know, I know (personally)		11
content/triste	happy/sad		1
se coucher, je me couche	to go to bed, I go to bed		14
courir, je cours	to run, I run		8
course (f.)	race		8
d'accord	OK, as in "OK, I agree," *not* as in "Are you OK?"		9 (CJ)
dame (f.)	lady		6
dans	in	4	
de	of, from	2	
de rien	you're welcome	9 (CJ)	
dégoûtant	disgusting		6
déjà	already		8 (CJ)
délicieux	delicious	12	
demain	tomorrow		11
dent	tooth		14

Français (French)	**Anglais** (English)	**Chapitre** (Chapter) *FFCA*	*FFCB*
se dépêcher, je me dépêche	to hurry, I hurry		15
derrière	behind	7	
désolé	sorry	3 (CJ)	
deux	two	8	
devant	in front of	6	
devoir (m.)	homework	2	
devoir, je dois	to have to, should; I have to, I should		7
difficile/simple	difficult/simple		1
dire, je dis	to say, I say		12
dix	ten	8	
dormir, je dors	to sleep, I sleep		8
dos (m.)	back	15	
douze	twelve	8	
eau (f.)	water	11	
école (f.)	school	2	
enchanté	nice to meet you	4 (CJ)	
encore	again, more		4
s'endormir, je m'endors	to fall asleep, I fall asleep		15
endroit (m.)	place		1
enfant (m.)	child	8	
ensemble	together		1
ensuite	then, next		12
entre nous	between us *or* just between us (Note preposition **entre**, which means "between.")		13 (CJ)
entrer, j'entre	to enter, I enter		4
Entrez!	Come in!, Enter!		4 (CJ)
épaule (f.)	shoulder	15	
espérer [que], j'espère [que]	to hope [that], I hope [that]	3	
et	and	1	
être d'accord, je suis d'accord	to agree, I agree		4
être, je suis	to be, I am		1
étudier, j'étudie	to study, I study	1	
excusez-moi	excuse me	11 (CJ)	

Français (French)	**Anglais** (English)	**Chapitre** (Chapter) *FFCA*	*FFCB*
facile	easy	12	
faire attention	to pay attention (ex. **Je fais attention** = I pay attention)		11 (CJ)
faire une pause, je fais une pause	to take a break, I take a break		13
faire, je fais	to do/to make, I do/I make		6
famille (f.)	family	8	
fatigué	tired		4
Félicitations!	Congratulations!		13 (CJ)
femme (f.)	woman, wife	13	
ferme (f.)	farm	6	
fermer, je ferme	to close, I close		13
fille (f.)	girl, daughter	8, 13	
fils (m.)	son	13	
fin (f.)	end		13
finalement	finally		12
finir, je finis	to finish, I finish	3	
fleur (f.)	flower	7	
fleuve (m.)	river	11	
foire (f.)	fair		2
forêt (f.)	forest	2	
fort	strong (can also mean "good" or "capable" as a more familiar, colloquial expression)		15
fou	crazy		8
fraise (f.)	strawberry		7
français (m.)	French	1	
frère (m.)	brother	8	
fromage (m.)	cheese	6	
fruit (m.)	fruit		4
gagner, je gagne	to win, I win		11
garçon (m.)	boy	8	
Génial!	Great!		7 (CJ)
genou (m.)	knee	15	
gentil	nice/kind	12	
grand	big	14	
grange (f.)	barn	6	
s'habiller, je m'habille	to get dressed, I get dressed		14

Français (French)	**Anglais** (English)	**Chapitre** (Chapter) *FFCA*	*FFCB*
habiter, j'habite	to live, I live	4	
heureux	happy	13	
hier	yesterday		11
homme (m.)	man	13	
huit	eight	8	
ici	here	4	
idée (f.)	idea		1
il y a	there is/there are		14
Incroyable!	Unbelievable!		12 (CJ)
s'inquiéter (de), je m'inquiète (de)	to worry (about), I worry (about)		15
intelligent/bête	smart/dumb		1
intéressant	interesting	12	
J'espère que oui.	I hope so.	6 (CJ)	
jamais	never		12
jambe (f.)	leg	15	
jaune	yellow	12	
je m'appelle	my name is	4 (CJ)	
Je pense que oui.	I think so.	6 (CJ)	
je suis sûr	I'm sure		7 (CJ)
jeu (m.)	game	9	
jeune	young	14	
jouer, je joue	to play, I play	6	
les jours de la semaine	days of the week (Note that to say in French, "Today is Thursday"—or Friday, or Monday, etc.—we often say, "**Aujourd'hui, nous sommes jeudi**," which means "Today *we are* Thursday.")		11 (CJ)
là	there (as in a place right around where you are speaking—"What are you doing *there*? That's my seat!" *not* "over there" [**là-bas**], which is farther away)		6 (CJ)
La vache!	Holy cow!	8 (CJ)	
là-bas	over there	13 (CJ)	
se laver, je me lave	to wash (oneself), I wash myself		14
lac (m.)	lake	11	
Laisse tomber!	Forget it! (literal translation: "Let it fall!")		12 (CJ)
laisser, je laisse	to leave (something or someone), I leave (something or someone)	13	

Français (French)	**Anglais** (English)	**Chapitre** (Chapter) *FFCA*	*FFCB*
légume (m.)	vegetable		4
se lever, je me lève	to get up, I get up		14
loin (de)	far (from)	7	
loup (m.)	wolf		2
Lundi, Mardi, Mercredi, Jeudi, Vendredi, Samedi, Dimanche	Monday, Tuesday, Wednesday, Thursday, Friday, Saturday, Sunday		11 (CJ)
mademoiselle	miss (as in "Excuse me, miss.")		11 (CJ)
magasin (m.)	store		13
magnifique	magnificent, wonderful	12	
main/mains (f.)	hand/hands	15	
maintenant	now	12 (CJ)	
mais	but	9	
maison (f.)	house, home	2	
manger, je mange	to eat, I eat	3	
manière (f.)	way, manner		3
manteau (m.)	coat		2
marché (m.)	market		4
marcher, je marche	to walk, I walk	2	
matin (m.)	morning		11
mauvais	bad	14	
méchant	mean	12	
même	same		14
mer (f.)	sea	11	
merci	thank you	7 (CJ)	
mère (f.)	mother	8	
mieux	better		15
mignon	cute	13	
Mince!	Darn!		13 (CJ)
moche	ugly	13	
moi	me	12 (CJ)	
montagne (f.)	mountain	7	
mouton (m.)	sheep		2
musée (m.)	museum		12

Français (French)	**Anglais** (English)	**Chapitre** (Chapter)	
		FFCA	***FFCB***
N'est-ce pas?	Right? as in "You're coming, *right*?" or "They won, *right*?"		8 (CJ)
nager, je nage	to swim, I swim	11	
neuf	nine	8	
nez (m.)	nose	14	
noir	black	12	
non	no	1 (CJ)	
non plus	neither/either, as in "Me neither" or "They don't understand either."		9 (CJ)
normal	normal		13
s'occuper de, je m'occupe de	to take care of, I take care of		15
œil/yeux (m.)	eye/eyes	14	
œuf (m.)	egg		6
oiseau (m.)	bird	7	
omelette (f.)	omelet		6
onze	eleven	8	
orange	orange	12	
oreille/oreilles (f.)	ear/ears	14	
ou	or	3	
où?	where?		1 (CJ)
oui	yes	1 (CJ)	
pain (m.)	bread		3
pantalon (m.)	pants		2
parce que	because	9 (CJ)	
paresseux	lazy	12	
parfait	perfect		14 (CJ)
parler, je parle	to speak, I speak	1	
partir, je pars	to leave, I leave (location)		9
Pas de problème.	no problem		7 (CJ)
pas du tout	not at all		3 (CJ)
pas grand-chose	nothing much		8 (CJ)
patte (f.)	paw, hoof, foot		3
pêche (f.)	peach		7
penser [que], je pense [que]	to think [that], I think [that]	4	

V

Français (French)	**Anglais** (English)	**Chapitre** (Chapter) *FFCA*	*FFCB*
père (m.)	father	8	
petit	small	14	
peut-être	perhaps, maybe	12 (CJ)	
pied (m.)	foot	15	
plage (f.)	beach	11	
poire (f.)	pear		8
poisson (m.)	fish	11	
pomme (f.)	apple		7
pomme de terre (f.)	potato		7
pommier (m.)	apple tree		9
porter, je porte	to carry, I carry *or* to wear, I wear	15	
pour	for	2	
pourquoi?	why?	15 (CJ)	
pouvoir, je peux	to be able to, I can		7
préférer, je préfère	to prefer, I prefer	4	
prendre, je prends	to take, I take		9
près (de)	near (to), close (to)	11	
problème (m.)	problem	9	
se promener, je me promène	to go for a walk, I go for a walk		14
puisque	since (ex., "We're tired *since* we didn't sleep last night.")		3 (CJ)
purée!	an exclamation of surprise such as "Oh man!" or "Holy smokes!"		15 (CJ)
Quand?	When?		4 (CJ)
quatre	four	8	
Quel âge as-tu?	How old are you?	14 (CJ)	
quelque chose	something/anything		14
queue (f.)	tail		3
qui?	who?	13 (CJ)	
quoi?	what?	13 (CJ)	
raisin (m.)	grape		9
rat (m.)	rat		6
regarder, je regarde	to look (at), I look (at)	1	
région (f.)	region		9
renard (m.)	fox	6	

Français (French)	**Anglais** (English)	**Chapitre** (Chapter) *FFCA*	*FFCB*
rencontrer, je rencontre	to meet, I meet		12
restaurant (m.)	restaurant		12
rester, je reste	to stay, I stay	3	
retourner, je retourne	to return, I return		12
réussir, je réussis	to succeed, I succeed	3	
rouge	red	12	
route (f.)	road		13
s'il te plaît	please (informal)	8 (CJ)	
s'il vous plaît	please (formal or group)		6 (CJ)
sac (m.)	bag		3
sans	without		13
savoir, je sais	to know, I know (facts or abilities)		9
semaine (f.)	week		11
se sentir, je me sens	to feel, I feel		15
sept	seven	8	
serpent (m.)	snake	6	
seulement	only		12
si	if, so (as in "*so* nice" *or* "*so* sad")	9	7
six	six	8	
sœur (f.)	sister	8	
soir (m.)	evening		11
souris (f.)	mouse	1	
sous	under		13
se souvenir (de), je me souviens (de)	to remember (**de** + something), I remember (**de** + something)		15
souvent	often		9
sur	on, on top of	7	
sympathique (sympa)	nice	12	
tard	late		11
terminer, je termine	to terminate/finish, I terminate/finish		4
tête (f.)	head	14	
tirer, je tire	to pull, I pull		6
tomate (f.)	tomato		7
tomber, je tombe	to fall, I fall	7	
toujours	always	9	
tout	everything, all	11	

Français (French)	**Anglais** (English)	**Chapitre** (Chapter) *FFCA*	*FFCB*
tout le monde	everyone, everybody	14 (CJ)	
travailler, je travaille	to work, I work	2	
très	very	13	
très bien	very good		2 (CJ)
trois	three	8	
trop	too (as in "too much," not as in "also")	15	
trouver, je trouve	to find, I find	4	
se trouver, je me trouve	to be located, I am located		14
un	one	8	
un peu	a little (For example, "I know a *little* German.")		1 (CJ)
vache (f.)	cow	1	
Vas-y!/Allez-y!	Go ahead!/Go on!/Keep going! (a kind of encouragement)		2 (CJ)
venir, je viens	to come, I come		8
vent (m.)	wind	7	
vers	toward	4	
vert	green	12	
vêtements (m.)	clothes		3
vieux	old	14	
vigne (f.)	vine		9
village (m.)	village	6	
ville (f.)	city	6	
violet	purple	12	
visiter, je visite	to visit, I visit		1
vite/lent	fast/slow		8
voilà	there it is, there you have it, there is, there we go	6 (CJ)	
voir, je vois	to see, I see		9
voiture (f.)	car	3	
voler, je vole	to fly, I fly	7	
vouloir, je veux	to want, I want		7
voyage (m.)	trip, voyage		13
voyager, je voyage	to travel, I travel		1
vraiment	really	13 (CJ)	
zoo (m.)	zoo	4	

Appendix A

Dialogue Translations

Chapitre 1

Dialogue [01_01/Tr. 1]

In case you're just joining us or can't quite recall what was happening in the dialogue sections in FFCA*, we have been following the story of Jean, a field mouse, and Aurélie, a dairy cow, who were mistakenly released into the wild after zookeepers mistook them for protected species. They have been trying to find their way back to the zoo and at this point in the story have joined up with a somewhat eccentric village miller and his son. The miller and his son are on their way to the local fair, which happens to be on the way to the city.*

Aurélie, Jean, the miller's son, and the miller—still carrying his donkey—set off for the fair. The miller manages to walk at a surprising pace, given his load, and soon he has gone some distance ahead of the others. Jean and Aurélie begin talking with the boy as the miles go by.

JEAN, *speaking to the miller's son.* **Alors! Comment t'appelles-tu?** (So! What's your name?)

THIBAULT. **Je m'appelle Thibault—et vous? Comment vous appelez-vous?** (My name is Thibault—and you? What are your names?)

JEAN. **Moi, je m'appelle Jean.** (Me, my name is Jean.)

AURÉLIE. **Et je suis Aurélie—enchantée!** (And I'm Aurélie—pleased to meet you!)

THIBAULT. **Enchanté! Je suis content de marcher avec vous.** (Pleased to meet you! I'm happy to walk with you.)

JEAN. **Nous sommes contents aussi.** (We're happy, too.) The road is a long one, and we're glad for the company. Plus, we weren't quite sure we could trust your dad's . . . errr . . . well . . . judgment. . . . *Jean points ahead to the miller, who is still huffing and puffing as he carries his donkey.*

THIBAULT. **Ah non, ça va, ça va. Il aime ses animaux, c'est tout. Et il aime beaucoup son âne!** (Oh, no, it's OK, it's OK. He loves animals, that's all. And he really loves his donkey!) He's just making sure it doesn't get too tired.

JEAN. Well, it's still nice to go along with you.

AURÉLIE. **Et vraiment . . . nous avons un peu peur de voyager . . . nous habitons dans le zoo!** (And really . . . we're a little scared of traveling . . . we live in the zoo!)

JEAN. Yes, you see, and we are not used to traveling like most folks. **Toi, tu voyages beaucoup?** (Do you travel a lot?)

THIBAULT. **Non. C'est dommage. J'ai envie de voyager. J'ai envie de visiter beaucoup d'endroits.** (No. It's too bad. I want to travel. I want to visit lots of places.)

AURÉLIE, *not believing that people actually want to travel on purpose.* ***Vraiment? Où?*** (*Really? Where?*)

THIBAULT. Oh, I don't know. **Beaucoup d'endroits sont intéressants . . . la plage, les montagnes . . . la ville, peut-être? Tout le monde dans mon village parle de la grande ville. "Oh, la ville, elle est magnifique!"** (Lots of places are interesting . . . the beach, the mountains . . . the city, maybe? Everyone in my village talks about the big city. "Oh, the city, it's great!") They say, **"La ville, elle est grande et belle!** (The city, it's big and beautiful!)" The farthest I've been, though, is just the next town over where the market is, so how should I know? **Mais vous, vous êtes de là-bas. Vous pensez que la ville est si belle?** (But you, you're from there. Do you think the city is so beautiful?)

JEAN. **Hmmm . . . tu as des bonnes questions.** (Hmmm . . . you have good questions.) You know, it's been so long since I was out walking around there. **Nous sommes toujours dans le zoo, alors c'est difficile pour nous d'avoir une idée.** (We're always in the zoo, so it's hard for us to have any idea.)

AURÉLIE. **J'ai une idée.** (I have an idea.)

THIBAULT AND JEAN. What is it?

AURÉLIE. **Nous visitons la ville ensemble!** (We visit the city together!)

THIBAULT. Hey, Jean, what do you think of that?

JEAN. **Oui! Je pense que c'est une bonne idée. Aurélie, tu es une vache intelligente!** (Yes! I think it's a good idea. Aurelie, you're an intelligent cow!) But I'm afraid it will be quite a challenge getting back . . . **si nous réussissons** (if we succeed), I'll be glad to see the city **avec toi, Thibault! Allons-y!** (with you, Thibault! Let's go!)

Chapitre 2

Dialogue [02_01/Tr. 8]

Suddenly, the miller stops dead in his tracks and cries out. The three companions soon catch up and see, approaching in the distance, the outline of a wolf walking toward them. As he nears, however, the four travelers realize that this is no ordinary predator.

THIBAULT. **Bonjour, Monsieur le Loup. Ça va?** (Hello, Mr. Wolf. How's it going?)

Monsieur le Loup. **Ça va très bien, merci! Et vous, les amis? Vous allez où aujourd'hui? Vous allez aussi aux champs, peut-être?** (Very well, thank you! And you, friends? Where are you going today? You're going to the fields, too, perhaps?)

Jean. **Aux champs? Non . . . nous allons à la foire . . .** (To the fields? No . . . we're going to the fair.)

Monsieur le Loup, *relieved.* **Aha! Ça c'est *très, très* bien.** (Aha! That's *very, very* good.) The fields are so boring, anyway.

Aurélie. **Mais, monsieur? Alors, pourquoi vous allez aux champs?** (But, sir? Then why are you going to the fields?)

Monsieur le Loup. **Moi? Euh . . . je vais aux champs pour . . . euh . . . pour le business . . . oui, c'est ça.** (Me? Um . . . I'm going to the fields for . . . um . . . for business . . . yes, that's it.)

Jean, *noticing the wolf's peculiar attire.* I see. **Mais j'ai une question. Pourquoi portez-vous un manteau?** (But I have a question. Why are you wearing a coat?)

Monsieur le Loup. **Ah, mon manteau . . . alors . . . ça . . .** (Oh, my coat . . . well . . . that . . .)

Thibault. **Oui, Monsieur le Loup . . . et vous portez aussi un chapeau? Les loups portent des chapeaux?** (Yes, Mr. Wolf . . . and you're also wearing a hat? Do wolves wear hats?)

Monsieur le Loup. **Mon chapeau? Alors, c'est pour . . . euh . . .** (My hat? Well, it's for . . . um . . .)

Thibault. And it looks like something's written on your hat, too—**"Je suis Guillaume, le berger des moutons." Monsieur? Vous êtes berger?** ("I'm William, the shepherd of the sheep." Sir? You're a shepherd?)

Monsieur le Loup. **Oui . . . euh . . . oui! Et bien sûr, je m'appelle . . . Gérald—non—Guillaume! Je vais aux champs pour regarder mes moutons.** (Yes . . . um . . . yes! And of course my name is . . . Gerald—no—William! I'm going to the fields to look at my sheep.)

Aurélie. **Oh, il est très intéressant, le loup. J'ai envie d'aller avec Guillaume!** (Oh, he's very interesting, this wolf. I'd like to go with William!)

Monsieur le Loup. **Avec qui? Ah, non, non, non! C'est une mauvaise idée** . . . (With who? Oh, no, no, no! That's a bad idea . . .) besides, **tu vas à la foire** (you're going to the fair); I don't want to make you late . . . **vas-y, vas-y** (go on, go on)!

Jean, *growing more and more suspicious.* **Alors, Guillaume. Vous aimez être berger?** (So, William. Do you like being a shepherd?)

Monsieur le Loup. **Moi? Ah oui.** (Me? Oh yes.) [*smiles*] **J'aime les moutons. Ils sont filets mignons—mmm ahem—** (I like the sheep. They're filets mignons—ahem—) [*coughs*] **excusez-moi—*très* mignons . . .** (excuse me—*very* cute . . .)

Chapitre 3

Dialogue [03_01/Tr. 14]

Jean, *who has had enough of the wolf's story.* **Monsieur le Loup, excusez-moi, mais nous ne sommes pas bêtes. Vous n'êtes pas berger.** (Mr. Wolf, excuse me, but we're not dumb. You're not a shepherd.)

Monsieur le Loup, *laughing nervously.* **Bien sûr, vous n'êtes pas bêtes, ou stupides** . . . (Of course, you aren't dumb, or stupid . . .) but you really don't think that I'm a shepherd? **Ha ha . . . alors, pourquoi pensez-vous que je ne suis pas berger?** (Ha ha . . . so, why do you think I'm not a shepherd?)

Le meunier. Well, your appearance, for one. **Vous n'avez pas l'air d'un berger.** (You don't seem like a shepherd.)

Monsieur le Loup. I don't seem like a shepherd? **Aha . . . ben, c'est normal . . . puisque je suis nouveau. . . .** (Aha . . . well, that's normal . . . because I'm new at it. . . .)

Thibault. Hmm . . . I'm not sure I believe that one, either. **En plus, vous ne marchez pas comme un berger. Ce n'est pas leur manière de marcher à quatre pattes.** (And furthermore, you aren't walking like a shepherd. It's not their style to walk on four paws.)

Monsieur le Loup. Vraiment . . . euh . . . (Really . . . um . . .)

Jean. **Vous ne portez pas des vêtements de berger. Votre manteau, c'est un grand sac! Où est votre pantalon? Où sont vos chaussures?** (You're not wearing shepherd's clothes. Your coat, it's a big bag! Where are your pants? Where are your shoes?)

Monsieur le Loup. Well, I mean, I have them, they're just back in my—

Aurélie, *realizing what's happening.* **Oh là là! Vous ne parlez pas comme un berger! Pas du tout!** (Oh my! You don't speak like a shepherd! Not at all!)

Monsieur le Loup. Je ne parle pas comme un berger? Comment? (I don't speak like a shepherd? Excuse me?) How do you know that?

Aurélie. **Puisque votre manière de parler n'est pas gentille.** (Because your way of talking isn't nice.)

Monsieur le Loup, *backing away slowly.* Well, friends, you'll have to excuse me—I really must be going. **Mes moutons sont délicieux—**ahem!**—un peu vieux, et ils ont besoin de moi pour trouver la grange . . .** (My sheep are delicious—ahem!—a little old, and they need me to find the barn . . .)

Jean. **Bien sûr.** (Of course.) Be off! But don't think that your costume is going to fool any sheep—let alone a real shepherd and his dogs. Besides, **les bergers n'ont pas de queue** (shepherds don't have tails)**!**

Monsieur le Loup, *shouts as he is running away.* We'll see! **J'espère que les moutons ne sont pas intelligents comme vous!** (I hope that the sheep aren't intelligent like you!)

Chapitre 4

Dialogue [04_01/Tr. 26]

At the end of the first leg of their long journey, the four travelers finally reach the town hosting the market. But even as they approach, the gatekeeper at the main entrance grows increasingly suspicious. He doesn't like the look of our four voyagers, and he has no shortage of questions for them upon their arrival. . . .

Le gardien (The Gatekeeper), *motions to the travelers to come off the road next to his watchtower; a huge, growling dog stands at his side.* Over here, **s'il vous plaît!** (please!)

Aurélie, *whispers to Jean.* **Oh là là, il a l'air méchant.** (Oh my, he seems mean.)

Jean, *whispering back.* **Je suis d'accord!** (I agree!)

Le gardien. Quoi!? Est-ce que tu parles de moi? (What!? Are you talking about me?)

Jean. **Non, monsieur.** (No, sir.)

Le gardien. J'espère que non. (I hope not.)

Jean. **Elle . . . elle . . . elle parle de votre chien. Elle pense qu'il est mignon.** (She . . . she . . . was talking about your dog. She thinks he's cute.)

Le gardien. Bruno!? Mignon!? Hmph . . . (Bruno!? Cute!? Hmph . . .), *forgetting his job for a moment,* **Je ne pense pas, mais peut-être. Il a des beaux yeux. Et ses pattes . . . elles sont mignonnes . . . Hum hum!** (I don't think so, but maybe. He has beautiful eyes. And his paws . . . they're cute . . . Ahem!) *remembering his duty,* **Où est-ce que vous allez?** (Where are you going?)

Le meunier. Ben, nous allons au marché, monsieur. (Well, we're going to the market, sir.)

Le gardien. Et pourquoi est-ce que vous allez à notre marché? (And why are you going to our market?)

Le meunier. Parce que nous avons envie d'acheter des choses ici. S'il vous plaît, Monsieur, quand est-ce que le marché termine aujourd'hui? (Because we want to buy things here. Please, sir, when does the market end today?)

Le gardien. Hmmm . . . bientôt! Mais, vous avez l'intention d'acheter quoi ici? Des chevaux? Des vaches? Nous n'avons pas beaucoup de chevaux et de vaches! (Hmmm . . . soon! But, what are you planning to buy here? Horses? Cows? We don't have a lot of horses and cows!)

THIBAULT. **Non, non. Nous avons besoin d'acheter des fruits et des légumes, c'est tout.** (No, no. We need to buy fruit and vegetables, that's all.)

LE GARDIEN, *turning his attention back to* ***le meunier***. **Et vous, monsieur. Pourquoi est-ce que vous portez votre âne sur la tête?** (And you, sir. Why are you carrying a donkey on your head?)

LE MEUNIER, *who has been getting tired of so many questions, especially the last one, replies.* **Encore une question! C'est assez! Oui, je porte mon âne sur la tête. Est-ce que c'est un problème!? Et vous, pourquoi est-ce que vous ne portez pas votre chien sur la tête? Combien de questions est-ce que vous avez? Nous sommes fatigués! Nous avons faim! Nous avons envie d'entrer!** (Another question! That's enough! Yes, I'm carrying my donkey on my head. Is that a problem!? And you, why aren't you carrying your dog on your head? How many questions do you have? We're tired! We're hungry! We want to come in!)

LE GARDIEN, *surprised*. **Bon, euh, je suis désolé. Entrez, entrez!** (Oh, um, I'm sorry. Come in, come in!)

Chapitre 6

Dialogue [06_01/Tr. 27]

The miller immediately sets off to start bargaining, leaving Jean, Aurélie, and Thibault to wander around the bustling streets of the market town. Before long, they stumble upon a strange sight.

THIBAULT. **Jean, Aurélie? Est-ce que vous regardez les deux rats là-bas? Qu'est-ce qu'ils font?** (Jean, Aurélie? Are you looking at the two rats over there? What are they doing?)

JEAN. I have no idea . . . **mais ça a l'air bizarre** (but it seems strange)**!**

AURÉLIE. **Hé, ho! Les rats! Qu'est-ce que vous faites là? Qu'est-ce que vous avez?** (Hey! Rats! What are you doing there? What do you have?)

RAT #1, *quietly*. **Chut! C'est un œuf! Mais chut! Le renard arrive! Il aime manger nos œufs.** (Shh! It's an egg! But shhh! The fox is coming! He likes to eat our eggs.)

AURÉLIE, *whispering*. **OK, mais pourquoi est-ce que tu es sur ton dos avec l'œuf dans les pattes?** (OK, but why are you on your back with the egg in your paws?)

JEAN, *to the other rat*. **Oui! Et, pourquoi est-ce que tu tires ton ami par la queue?** (Yes! And, why are you pulling your friend by the tail?)

RAT #1, *in a hushed voice*. **Chuuuuut! Nous n'avons pas envie de casser notre œuf . . .** (Shhhhhhh! We don't want to break our egg . . .)

RAT #2. **Mais nous avons besoin de cacher notre œuf parce que le renard arrive.** (But we need to hide our egg because the fox is coming.)

THIBAULT, *speaking normally.* **C'est *votre* œuf?** (It's *your* egg?)

RAT #2. **CHUUUT! S'IL VOUS PLAÎT!! . . . Mais oui! Les gentilles dames ici au marché laissent toujours des œufs pour nous . . .** (SHHHH! PLEASE!! . . . Of course! The nice ladies here in the market always leave eggs for us . . .)

JEAN. Hmm . . . I've heard that kind of story before . . .

RAT #1. **C'est vrai! Elles font toujours ça, les vieilles dames du marché.** (It's true! They always do that, the old ladies from the market.)

THIBAULT. **C'est bizarre, votre manière de porter un œuf.** (It's strange, your way of carrying an egg.) But I guess so is *eating* raw egg . . .

RAT #2, *forgetting his fear, his pride now wounded.* **Ah mais, nous ne mangeons pas les œufs comme ça! Nous faisons des omelettes.** (Oh, but we don't eat eggs like that! We make omelets.)

RAT #1. **Oh là là, nous faisons des omelettes délicieuses.** (Oh my, we make delicious omelets.)

RAT #2. **Et mon ami fait des gâteaux supers!** (And my friend makes amazing cakes!)

RAT #1. **Ça va, ça va, ils ne sont pas si bons . . .** (Oh, they're not that good . . .)

RAT #2, *turning to his friend.* **Tu fais des gâteaux magnifiques!** (You make magnificent cakes!)

RAT #1. **Ah, ben, merci . . . c'est gentil.** (Oh, well, thanks . . . that's nice.)

RAT #2. **Non, mais vraiment, je trouve tes gâteaux très, très bien. Quand tu fais le gâteau au vieux fromage—OH! Ça, j'aime beaucoup. Ah, et ton gâteau aux têtes de poissons—super!** (No, but really, I think your cakes are really, really good. When you make the cake with old cheese—OH! I like that one a lot. Oh, and your fish head cake—amazing!)

AURÉLIE, JEAN, AND THIBAULT, *under their breath.* **Dégoûtant!** (Disgusting!)

Chapitre 7

Dialogue [07_01/Tr. 33]

THIBAULT. **Alors, je veux aller à la ville avec vous, mais je dois parler avec mon père.** (So, I want to go to the city with you, but I have to speak with my father.) If he thinks it's all right, then we can leave right from here—this gate leads right out to the city.

AURÉLIE. **Est-ce qu'il est près d'ici, ton père?** (Is your father near here?)

THIBAULT, *pointing at the stand of one of last merchants before the gate.* **Oui! Il est là-bas.** (Yes! He's over there.) I think he's trying to trade our donkey. *They approach from behind and begin to pick up snippets of the conversation.*

Le meunier. . . . un sac de pommes, cinq sacs de fraises, cinq sacs de pêches, et trois bons fromages? (. . . a bag of apples, five bags of strawberries, five bags of peaches, and three good cheeses?)

La dame. Non monsieur! Je ne peux pas! C'est trop. (No, sir! I can't! It's too much.)

Le meunier, *getting frustrated*. **Alors, je veux un sac de pommes, un de pommes de terre, un de tomates et trois fromages . . . ça, ça va?** (So, I want a bag of apples, one of potatoes, one of tomatoes and three cheeses . . . does that work?)

La dame. **Ben non, monsieur**. (No, sir.)

Le meunier. S'il vous plaît! (Please!)

La dame. **Vous ne pouvez pas avoir les fruits, les légumes, *et* le fromage tout pour votre petit âne . . .** (You can't have fruit, vegetables, *and* cheese all for your little donkey . . .) This cheese costs more than your donkey alone! **Il est de la ville, mon fromage. C'est très cher!** (My cheese is from the city. It's very expensive!)

Le meunier. And you think my donkey isn't expensive? Just look at him! **Regarde sa tête! Regarde ses pattes! Sa queue! Son dos!** (Look at his head! Look at his feet! His tail! His back!) He's worth a fortune!

Thibault, *interrupting*. **Papa, Aurélie et Jean veulent aller à la ville maintenant. Est-ce que nous pouvons aller ensemble?** (Papa, Aurélie and Jean want to go to the city now. Can we go together?)

Le meunier. Hmmm . . . vous voulez aller ensemble? Je ne suis pas sûr . . . la ville est loin. Ben . . . (Hmmm . . . you want to go together? I'm not sure . . . the city is far. Well . . .), *seeing the woman scowling at him from behind her cheeses*. If you can bring back **trois bons fromages de la ville . . . oui, tu peux aller avec Jean et Aurélie** (three good cheeses from the city . . . yes, you can go with Jean and Aurelie). You'd make your mother quite happy, too, seeing as I won't be bringing any home . . . **puisque le fromage ici est si cher . . .** (since the cheese here is so expensive . . .), *he scowls back at the woman*.

Thibault. **Génial! Merci, Papa!** (Great! Thanks, Papa!)

Jean and Aurélie. **Merci, monsieur!** (Thanks, sir!)

Jean. **Nous pouvons trouver les fromages, pas de problème. Allons-y!** (We can find cheese, no problem. Let's go!)

Chapitre 8

Dialogue [08_01/Tr. 39]

Striking out on the road again, the travelers swap stories about zoo life and village life, the city and the country, people and animals alike. The long, flat road takes a straight course to the city, and eventually the fields begin to give way to more and more trees. It is under one of these that the travelers meet our next curious—but probably familiar—character.

Le lapin (The Rabbit). **Excusez-moi, les amis. Quelle heure est-il?** (Excuse me, friends. What time is it?)

Thibault. **Bonjour petit lapin! Il est onze heures. Mais qu'est-ce que tu fais là?** (Hello, little rabbit! It's eleven o'clock. But what are you doing there?)

Le lapin. Pas grand-chose. (Not much.) Just relaxing, catching a few winks. You should try it. **Vous marchez trop vite! D'où est-ce que vous venez?** (You're walking too fast! Where are you coming from?)

Thibault. **Nous venons du village. Et toi?** (We're coming from the village. And you?)

Le lapin. Je viens aussi du village! J'attends mon amie, la tortue. Elle arrive, je suis sûr. Nous faisons une course à pied. (I'm coming from the village, too! I'm waiting for my friend, the Turtle. She's coming, I'm sure. We're racing.)

Aurélie. **Vous faites une course à pied . . . et tu dors?** (You're racing . . . and you're sleeping?)

Le lapin. Bien sûr, je dors! Il est onze heures! (Of course, I'm sleeping! It's eleven o'clock!) It's still early! How am I supposed to run so fast without a few *zzzzs* every so often?

Aurélie. **Tu dois courir! Pourquoi est-ce que tu attends ton amie?** (You should run! Why are you waiting for your friend?)

Le lapin. Oh, je n'ai pas peur de mon amie, la tortue. Je cours très vite. Mais les tortues? Elles sont très lentes! (Oh, I'm not afraid of my friend, the Turtle. I run very fast. But turtles? They're very slow!)

Jean. **Aurélie, il a raison.** (Aurélie, he's right.) Turtles are pretty slow. But I'm sure that you will be on your way soon, right?

Le lapin. Ben, non. (Well, no.) After my nap I was going to pick some fruit around here. **Les arbres ici sont magnifiques, n'est-ce pas? C'est délicieux, toutes les poires, les cerises! Alors, aujourd'hui, je dors et je mange.** (The trees here are amazing, aren't they? The pears and cherries are delicious! So, today, I'm sleeping and I'm eating.) Maybe I'll run tomorrow.

Aurélie. **Mais tu es fou!** (You're crazy!)

Thibault, *also dumbfounded.* **Bon, ben . . . bonne chance.** (Well, then . . . good luck.) We need to be continuing on!

Le lapin. Au revoir! (Good-bye!)

Jean. **Bon appétit!** (Enjoy your meal!)

Chapitre 9

Dialogue [09_01/Tr. 45]

The travelers' path dips and bends through stretches of orchards and gardens with small houses set back from the road. Before long, they can't resist the temptation to stray from the road and explore the fruit trees and vines.

THIBAULT. **Ouah, nous n'avons pas de fruit comme ça chez moi.** (Wow, we don't have fruit like that where I come from.)

JEAN. **Nous non plus. Est-ce que vous voyez tous les pommiers et les cerisiers?!** (Us neither.[1] Do you see those apple trees and cherry trees?!)

AURÉLIE. **Et les vignes avec tous les raisins! Ils ont l'air délicieux!** (And the vines with all the grapes! They look delicious!)

LE RENARD BOUDEUR (THE MOPEY FOX), *surprising the three friends from behind.* **Oh, vous allez manger les raisins?** (You're going to eat the grapes?)

AURÉLIE. **Ouah! Encore un renard!** (Wow! Another fox!)

THIBAULT. **Bonjour, mon ami. Oui, oui. Nous allons manger les raisins—pourquoi?** (Hello, my friend. Yes, yes. We're going to eat the grapes—why?) They don't belong to you, do they? They're just growing wild here, it seems.

LE RENARD BOUDEUR. Non, non, ce ne sont pas mes raisins. Mais ce n'est pas une bonne idée. Vous n'allez pas aimer les raisins. (No, no, they aren't my grapes. But it's not a good idea. You're not going to like those grapes.)

JEAN. **Ah, est-ce que les raisins ne sont pas bons?** (Oh, the grapes aren't good?)

LE RENARD BOUDEUR. Non. (No.)

THIBAULT. **D'accord, je comprends maintenant. Est-ce que tu viens d'ici?** (OK, I understand now. Are you from around here?)

LE RENARD BOUDEUR. Non. (No.)

THIBAULT. **Mais tu manges souvent les raisins ici, alors?** (But you eat the grapes here often, then?)

LE RENARD BOUDEUR. Non. (No.)

THIBAULT. **Euh . . . alors, je ne comprends pas. Comment est-ce que tu sais que les raisins sont mauvais?** (Um . . . then, I don't understand. How do you know the grapes are bad?) Have you ever tried them?

LE RENARD BOUDEUR. Je ne peux pas. (I can't.) They're too high for me to pick them.

1. A more standard way to say this in English would be, "We don't either" or "Neither do we."

THIBAULT. You mean you can't reach the grapes, **mais tu sais qu'ils sont mauvais** (but you know they're bad)?

LE RENARD BOUDEUR. **Si je ne peux pas manger les raisins, ils ne peuvent pas être très bons.** (If I can't eat the grapes, they can't be very good.) I'm just warning you. **Mais j'ai faim. Je vais chercher les œufs de la ferme... vous pouvez manger les raisins si vous voulez. Moi, je pars.** (But I'm hungry. I'm going to go look for the eggs from the farm . . . you can eat the grapes if you want. Me, I'm leaving.)

JEAN, *as* ***Le renard boudeur*** *shuffles away.* That fox had some strange ideas about grapes, I dare say.

THIBAULT. I agree. I'm not quite sure what to make of all this, but I bet I know what Aurélie is thinking. **Tu vas manger les raisins, n'est-ce pas?** (You're going to eat the grapes, right?)

AURÉLIE. **Bien sûr!** (Of course!)

Chapitre 11

Dialogue [11_01/Tr. 56]

Full of fresh fruit, our travelers spend a pleasant night under the stars. The distant lights of the city appear faintly on the horizon. The next morning, traffic on the road begins to pick up, and among the many wagons and carts rolling along, the three companions happen upon a rather slow-moving voyager.

AURÉLIE. **Hé oh! Je vois une tortue, là-bas. C'est peut-être l'amie du lapin!** (Hey! I see a turtle over there. Maybe it's the rabbit's friend!)

THIBAULT. **Je pense que tu as raison, Aurélie.** (I think you're right, Aurélie.) Let's go talk to her—we can at least tell her that she's winning their race by a long shot. **Elle va être contente.** (She's going to be happy.)

They catch up to the tortoise.

JEAN. **Bonjour, mademoiselle la tortue!** (Hello, Miss Turtle!)

MADEMOISELLE LA TORTUE. **Bonjour, bonjour! Comment allez-vous?** (Hello, hello! How are you?)

JEAN. **Ben, très bien, merci.** (Well, fine, thank you.)

AURÉLIE. **Est-ce que tu es l'amie du petit lapin du village?** (Are you the friend of the little rabbit from the village?)

MLLE LA TORTUE. **Ah! Vous connaissez Monsieur le lapin!? Oui, bien sûr, je suis une de ses amis. Nous faisons une course cette semaine. Nous avons commencé dimanche.** (Oh!

You know Mr. Rabbit!? Yes, of course, I'm one of his friends. We are doing a race this week. We started Sunday.)

JEAN. **Oui, oui, nous savons. Nous avons vu ton ami le lapin.** (Yes, yes, we know. We saw your friend the rabbit.) He was a few miles back. **Il dort, il mange—mais il ne court pas beaucoup.** (He's eating, he's sleeping—but he isn't running very much.)

MLLE LA TORTUE. Ah bon? Ça c'est intéressant! *Très* intéressant! (Really? That's interesting! *Very* interesting!)

JEAN. **Je pense que tu vas gagner, mademoiselle!** (I think you're going to win, young lady!)

MLLE LA TORTUE. Hmmm . . . tu as raison, peut-être. (Hmmm . . . you might be right.) Even if he runs his fastest, I don't think he can catch me now. **Quand est-ce que vous avez parlé avec mon ami?** (When did you talk to my friend?)

THIBAULT. **Aujourd'hui, nous sommes mardi, n'est-ce pas?** (Today is Tuesday, right?)

MLLE LA TORTUE. Oui. (Yes.)

THIBAULT. **Alors, nous avons vu le lapin hier, lundi. Oui, hier après-midi.** (So, we saw the rabbit yesterday, Monday. Yes, yesterday afternoon.) About seven miles behind.

MLLE LA TORTUE. Ah bon!? Alors, il ne va pas arriver à la ville avant le soir. (Really!? Then he won't get to the city before evening.)

AURÉLIE. **Mais peut-être qu'il a fini de dormir! Peut-être qu'il a fini de manger! Peut-être qu'il va arriver demain matin . . . attention!** (But maybe he finished sleeping! Maybe he's done eating! Maybe he'll get there tomorrow morning . . . be careful!)

MLLE LA TORTUE. Attention? Pourquoi est-ce que je dois faire attention? Je n'ai pas peur! Il va arriver trop tard. (Careful? Why should I be careful? I'm not afraid! He's going to arrive too late.)

AURÉLIE. **Ah bon? Trop tard? Comment?** (Really? Too late? What?)

MLLE LA TORTUE. Vous marchez aussi vers la ville, n'est-ce pas? (You're walking to the city, too, right?)

JEAN. **Oui, et alors?** (Yes, so?)

MLLE LA TORTUE. Eh ben, nous allons arriver ce soir! (Well, we are going to arrive tonight!)

Chapitre 12

Dialogue [12_01/Tr. 62]

The road is getting busier with each passing hour, so the four travelers shift toward the shoulder of the road. ***Mademoiselle la Tortue*** *peppers Jean, Aurélie, and Thibault with questions about their trip to the city . . .*

Mlle la Tortue. So, exactly how far have you all come? Are you just on your way up from the orchards?

Jean. **Pas du tout! Nous avons commencé dans la forêt. Nous avons marché de la forêt aux montagnes. Ensuite, nous avons marché des montagnes au fleuve. Du fleuve, nous sommes entrés au village.** (Not at all! We started in the forest. We walked from the forest to the mountains. Then, we walked from the mountains to the river. From the river, we went into the village.)

Thibault. That's when I first saw them. **J'ai rencontré Aurélie et Jean dans le village.** (I met Aurélie and Jean in the village.)

Aurélie. **Et finalement, nous sommes partis pour la ville.** (And finally, we left for the city.)

Mlle la Tortue. Ouah! Incroyable! Vous avez fait un grand voyage! Vous marchez très, très vite! (Wow! Incredible! You've had a long journey! You walk very, very fast!)

Jean. **Oui, et nous n'avons pas fini. Nous retournons chez nous—au zoo.** (Yes, and we haven't finished. We're going back to our home—in the zoo.)

Mlle la Tortue, *turning to Thibault*. You . . . you don't look like you live in the zoo.

Thibault. **Oui, tu as raison. J'habite dans mon village. Mais je ne suis jamais parti du village, alors j'ai voulu voir la ville.** (Yes, you're right. I live in my village. But I've never left the village, so I wanted to see the city.) When Aurélie and Jean told me about their plans to go back, **j'ai eu envie de venir** (I wanted to come)!

Mlle la Tortue. Ah! Tu n'as jamais vu la ville? Tu vas beaucoup aimer la ville. C'est chouette! (Oh! You've never seen the city? You're really going to like the city. It's cool!)

Thibault. **Tout le monde dit ça!** (Everyone says that!)

Mlle la Tortue. Qu'est-ce que vous allez faire là-bas? Seulement visiter le zoo? (What are you going to do there? Just visit the zoo?)

Thibault. Well, aside from Aurélie and Jean getting back home, **nous avons une chose très importante à faire** (we have something very important to do).

Mlle la Tortue. Hmmm . . . voir les musées? (Hmmm . . . see the museums?)

THIBAULT. **Non. Nous n'allons pas voir les musées . . .** (No. We're not going to see the museums . . .)

MLLE LA TORTUE. Aller au restaurant? (Go to a restaurant?)

JEAN. **Non. Les vaches ne peuvent pas manger dans les restaurants.** (No. Cows can't eat in restaurants.)

AURÉLIE, *hurt*. **Et les souris!?** (And mice can!?)

MLLE LA TORTUE. Hmmm . . . alors, faire du shopping? (Hmmm . . . then, go shopping?)

THIBAULT. **Pas vraiment . . .** (Not really . . .)

MLLE LA TORTUE. Ben, je ne sais pas, alors. Quoi? (Well, I don't know then. What?)

THIBAULT. **Nous allons acheter du fromage.** (We're going to buy cheese.)

Chapitre 13

Dialogue [13_01/Tr. 68]

The travelers finally reach the city's gate and enter triumphantly.

THIBAULT. **Nous sommes arrivés! Après deux jours!** (We're here! After two days!)

MLLE LA TORTUE. Oui, félicitations! Vous avez réussi votre voyage. (Yes, congratulations! You finished your journey.)

AURÉLIE. **Et félicitations à toi aussi, mademoiselle la Tortue: tu as gagné la course avec ton ami le lapin. Sans courir!** (And congratulations to you, too, Miss Turtle: You've won the race with your friend the rabbit. Without running!)

MLLE LA TORTUE. Oui, mais aussi je suis venue à la ville sans faire de pause (Yes, but I've also come to the city without stopping)—that's what counts. **Vous voyez** (You see), I didn't really dilly-dally **comme mon ami: je ne suis pas restée sous les arbres à côté de la route comme lui, je n'ai pas mangé de fruits comme lui** (like my friend: I didn't stay under the trees beside the road like him, I didn't eat fruit like him). And above all, **je n'ai jamais dormi au milieu de l'après-midi comme lui** (I never slept in the middle of the afternoon like him)!

JEAN. **Très bien!** (Very good!) So. Where to now, **mes amis** (my friends)?

MLLE LA TORTUE. Moi, je vais attendre mon ami ici, donc, je pense que je vais dire "au revoir" maintenant. J'ai été contente de marcher avec vous! (I'm going to wait for my friend here, so I think I'll say good-bye now. I'm happy to have walked with you!)

THIBAULT. **Nous aussi! Merci . . . et à bientôt, nous espérons.** (Us, too! Thanks . . . and see you soon, we hope.)

JEAN, AURÉLIE. **Bonne soirée!** (Have a nice evening!)

Thibault, Aurélie, and Jean wander into the city, where shops and businesses are closing down for the night.

Jean. **Hmm . . . Quelle heure est-il?** (Hmm . . . What time is it?)

Thibault. **Je ne sais pas—il est six heures, ou sept heures peut-être. Les magasins ferment.** (I don't know—it's six o'clock, or maybe seven o'clock. The stores are closing.)

Aurélie. **Mince! Nous devons aller vite, alors. Le zoo ferme à huit heures. Thibault, est-ce que nous pouvons acheter ton fromage demain?** (Oh no! We should go quickly, then. The zoo closes at eight o'clock. Thibault, can we buy your cheese tomorrow?)

Thibault. **Pas de problème.** (No problem.)

Jean. **Et est-ce que ça va pour toi de dormir avec tous les animaux?** (And is it OK with you to sleep with all the animals?)

Thibault. **Oui, oui, je peux dormir avec eux.** (Yes, yes, I can sleep with them.) Honestly, I'm so tired I could sleep anywhere at this point!

Aurélie. **Moi aussi.** (Me, too.)

Jean. **Je suis d'accord.** (I agree.) *The three head off down the street. After a short distance, Jean pauses and whispers to Aurélie . . .* **Mais, entre nous, est-ce que tu sais pourquoi je suis vraiment content de retourner chez nous?** (But, between us, do you know why I'm really happy to get home?)

Aurélie. **Non, pourquoi?** (No, why?)

Jean. **Parce que finalement, après notre grand voyage, nous allons être avec des animaux normaux!** (Because finally, after our long journey, we'll be with animals that are normal!)

Chapitre 14

Dialogue [14_01/Tr. 75]

Jean, Aurélie, and Thibault are searching for a place in the zoo to sleep for the night.

Jean. **Alors, Aurélie, où est-ce que nous dormons ce soir?** (So, Aurélie, where are we sleeping tonight?)

Aurélie. **Je vais me coucher avec mes amies, les vaches. Elles se trouvent pas loin d'ici. Vous pouvez venir si vous voulez!** (I am going to sleep with my friends, the cows. They are located not far from here. You can come if you want!)

Thibault. **Parfait!** (Perfect!)

Jean. **Parfait!** (Perfect!)

THIBAULT. I didn't plan to spend my first night in the city sleeping with cattle, but it's as good a place as any. Where can I brush my teeth?

AURÉLIE. **Eeeuuhhh . . . les vaches ne se brossent pas les dents.** (Ummm. . . . Cows do not brush their teeth.)

THIBAULT. **Ah bon? Ben . . . d'accord.** (Oh really? Well . . . OK.) Where can I wash up, then?

AURÉLIE. **Eeeuuhh, désolée. Les vaches ne se lavent pas non plus.** (Ummm . . . sorry. Cows do not wash up either.)

THIBAULT. **Ça alors!** (Well then!)

JEAN. Well, that simplifies things, I guess. **À quelle heure est-ce que nous nous levons demain?** (What time are we waking up tomorrow?)

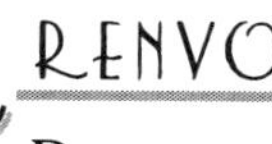

RENVOI

Do you remember how to tell time in French? If not, take a look back at **chapitre** 8 to refresh your memory.

THIBAULT. Not terribly early, I say. I won't need time to wash up or brush my teeth, after all. Ahem! *Thibault looks jokingly at Aurélie.* **Je pense que ça va si nous nous levons à neuf heures. Nous nous couchons tôt ce soir, donc ça ne doit pas être un problème.** (I think it is fine if we wake up at nine o'clock. We are going to bed early this evening, so it should not be a problem.)

JEAN. **Parfait! Comme ça, nous allons avoir le temps d'acheter tes fromages, Thibault. Ensuite, nous pouvons nous promener dans la ville ensemble.** (Perfect! That way, we will have the time to buy your cheeses, Thibault. Then, we can go for a walk in the city together.) We'll see lots of beautiful sights.

THIBAULT. **Génial! Mais d'abord, j'ai *très* faim—est-ce qu'il y a quelque chose à manger dans le zoo?** (Great! But first, I am very hungry. Is there something to eat in the zoo?)

JEAN. **Mmm . . . j'ai eu la même idée, Thibault! Je veux manger avant de me coucher!** (Mmm . . . I had the same idea, Thibault! I want to eat before going to bed!)

AURÉLIE. **Eh ben, vous devez venir avec moi pour rencontrer les vaches! Nous ne nous brossons pas les dents, et nous ne nous lavons pas, mais *manger*! ça, nous savons faire.** (Well, you should come with me to meet the cows! We don't brush our teeth, and we don't wash up, but *eat*! that we know how to do.)

Chapter 15

Dialogue [15_01/Tr. 81]

Following a good meal and a solid night's sleep, the three companions slip out of the zoo to see the city. After a full day of sightseeing, delicacy tasting, and memory making, Aurélie expresses concern.

Aurélie. **Allons-y les amis! Nous devons nous dépêcher si nous voulons acheter les fromages. Il est déjà huit heures!** (Let's go, friends! We should hurry if we want to buy the cheeses. It is already eight o'clock!)

Jean. **Mince! Aurélie a raison!** (Shoot! Aurélie is right.) They may have already sold out.

Thibault, *smiling*. **Pourquoi est-ce que vous vous inquiétez? Je me suis occupé de ça! J'ai appelé ce matin** (Why are you worrying? I took care of that! I called this morning)—I reserved three big wheels. As soon as I woke up, **je me suis souvenu** (I remembered)!

Aurélie. **Oh purée, il est fort, Thibault!** (Holy smokes! He's good, that Thibault!)

The three friends head to the shop to pick up Thibault's order. Upon leaving, Jean reflects.

Jean. **Tu sais, Thibault, nous ne rencontrons pas souvent des garçons comme toi au zoo. Nous allons nous souvenir de toi!** (You know, Thibault, we do not often meet boys like you at the zoo. We will remember you!)

Thibault. **Et moi, je vais me souvenir de vous. Nous nous sommes amusés ensemble!** (And I will remember you. We had fun together!)

Aurélie. **Est-ce que tu vas te souvenir de comment retourner au zoo?** (Will you remember how to return to the zoo?)

Thibault. **Bien sûr! Et je vais venir avec toute ma famille.** (Of course! And I will come with all my family.)

Jean. **Super. Je pense que Aurélie et moi, nous préférons rester dans la ville maintenant—la campagne, c'est bien, mais nous nous sentons mieux au zoo!** (Super. I think that Aurélie and I, we prefer to stay in the city now—the countryside is fine, but we feel better at the zoo!)

Thibault. **Et moi, je me sens bien à la campagne.** (And I feel better in the countryside.) But visiting friends is always worth a journey!

Jean. And so is a **bon fromage** (good cheese)!

Appendix B

Chant Translations

Chapitre 1

To Be or Not to Be [01_02/Tr. 2]

Chant (ahem, rap)	Translation
Les garçons: Je suis beau. (Yo!)	The boys: I am handsome. (Yo!)
Les filles: Je suis belle. (Belle!)	The girls: I am beautiful. (Beautiful!)
Tu es beau. (Yo!)	You are handsome. (Yo!)
Tu es belle. (Belle!)	You are beautiful. (Beautiful!)
Il est beau. (Yo!)	He is handsome. (Yo!)
(Et elle est belle, belle, belle, belle!)	(And she is beautiful, beautiful, beautiful, beautiful!)
Nous sommes beaux. (Yo!)	We are handsome. (Yo!)
Vous êtes beaux. (Yo!)	You are handsome. (Yo!)
Vous êtes belles. (Belles!)	You are beautiful. (Beautiful!)
Ils sont beaux (Yo, yo!)	They are handsome. (Yo, yo!)
(Et elles sont belles, belles, belles, belles!)	(And they are beautiful, beautiful, beautiful, beautiful!)

Être (to be) [01_03/Tr. 3]

Person	Singular	Plural
1st Person	**je suis** (I am)	**nous sommes** (we are)
2nd Person	**tu es** (you are)	**vous êtes** (you are)
3rd Person	**il/elle est** (he/she/it is)	**ils/elles sont** (they are)

Chapitre 2

Aller (to go) [02_02/Tr. 9]

Person	Singular	Plural
1st Person	**je vais** (I go)	**nous allons** (we go)
2nd Person	**tu vas** (you go)	**vous allez** (you go)
3rd Person	**il/elle va** (he/she/it goes)	**ils/elles vont** (they go)

Chapitre 3

Je ne mange pas de fromage. (I don't eat cheese.) [03_02/Tr. 15]

A lost poem from the miller's wife from her childhood (before imported cheese) . . .

Chant	Translation
Je ne mange pas de fromage.	I do not eat cheese.
Il n'est pas bon dans mon village.	It is not good in my village.
Puisque je n'aime pas marcher loin,	Since I do not like to walk far,
Je reste ici, et mange le pain.	I stay here, and eat the bread.

Chapitre 4

Est-ce que tu chantes? (Do you sing?) [04_02/Tr. 21]

Chant	Translation
Est-ce que tu chantes? *Oui, beaucoup.*	Do you sing? *Yes, a lot.*
Et tu chantes quoi? *Je chante le blues.*	And what do you sing? *I sing the blues.*
Pourquoi est-ce que tu chantes? *Je ne suis pas content!*	Why do you sing? *I'm not happy!*
Quand est-ce que tu chantes? *Maintenant!*	When are you singing? *Now!*
Ah . . . au revoir, alors!	Ah . . . goodbye, then!

Chapitre 6

Faire (to do/make) [06_02/Tr. 28]

Person	Singular	Plural
1st Person	**je fais** (I do/I make)	**nous faisons** (we do/we make)
2nd Person	**tu fais** (you do/you make)	**vous faites** (you do/you make)
3rd Person	**il/elle fait** (he/she/it does; he/she/it makes)	**ils/elles font** (they do/they make)

Chapitre 7

Pouvoir (to be able to/can) [07_02/Tr. 34]

Person	Singular	Plural
1st Person	**je peux** (I can)	**nous pouvons** (we can)
2nd Person	**tu peux** (you can)	**vous pouvez** (you can)
3rd Person	**il/elle peut** (he/she/it can)	**ils/elles peuvent** (they can)

Chapitre 8

Il est sept heures. (It is seven o'clock.) [08_02/Tr. 40][1]

Chant	Translation
Il est sept heures, déjà, alors, il est sept heures, et toi tu dors.	It is seven o'clock, already, so, it is seven o'clock, and you, you are sleeping.
Il est huit heures, déjà, alors, il est huit heures et toi tu dors.	It is eight o'clock, already, so, it is eight o'clock and you, you are sleeping.
Il est neuf heures, déjà, alors! Il est neuf heures, et toi tu dors.	It is nine o'clock, already, so! It is nine o'clock and you, you are sleeping.
Il est dix heures, déjà! Alors! Il est dix heures, tu dors encore!	It is ten o'clock, already! So! It is ten o'clock, you are still sleeping![1]
Tout ça n'est pas très amusant: toi tu dors, et moi j'attends!	All that is not very funny: you, you're sleeping, and me, I'm waiting!

Chapitre 9

The Future Tense—Starring the Verb Manger (to eat) [09_02/Tr. 46]

Person	Singular	Plural
1st Person	**je vais manger** (I will eat)	**nous allons manger** (we will eat)
2nd Person	**tu vas manger** (you will eat)	**vous allez manger** (you will eat)
3rd Person	**il/elle va manger** (he/she/it will eat)	**ils/elles vont manger** (they will eat)

1. In **chapitre** 4, the word **encore** was translated as "again" or "another." When used with a verb (as in this chant), it can also mean "still," as in "You're *still* sleeping!" (**Tu dors encore!**) or "You're still eating!" (**Tu manges encore!**).

Chapitre 11

Le passé composé: avoir + the Past Participle [11_02/Tr. 57]

Person	Singular	Plural
1st Person	**j'ai chanté** (I sang)	**nous avons chanté** (we sang)
2nd Person	**tu as chanté** (you sang)	**vous avez chanté** (you sang)
3rd Person	**il/elle a chanté** (he/she/it sang)	**ils/elles ont chanté** (they sang)

Chapitre 12

Mini Tour de France [12_02/Tr. 63]

Chant	Translation
Paris, c'est beau, Paris—je suis retourné.	Paris, it's beautiful, Paris, I returned.
L'Alsace est belle, très belle—il est retourné.	Alsace is beautiful, very beautiful—he returned.
La Provence est superbe, ah oui, superbe—elle est retournée.	Provence is superb, ah yes, superb—she returned.
Et la Bretagne, la Normandie? Magnifique, magnifique!—ils sont retournés . . .	And Brittany? Normandy? Magnificent! Magnificent!—they returned . . .
elles sont retournées, nous sommes retournés, vous êtes retournés!	they returned, we returned, you returned!
Et toi, tu es retourné?	And you, you returned? *or* And you, did you return?

Le passé composé II: être + the past participle [12_03/Tr. 64]

Person	Singular	Plural
1st Person	**je suis retourné** (I returned)	**nous sommes retournés** (we returned)
2nd Person	**tu es retourné** (you returned)	**vous êtes retournés** (you returned)
3rd Person	**il est retourné** (he/it returned) **elle est retournée** (she/it returned)	**ils sont retournés** (they returned) **elles sont retournées** (they, f. returned)

Chapitre 13

Stressed Pronouns: Moi, je suis beau! (I'm handsome!) [13_02/Tr. 70][2]

Chant	Translation
Moi, je suis beau!	Me, I am handsome!
Moi, je suis intelligent!	Me, I am intelligent!
Moi, je suis magnifique!	Me, I am magnificent!
Moi, je suis sympathique!	Me, I am nice!
Hmmm . . . toi, tu es orgueilleux!!![2]	Hmmm . . . You, you are proud!

Person	Singular	Plural
1st Person	**moi** (me)	**nous** (we)
2nd Person	**toi** (you)	**vous** (you)
3rd Person	**lui/elle** (him/her/it)	**eux/elles** (them)

Chapitre 14

Pronominal Verbs—Je me lève (I get up) [14_02/Tr. 77]

Person	Singular	Plural
1st Person	**je me lève** (I get up)	**nous nous levons** (we get up)
2nd Person	**tu te lèves** (you get up)	**vous vous levez** (you get up)
3rd Person	**il/elle se lève** (he/she/it gets up)	**ils/elles se lèvent** (they get up)

Chapitre 15

Past-Tense Pronominals—Je me suis amusé. (I had fun.) [15_02/Tr. 83]

Person	Singular	Plural
1st Person	**je me suis amusé(e)** (I had fun)	**nous nous sommes amusé(e)s** (we had fun)
2nd Person	**tu t'es amusé(e)** (you had fun)	**vous vous êtes amusé(e)(s)** (you had fun)
3rd Person	**il s'est amusé/elle s'est amusée** (he had fun/she had fun)	**ils se sont amusés/elles se sont amusées** (they had fun)

2. **Orgueilleux** means "proud" or "self-centered" in English.

Appendix C

Verbs

Regular Verbs

-er Verbs

(All **-er** verbs will have the same conjugation pattern as **parler**.)

Parler *(to speak/talk)* (FFCA chapitre *1)*

Person	Singular	Plural
1st Person	**je parle** (I speak/talk)	**nous parlons** (we speak/talk)
2nd Person	**tu parles** (you speak/talk)	**vous parlez** (you [all] speak/talk)
3rd Person	**il/elle parle** (he/she/it speaks/ talks)	**ils/elles parlent** (they, masculine/ they, feminine speak/talk)
p.p. **parlé**		

-ir Verbs

(All *regular*[1] **-ir** verbs will have the same conjugation pattern as **finir**.)

Finir *(to finish)* (FFCA chapitre *3)*

Person	Singular	Plural
1st Person	**je finis** (I finish)	**nous finissons** (we finish)
2nd Person	**tu finis** (you finish)	**vous finissez** (you all finish)
3rd Person	**il/elle finit** (he/she/it finishes)	**ils/elles finissent** (they finish)
p.p. **fini**		

1. Some **-ir** verbs are irregular, such as **dormir**, which is also in this appendix.

Irregular Verbs

Attendre *(to wait)* (FFCB chapitre *8)*

Person	Singular	Plural
1st Person	**j'attends** (I wait)	**nous attendons** (we wait)
2nd Person	**tu attends** (you wait)	**vous attendez** (you wait)
3rd Person	**il/elle attend** (he/she/it waits)	**ils/elles attendent** (they wait)
p.p. **attendu**		

Avoir *(to have)* (FFCA chapitre *8)*

Person	Singular	Plural
1st Person	**j'ai** (I have)	**nous avons** (we have)
2nd Person	**tu as** (you have)	**vous avez** (you have)
3rd Person	**il/elle a** (he/she/it has)	**ils/elles ont** (they have)
p.p. **eu**		

Courir *(to run)* (FFCB chapitre *8)*

Person	Singular	Plural
1st Person	**je cours** (I run)	**nous courons** (we run)
2nd Person	**tu cours** (you run)	**vous courez** (you run)
3rd Person	**il/elle court** (he/she/it runs)	**ils/elles courent** (they run)
p.p. **couru**		

Connaître *(to know)* (FFCB chapitre *11)*

Person	Singular	Plural
1st Person	**je connais** (I know)	**nous connaissons** (we know)
2nd Person	**tu connais** (you know)	**vous connaissez** (you know)
3rd Person	**il/elle connaît** (he/she/it knows)	**ils/elles connaissent** (they know)
p.p. **connu**		

Dormir *(to sleep)* (FFCB chapitre *8)*

Note that the conjugation of ***s'endormir*** *(to fall asleep) is based on* ***dormir****—just add* ***en****!*

Person	Singular	Plural
1st Person	**je dors** (I sleep)	**nous dormons** (we sleep)
2nd Person	**tu dors** (you sleep)	**vous dormez** (you sleep)
3rd Person	**il/elle dort** (he/she/it sleeps)	**ils/elles dorment** (they sleep)
p.p. **dormi**		

Être *(to be)* (FFCB chapitre *1)*

Person	Singular	Plural
1st Person	**je suis** (I am)	**nous sommes** (we are)
2nd Person	**tu es** (you are)	**vous êtes** (you are)
3rd Person	**il/elle est** (he/she/it is)	**ils/elles sont** (they are)
p.p. **été**		

Faire *(to do/make)* (FFCB chapitre *6)*

Person	Singular	Plural
1st Person	**je fais** (I do/make)	**nous faisons** (we do/make)
2nd Person	**tu fais** (you do/make)	**vous faites** (you do/make)
3rd Person	**il/elle fait** (he/she/it does/makes)	**ils/elles font** (they do/make)
p.p. **fait**		

Partir *(to leave)* (FFCB chapitre *9)*

Person	Singular	Plural
1st Person	**je pars** (I leave)	**nous partons** (we leave)
2nd Person	**tu pars** (you leave)	**vous partez** (you leave)
3rd Person	**il/elle part** (he/she/it leaves)	**ils/elles partent** (they leave)
p.p. **parti**		

Pouvoir *(to be able to/can)* (FFCB chapitre *7)*

Person	Singular	Plural
1st Person	**je peux** (I can)	**nous pouvons** (we can)
2nd Person	**tu peux** (you can)	**vous pouvez** (you can)
3rd Person	**il/elle peut** (he/she/it can)	**ils/elles peuvent** (they can)
p.p. **pu**		

Prendre *(to take)* (FFCB chapitre *9)*

Person	Singular	Plural
1st Person	**je prends** (I take)	**nous prenons** (we take)
2nd Person	**tu prends** (you take)	**vous prenez** (you take)
3rd Person	**il/elle prend** (he/she/it takes)	**ils/elles prennent** (they take)
p.p. **pris**		

Savoir *(to know)* (FFCB chapitre *9)*

Person	Singular	Plural
1st Person	**je sais** (I know)	**nous savons** (we know)
2nd Person	**tu sais** (you know)	**vous savez** (you know)
3rd Person	**il/elle sait** (he/she/it knows)	**ils/elles savent** (they know)
p.p. **su**		

Venir *(to come)* (FFCB chapitre *8)*

Note that the conjugation of **se souvenir** *(to remember) is based on* **venir***—just add* **sou***.*

Person	Singular	Plural
1st Person	**je viens** (I come)	**nous venons** (we come)
2nd Person	**tu viens** (you come)	**vous venez** (you come)
3rd Person	**il/elle vient** (he/she/it comes)	**ils/elles viennent** (they come)
p.p. **venu**		

Voir *(to see)* (FFCB chapitre *9)*

Person	Singular	Plural
1st Person	**je vois** (I see)	**nous voyons** (we see)
2nd Person	**tu vois** (you see)	**vous voyez** (you see)
3rd Person	**il/elle voit** (he/she/it sees)	**ils/elles voient** (they see)
p.p. **vu**		

Devoir *(to have to, should)* (FFCB chapitre *7)*

Person	Singular	Plural
1st Person	**je dois** (I have to)	**nous devons** (we have to)
2nd Person	**tu dois** (you have to)	**vous devez** (you have to)
3rd Person	**il/elle doit** (he/she/it has to)	**ils/elles doivent** (they have to)
p.p. **dû**		

Vouloir *(to want)* (FFCB chapitre *7)*

Person	Singular	Plural
1st Person	**je veux** (I want)	**nous voulons** (we want)
2nd Person	**tu veux** (you want)	**vous voulez** (you want)
3rd Person	**il/elle veut** (he/she/it wants)	**ils/elles veulent** (they want)
p.p. **voulu**		

Dire *(to say)* (FFCB chapitre *12)*

Person	Singular	Plural
1st Person	**je dis** (I say)	**nous disons** (we say)
2nd Person	**tu dis** (you say)	**vous dites** (you say)
3rd Person	**il/elle dit** (he/she says)	**ils/elles disent** (they say)
p.p. **dit**		

S'inquiéter *(to worry)* (FFCB chapitre *15)*

Person	Singular	Plural
1st Person	**je m'inquiète** (I worry)	**nous nous inquiétons** (we worry)
2nd Person	**tu t'inquiètes** (you worry)	**vous vous inquiétez** (you worry)
3rd Person	**il/elle s'inquiète** (he/she/it worries)	**ils/elles s'inquiètent** (they worry)
p.p. **inquiété**		

Appendix D

Past Participles

Infinitive	Past Participle
parler[1]	**parlé**
finir[2]	**fini**
attendre	**attendu**
avoir	**eu**
courir	**couru**
connaître	**connu**
dormir	**dormi**
être	**été**
faire	**fait**
partir	**parti**
pouvoir	**pu**
prendre	**pris**
savoir	**su**
venir	**venu**
voir	**vu**
devoir	**dû**
vouloir	**voulu**
dire	**dit**
s'endormir	**endormi**
se souvenir	**souvenu**
s'inquiéter	**inquiété**

1. The past participle of all **-er** verbs will end in **-é**.
2. The past participle of all **-ir** verbs will end in **-i**.

Appendix E

Prepositions

Français (French)	**Anglais** (English)	Book/**Chapitre**
à	to, at	A/1
à côté de	next to	A/6
après	after	B/12
avant	before	B/11
avec	with	A/1
dans	in	A/4
de	of, from	A/2
derrière	behind	A/7
devant	in front of	A/6
loin (de)	far (from)	A/7
pour	for	A/2
près (de)	near (to), close (to)	A/11
sans	without	B/13
sous	under	B/13
sur	on, on top of	A/7
vers	toward	A/4